MW00782232

Constitutional
Morality and the Rise
of Quasi-Law

BRUCE P. FROHNEN and GEORGE W. CAREY

Constitutional Morality and the Rise of Quasi-Law

Harvard University Press

Cambridge, Massachusetts, and London, England

2016

Second printing

Library of Congress Cataloging-in-Publication Data

Frohnen, Bruce, author.
  Constitutional morality and the rise of quasi-law / Bruce P. Frohnen, George W. Carey.
    pages cm
  Includes bibliographical references and index.
  ISBN 978-0-674-08887-0 (hardcover)
  1. Constitutional law—United States. 2. Constitutional history—United States. 3. Rule of
law—United States. 4. Executive power—United States. 5. Delegated legislation—United
States. 6. Progressivism (United States politics) 7. Political ethics—United States. I. Carey,
George W. (George Wescott), 1933–2013, author. II. Title.
  KF4550.F76 2016
  342.73—dc23   2015034453

for my Antonia

eres el amor de mi vida

BPF

Contents

Constitutional
Morality and the Rise
of Quasi-Law

Introduction

A Conflict of Expectations

A CADEMICS HAVE A BAD HABIT of describing political conflicts in terms of crisis. This is understandable as it highlights the importance of one's topic. But not every conflict is a crisis in the sense of presenting the possibility of revolutionary change or systemic collapse. Empires, nations, and regimes are more likely to succumb over time to multiple ailments than to suffer dramatic demise from a single blow. This does not mean, however, that internal conflicts and tensions are unimportant, for they may weaken the system to the point where a relatively small shock proves fatal.

In this light, seemingly constant expressions of concern in recent years over "deadlock" between Congress and the president in Washington may be seen as overwrought but not unimportant. These fears, exaggerated no doubt for political effect, stem from disappointed expectations concerning the power of officers within the federal government to agree upon and take meaningful action aimed at reshaping important institutions and policies. In this book we are concerned less with the lack of systemic policy changes than with the conflict between expectations and practice in American politics. We believe this conflict stems from misunderstandings concerning the role of the federal government provided for in our Constitution and, as important, deep-seated disagreements concerning how political actors should conduct themselves—what they should strive to achieve in government and how. These disagreements both point to and exacerbate tensions among citizens and political actors concerning the nature of their constitution and the government it provides. And disagreements of this sort can, in

1

fact, undermine a regime, precipitating crisis, collapse, or a process of sustained disintegration.

The problem of American government today can be stated in simple terms: America's written and unwritten constitutions no longer fit one another. As a result, the written Constitution no longer means what it says to the people it is supposed to govern and our regime no longer acts according to the rule of law. Put another way, the rules of the game no longer apply as written, and none of the players has a good enough conception of the unwritten rules to predict with relative certainty what will earn points and what will earn penalties. The result is a regime that is losing legitimacy, efficacy, and the ability to make rational, sustainable policies. Reasons for this situation are many, but center on changes in habits and beliefs shaping how the words of the Constitution are put into action not only by courts, but by political actors in general as they make law and public policy.

In mentioning habits and beliefs we may be seen as simply naming elements of the unwritten constitution. Indeed, to say that Americans' written Constitution is in tension with the manner in which it is put into practice may be seen as simply restating the old notion that the written Constitution is outdated and so must be made to change with the times. On this view an unwritten constitution is merely part of a "living" constitution needing constant reinterpretation to support social progress.

The "living constitution" holds a central position in American public discourse. Akhil Reed Amar, perhaps its most famous contemporary proponent, teaches at the Yale Law School and is a frequent participant in constitutional debates on television and various college campuses. Thus we can look to Amar's arguments in showing how the "living" constitution is constructed, as well as how this construction influences constitutional habits and beliefs.

In *America's Unwritten Constitution: The Precedents and Principles We Live By*, Amar argues that the Constitution's written words "only begin to map out the basic ground rules that actually govern our land." More than any mere distribution of political powers, rights, and duties, for Amar the Constitution taken as a whole constitutes a full-fledged ethical-political unity including rules of textual interpretation tied to fundamental principles and policy goals. The written Constitution is an important but gap-filled and unstable document that requires extratextual support to form "a single constitutional system."[1]

America's constitutional system, according to Amar, embodies the fundamental principles of equality and popular sovereignty. These principles are "unwritten" in that they do not appear in the text itself, but on Amar's reading are crucial parts of an ongoing conversation among interpreters, political actors, and the public. Over time, the play of unwritten with and against the written Constitution has marginalized inappropriate or unjust "extratextual practices and precedents" and embedded better ones doing "justice to the text," thereby making up an authoritative guide for determining what laws and policies to enact and uphold as "constitutional."[2]

Amar develops theories rooted in the work of Ronald Dworkin, who famously asserted that the Framers of the Constitution should be deemed to have chosen to express themselves through abstract principles focusing on the moral imperative of equality. Such principles, for Dworkin, require that constitutional language be reinterpreted to embody what he deems the best contemporary moral reasoning. The problem for Dworkin's theorizing has been the lack of any clear basis for his abstractions or the reformulation of texts and specifically limited, legal principles, in anything other than the preferences of particular persons and elites.[3] Amar seeks to shore up this weakness by constructing an interpretive device capable of achieving his desired results while maintaining sufficient connection with American constitutionalism to sustain his enterprise's legitimacy.

Amar's guide is complex, requiring intellectual expertise and proper values to master. This means that the unwritten constitution is in practice a set of interpretive materials available for use by scholars and judges. In determining the "meaning," or rather the operational requirements of the Constitution, interpreters must look, for example, to events surrounding adoption of various constitutional texts (the "enacted constitution"), modes of interpretation situated within a theory of judicial supremacy (the "doctrinal" constitution), and various ideological conceptions Amar finds to have added motive force to reform, such as the "feminist" constitution. There are eleven unwritten constitutions in all.

The fountainhead of Amar's unwritten constitution is the subject of his book's central chapter. Titled "Honoring the Icons," this chapter describes "America's Symbolic Constitution" and its role in glossing the written Constitution, earlier symbols, and the constitutional tradition as a whole. Amar begins with a seemingly eclectic set of a half dozen texts (the Declaration of Independence, the Northwest Ordinance, *The Federalist*, Lincoln's

Gettysburg Address, the Warren court's decision in the *Brown v. Board of Education* desegregation case, and Martin Luther King Jr.'s "I Have a Dream" speech). He deems these texts "privileged sources of meaning, inspiration, and guidance" that "set forth background principles that powerfully inform American constitutional interpretation."[4]

After an obligatory nod to the text of the written Constitution, Amar asserts that, in weighing possible interpretations of particular words or clauses, "interpreters should hesitate, and do in fact hesitate, to embrace any reading that would violate the clear letter and spirit of [his] other canonical texts." Indeed, to do otherwise would be positively un-American because "adherence to these texts helps *constitute* Americans as a distinct people among all the peoples of the Earth." This is not to say that the symbolic constitution presents a clear and obvious meaning, any more than does the written Constitution itself, for "once we move beyond this core set of texts, the outer boundaries of the canon are fuzzy. But then, so are the meaning-boundaries of many of the written Constitution's clauses, whose relatively solid core applications nestle inside blurred peripheries and penumbras."[5]

Nevertheless, the text cannot simply be made to say anything the interpreter wants: "America stands for certain things—things set forth in other texts that we, the people, as a people, hold dear." How do we find these things? For Amar the task begins with an imaginative understanding of his iconic texts, according to which later texts "regloss" earlier ones in keeping with progressive refinements of principles like equality and popular sovereignty. Utilizing these principles, Amar finds a specific narrative. As he puts it, "[T]hese texts form a symbolic network, a system. They connect not merely to the written Constitution but to each other." They form, over time and in the right hands, "the trajectory of the American constitutional project over the past two hundred years."[6]

As made clear by his use of the term *icons*, Amar emphasizes the transcendent nature of his texts—their status as symbols to which Americans should look in identifying who they as a people ought to be, as well as how they ought to act. This makes the resulting principles prescriptive; they are intended to prod Americans to change their behaviors and even deeply embedded constitutional practices. Thus, for example, Amar states as axiomatic that "all voters must count equally." Indeed, this principle, which he obliquely acknowledges would render illegitimate the United States

Senate, forms "the bedrock of the American system of government." As such, it has become universally accepted, according to Amar, as it has been used by courts in recent decades to eliminate not only racial but also geographically and historically rooted norms of apportionment operative for most of American history.[7]

Amar's icons tell and enforce a story of progress out of an oppressive past toward an increasingly egalitarian and just future. In accordance with this story, "the people" may create and approve new rules and even new rights not found in the written Constitution, if they are important to them and in keeping with the "trajectory of the American Constitutional project." These rights also may be discarded over time in accordance with that project, so long as the project's progressive nature is maintained.[8]

In this vein, Amar holds that the Fourteenth Amendment fundamentally altered American public law and life and portrays more cautious interpreters seeking to ground political practice in textual readings and longstanding political practice as defenders of retrograde interpretations and, with them, racial oppression.[9] He begins by observing that "only cranks" would question the legitimacy of the Fourteenth Amendment. One can safely assume that this particular issue, as Amar himself notes, has been settled. Nonetheless, he links discredited arguments to restrained readings of the Fourteenth Amendment, opining that they, in effect, question the legitimacy of Barack Obama's election to the presidency, along with even the most basic antidiscrimination policies. At the same time, Amar paints that amendment's ratification in stark, revolutionary terms. Here he references the role of Union troops in Southern states, emphasizing threats of force from those troops along with Congress's refusal to return voting rights and membership in the Union to these states until and unless they voted ratification. Amar then capitalizes on his revolutionary reading of ratification to assert a "new unwritten principle" arising not from the text but from the character of its ratification (the "doctrinal constitution"). The new principle: "the federal government would properly enjoy sweeping authority to hold state governments to the highest contemporary standards of democratic inclusiveness."[10] In this way Amar makes clear his belief that Americans face a stark choice: either side with racist confederates and other "cranks" or accept an interpretation of the Fourteenth Amendment that grants the federal government plenary power to nationalize issues of equality—not in relation to race alone, but also to sex, sexual orientation, and other potential categories and issues neither mentioned nor contemplated in the text of the Fourteenth Amendment.

Amar's "symbolic constitution" is intended to entrench a set of ideological principles rooted in his vision of justice as substantive equality and opposing attachment to history and tradition, which he identifies closely with racism and other forms of oppression. His unwritten constitution as a whole calls for the restructuring of attitudes and institutions to establish a society in keeping with his favored trajectory of rights and duties. His formulation of the unwritten constitution makes the Constitution a means to ends more important than itself, ends that in many cases command widespread support, but that continue to demand substantive reform.

Amar's ends and his concern to reshape constitutional practice both have roots in the Progressive movement of the late nineteenth and early twentieth centuries. That movement sought to overcome the formal structures and procedures at the core of the written Constitution in pursuit of laws and policies aimed at producing a more democratic society. But these ends—principally greater equality and individual rights enforced by the federal government against more local associations—are not the Constitution. And it is at least worth asking whether, in the drive to secure these ends by reglossing the Constitution, their proponents have not undermined not so much the "dead" text of that document as the living habits and beliefs of the people necessary for constitutional government and the rule of law.

For example, many people agree with the goals of President Obama's executive order granting "deferred action" to persons in the United States illegally who are parents of American citizens or who have been legal permanent residents in the country for five years, among others. Some also aver that this latest order has precedential support in executive orders issued by Presidents Reagan and George H. W. Bush.[11] Assuming for argument's sake that all this is true, we would ask whether the trend in recent decades toward executive actions with the force of law is in fact constitutional in any meaningful sense. That is, even if one agrees with various policies put into action by executive order, whether regarding immigration or executive war powers, the question remains whether establishing such policies by unilateral presidential action accords with the structures and procedures of the Constitution as written. If not, we submit that the action is not legal and harms our constitutional government by providing an example to both rulers and ruled of the successful exercise of arbitrary power.

Constitutionalism and Its Instrumental Virtues

Our argument is normative in a narrow sense. We are aware that terms like *morality* often are seen as too subjective for proper use in the study of politics and public institutions. However, norms or standards of behavior are what make constitutions, laws, and other social structures "live" in the sense of influencing concrete practice. These standards may be rooted in custom, religion, political ideology, or some combination of all three. In any event they set boundaries of conduct and grounds for deeming certain acts virtuous, or vicious.

We use the term *virtue* in the limited, Aristotelian sense of a certain excellence related to a given purpose: "The virtue of eyes, for instance, makes the eyes and their functioning excellent, because it makes us see well; and similarly, the virtue of a horse makes the horse excellent, and thereby good at galloping, at carrying its rider, and at standing steady in the face of the enemy."[12] An overlooked but fundamental virtue of special relevance here is that of obedience to law. Certainly this virtue can be overemphasized in the face of injustice. But constitutional government means rule according to law; it requires that rulers themselves be limited in the manner by which they may make law. This means constitutional government by nature depends on the virtue of law-abidingness. It is dangerous to constitutional government, then, for those in positions of power to lose the habit of following procedures for lawmaking laid out in the Constitution—including those often-deprecated requirements of bicameral legislative approval and presentment to the president for veto or signature. When such habits fray, officeholders begin to act in an arbitrary manner and the people, in turn, lose their ability to know what counts as a law and hence the ability to know and follow law on a regular, habitual basis.

Americans currently live under a political system that relies on what we term *quasi-laws*. By quasi-laws we mean directives with the force of law that lack crucial characteristics of genuine law. Emanating from all three branches of government, quasi-laws create rights and duties like laws but lack essential legal attributes such as promulgation through prescribed means and provision of predictable rules rather than mere delegation of discretionary power. Citizens today may find themselves charged with violating "rules" emanating from any branch of government (including, of course the fourth, administrative branch) without understanding their content or origins, even as rulers find it increasingly difficult to enforce effective policies in the face of unpredictable conflicts with members of other branches. Thus, the persistent breaking of constitutional rules has produced confusion, tension, and animosity among those making and following law.

It is important to note that our current situation is not the result of mere accident but of a combination of social and economic developments and an ideological commitment to face them through more systematic, positive government at the national level. In particular, Progressives beginning in the late nineteenth century attacked the procedures set down in the Framers' Constitution as producing only "the gridlock of democracy." In their view, adherence to the Constitution's formal, structural requirements kept state actors from "doing the people's business."

Constitutional formalism is inconsistent with the unwritten constitution taken as a set of interpretive ideological symbols. The separation of powers in particular requires too cumbersome a set of procedures for dynamic constitutional reglossing. How, then, to achieve substantive goals in the face of recalcitrant governmental machinery? This has been the question faced by Progressivism from its inception. The answer has been to alter the assumptions, habits, and expectations of political actors in particular so as to negate formal constitutional requirements and empower the various organs of the federal government to put Progressive policies into action.

There is an older, more deeply rooted understanding of the unwritten constitution that is fundamentally opposed to the Progressive conception. This cultural unwritten constitution is "the body of institutions, customs, manners, conventions, and voluntary associations which may not even be mentioned in the formal constitution, but which nevertheless form the fabric of social reality and sustain the formal constitution."[13] On this view, a society's unwritten constitution may include institutions as broad as the common law legal system and as seemingly divorced from debates over constitutional rights and duties as unions, churches, or business associations.

It encompasses political society and also social institutions and practices constituting a people's character and formative beliefs.

This cultural unwritten constitution determines, for example, whether certain kinds of laws will be obeyed. One relevant example here would be the widespread, violent opposition to Reconstruction in the post–Civil War South, with all the injustices that opposition brought. The cultural unwritten constitution also helps determine whether the people will look to their national, state, or local government—or to associations of civil society—for guidance in the interactions of daily life as well as for protection in difficult times.

The unwritten constitution understood as a people's political and constitutional culture shapes how and even whether a written constitution will be accepted and put into action.[14] It does not force the written constitution into any set, predetermined shape because its principles and goals are not summed up by any single ideological commitment, instead being dispersed in a variety of traditions and habits. It may be healthy or unhealthy, just or unjust, egalitarian or inegalitarian as judged by some set of universal standards, but it by nature forms the starting point for any constitution and limits the ability of written words and procedures to put particular policies into effect. And just as a written constitution will fail if it is inappropriate for a people's unwritten constitution, so changes to an unwritten constitution may render a formerly appropriate constitution no longer workable.

We have not here merely returned to the argument for a "living" constitution. Neither textual meaning nor political beliefs and habits are as malleable as living constitutionalists claim. The unwritten constitution does not simply change as directed by new interpretations. Such interpretations may, however, succeed in changing the habits and beliefs of political actors. In this way they are likely to create not a new constitution, but an ambiguous constitution producing confusion, animosity, and a breakdown of respect for law itself.

If law is to be maintained and violence avoided, culture and law must be rendered and maintained in sympathy with one another. Particularly important to this endeavor is the character of political actors. Good character in political actors involves virtuous habits and beliefs, especially in relation to the laws and constitution of one's people. This good character, then, rests on a specific, culturally conditioned constitutional morality.

We use the term *constitutional morality* to denote the felt duty of government officials in particular to abide by the restrictions and imperatives imposed on them by a constitution.[15] Such morality is only part of the wider unwritten constitution of a people. But it is of special importance because it holds, in a sense, the keys to the rule of law.

Constitutional morality requires that those holding office under a particular constitutional structure act with a requisite virtue, or set of virtues. We refer here not to an abstract conception of the virtuous "best person," but rather to the requirements for a good member of Congress, good Supreme Court justice, good president, or good administrator. The commonalities among these positions, in particular their relation to the functional and formalistic requirements of the Constitution's separation of powers, demand sufficiently similar virtues that it makes sense to talk about the virtue of a political official at the national level and a general constitutional morality. Moreover, these virtues must in some sense work together if they are to support the Constitution—the goal or natural end of constitutional morality.

Constitutional morality, then, does not entail universally necessary virtues. But its virtues are necessary for the proper functioning of the federal government. Political actors must have and apply them, lest they undermine the system.

The virtue of a good political actor under the Constitution was, as we will show in our discussion of the Framers' Constitution, one of restrained concern to protect the powers and position of one's branch within the framework of the separation of powers. Political actors within the three branches throughout most of American history recognized a duty to uphold their offices. Certainly out of fashion, this sense of duty should not look strange even to people today. Those giving testimony in court take oaths to tell the truth, and those admitted to legal practice take oaths to uphold the laws of the land and the Constitution, as do judges and politicians in numerous positions of public responsibility. While it may be fashionable to look at these oaths as meaningless remnants of a bygone era, we nonetheless should consider the roles they played in that era. Political officers often were corrupt, but a public ethic was sufficiently well maintained to ensure that habitual following of constitutional forms and procedures checked power, limited the damage done by bad actors, and maintained respect for law.

We will argue that contemporary cynicism regarding the possibility and necessity of virtue has proven debilitating to our constitutional morality. But this is not the sum of our argument. It also seems clear to us that the United States for some decades has been operating under an ideology according to which the centralized administrative state is the proper and necessary locus of power, indeed the only legitimate structure capable of bringing justice, order, and prosperity. This is, in fact, a relatively new and mistaken view of the organization of any good society, one that rejects the lessons of history, the facts of social science, and the logic of constitutionalism. It is a view that undermines law and with it the possibility of ordered liberty.

In his classic work *The Intellectual Crisis in American Public Administration*, Vincent Ostrom outlined two very different views of how a society must be administered, one monarchical and the other democratic.[16] Ironically, we currently are ruled by a monarchical system in the name of democracy. All societies have methods of distributing public goods. Even relatively primitive societies must come to an understanding of how roads, armed forces, and other necessities of social life will get built and their benefits distributed. Free markets themselves are a form of administration in that the legal system must enforce contracts for them to function. Some of these methods may be customary, some rooted in voluntary transactions, and some coercive or at least hierarchical in nature. Historically, most roads have been built by slaves or putatively free peasants conscripted for the task. In modern times, most people take pride in their liberties and look on the state as their servant. This made some sense when the state did not play much of a role in daily life—as when there were few public goods provided and the military was based in local militia. A governmental administration that is small and does not do much can be kept in check by an active, watchful community. But society, our demands on public administration, and the shape of that administration itself all have changed.

Now there is widespread belief that a centralized, "monarchical" form of bureaucracy is consistent with a free (for Ostrom, "democratic") society. Woodrow Wilson in particular helped institutionalize the view that democratic and authoritarian regimes differ principally in the source of political will directing them. In democratic nations politics aim to determine the will of the people, whereas in authoritarian nations the will of some person or group determines public policy. In either case, Wilson argued, administration ought to be the same, utilizing efficient, top-down procedures to translate the political will into public action.

In Hobbesian fashion, Wilson assumed a constant threat of disorder and violence that must be counteracted and contained by a single sovereign invested with the power to impose its will. Whatever the form of government, on this view, there must be some source of absolute, sovereign authority above the law. In a democratic state that authority is the legislature or, increasingly, a democratically elected president.

Ostrom emphasized the hostility of monarchical administrations toward local autonomy. Efficiency and prevention of various forms of discrimination require that all decision making occur at the highest, most "enlightened" level possible. And this means taking away from individual persons, families, voluntary associations, and local governments the freedom and authority necessary to maintain public participation and the ability to respond to local circumstances. In addition to eliminating local self-government, political systems rooted in Progressivism's extreme view of political sovereignty tend to eliminate the rule of law or, rather, to replace it with mere rule by law. Insistence that there must reside somewhere a final power to decide invests those with that power with the ability to decide that the laws they make should apply to others, but not to themselves. We see elements of this view in nations providing immunity from prosecution to political leaders, and also in the United States, where members of Congress exempt themselves and their offices from a variety of laws concerning, for example, labor regulations and Obamacare.

There is a further problem, however, in that rule by law exempts rulers from the limitations enshrined in the Constitution, both as text and as unwritten, cultural institution. Increasingly, a regime freed from the rule of law ceases to rule by law and comes to rule by something less than law. That something may be mere power. But it may also reside in quasi-laws. Such quasi-laws have the name and something of the form of law, but they fail to embody the elements necessary for what is called a law to fulfill its proper functions. They are used to undermine, tailor, and override preexisting laws and constitutional limitations, bringing forth incoherent, inconsistent, and surprising official government rules. The result is a regime that rules arbitrarily, with so much discretion that the people must abide by its will rather than known, settled rules. Defenders of such a regime may claim that it frees the state to provide us with more good things, including equality and justice. But a regime of quasi-law cannot provide actual law and over time will degenerate into arbitrary rule by decree.

The American Constitution rests on a very different set of assumptions regarding the nature of power and the requirements of a free society. Ostrom found in *The Federalist* principles of self-government essential to free government (but rejected by Wilson as mere literary theory). Of particular importance, according to Ostrom, is the Constitution's system of federalism and separation of powers. This structure produced a set of overlapping jurisdictions with overlapping constituencies and terms of office. And this multiplicity of authorities was necessary so that all citizens, by nature belonging to a variety of communities that administer public goods, could have their voices heard as administrators checked and balanced one another to prevent arbitrary power. Moreover, *The Federalist's* system relied on what Ostrom called "positive constitutional law," by which he meant the effective, lawlike nature of constitutional provisions limiting the power and scope of action of administrators and politicians. Fragmentation of authority is essential and must be maintained through "legally enforceable constitutional law."[17]

Of course, such a system entails the kind of "inefficient" discussion and low-level conflict anathema to Progressives. According to the prevailing theory of public administration, state and local governments are by nature inefficient; they bring about a fragmentation of authority "presumed to provide conflict, and create disorder and deadlock."[18] Only a single authority and chain of command can swiftly and fully turn political will into reality. But it was the polycentric, "inefficient" system "predicated upon the capacity of mankind for self-government" that was at the heart of the American experiment. In this light, Ostrom argued, "the Wilsonian theory of administration was no less than a counter-revolutionary doctrine."[19] Rooted in French revolutionary Jacobin theories of a general will and the proper powers of the state, Progressive public administration remains backward looking in the radical sense that it would undo centuries of constitutional development, returning us to an era in which the will of the state overrides the rights of persons and communities to govern themselves. Under such conditions, the vaunted claims of "the will of the people" merely serve to further empower a ruling class intent on imposing its own will on individual persons who, separated from their natural communities, are incapable of meaningful resistance to arbitrary power.

Argument of the Book

Our story concerns how Progressive ideology combined with a variety of socioeconomic factors to change, first, the manner in which the Constitution was perceived and applied and, second, the political culture itself, thereby undermining the constitutional morality without producing a corresponding change in the text or public meaning of the Constitution. American Progressives operating in a time of increased cultural and economic complexity in effect replaced habits appropriate for a constitution mediating among society's fundamental groups (rooted primarily in geography, ethnicity, religion, and economic activity) with habits appropriate for a constitution commanding the transformation of society to fit the demands of a particular vision of democracy. Being human artifacts, neither constitutional form is perfect. Mediating constitutions may be faulted for their intrinsic inability to address various forms of long-standing inequality and injustice because they respond to underlying cultural trends rather than attempting to instigate them. Commanding constitutions pose the danger of arbitrary action, especially on the part of executive officers responding to the impetus for swift, decisive action and the delegitimation of a constitutional morality of restraint. The central problem, in our view, is that the shift in habits, especially among political actors, has created conflict between the public meaning of the American Constitution and operational behaviors, undermining the efficacy and even legitimacy of the constitutional system.

Views among lawyers and political scientists concerning the nature and purpose of constitutionalism have changed dramatically over the last century. As evidence, one may consider the contrasting views of Carl J. Friedrich, the mid-twentieth-century constitutional scholar, and John Rawls, whose *A Theory of Justice* appeared near the end of Friedrich's career. Friedrich, a supporter of positive rights and other Progressive constitutional innovations, nonetheless continued to view constitutions themselves as "rules of the game" intended to restrain state power.[20] In contrast, Rawls began his *Theory of Justice* with an explication of justice as fairness, a combination goal and defining condition requiring political principles (such as the maximin principle) and constitutional structures (the veil of ignorance) intended to produce a society characterized by substantive equality.[21] That Rawls's paradigm continues to rule mainstream constitutional discourse may be seen in the use made of the veil of ignorance by the libertarian Richard Epstein. Epstein presents this veil as a constitutional principle ensuring fair (that is, disinterested) deliberations and a fair, disinterested constitution.[22] Meanwhile, in an overtly transformative but still Rawlsian vein, Cass Sunstein argues that constitutions must "create the conditions for a well-functioning democratic order." Constitutions will achieve this substantive goal, Sunstein argues, by transforming society in accordance with an "anticaste principle" and restructuring various opinion-forming groups to ensure diversity of rational viewpoints.[23]

The older conception of constitutions as frames of government and rules of the game has not regained favor even as transformative constitutional governments fail in numerous developing nations. In part this results from the now-prevalent view of laws and constitutions as by nature tools for shaping society in accordance with some vision of the common good. The change has not been, as some positivists argue, a delinking of law from morality. From the reputedly medieval notion that law, properly understood, includes only governmental rules meeting the demands of a higher, natural law, we have moved the relatively short distance to the conviction among both lawyers and political scientists that laws are expressions of the will of the state that must be justified by their utility in achieving results wise, Progressive scholars and jurists deem substantively just. The most important change in this realm has been the move from a procedural vision emphasizing the goods of peace, order, and the flourishing of social groups to an ideological concern for a specific, democratic political and social order.

In responding to the contemporary understanding of constitutionalism and law we look to both the effects and the intrinsic natures of law and constitutions in their substantive and procedural modes.

Chapter 1 begins by asking why we value the rule of law. Praised by all save those few who see law as intrinsically rooted in forms of oppression (one thinks, here, of the critical legal studies movement), the rule of law remains contested as to its nature and purposes. Taking account of—without rehashing—long-standing positivist/natural law debates, we build on the increasing recognition of law as by nature connected with moral claims and goals. We question both the neutrality of Rawlsian public reason and the connection between the contemporary civic republican pursuit of justice and its impact upon law. The rule of law, we argue, is a form of social order necessary for a civilized common life and necessary though not sufficient for establishing ordered liberty. Law is intrinsically connected with a procedural morality that recognizes the need for predictability if people are to lead decent lives, however defined. By nature, it cabins tyrannical impulses through its requirement of consistency and publication. It is not, however, infinitely malleable or capable of being used as a tool for whatever set of ends lawmakers may desire. In particular, acts of true evil are not conducive to lawlike implementation.

Chapter 2 applies this understanding of law to the "higher law" of a constitution. We argue that constitutions, as laws, are best adapted to setting general, largely procedural rules for mediation among a society's fundamental associations. We trace the very different historical, institutional, and cultural roots of mediating and commanding constitutions, showing the significant and deep conflicts among the habits and beliefs of each to the other.

Chapter 3 is a discussion of the U.S. Constitution as understood by its drafters. With special attention to arguments presented in *The Federalist*, we show the extent to which the Framers aimed to address a relatively limited set of "national" problems while seeking to prevent tyranny, principally through the separation of powers. Intended to fit the preexisting culture and people, the Constitution was set up to be a somewhat mechanical structure sitting atop more organic, preexisting states and other associations. The use of auxiliary precautions (checks and balances) as a means of maintaining the separation of powers was important, in this light, not only for itself but as an indicator of the central role of that very structural separation so disliked by the Constitution's later, Progressive detractors.

Chapter 4 deals with changes in ideology and administrative theory and the effects of these changes on constitutional morality. We examine a number of thinkers, including Woodrow Wilson and Herbert Croly, to show how the Progressive program of change and expansion of federal power emphasized the separation of politics from administration, with democratic accountability provided through centralization of authority in the president. The goal was greater efficiency and speed in implementing policy, with democratic input provided through direct presidential action and through participation in bureaucratic rulemaking, rather than open politics in the legislative branch.

Chapter 5 details the institutional and the operational changes wrought in our constitutional system under the influence of Progressivism. We focus on Wilson as the intellectual and practical godfather of reforms sought and implemented throughout the twentieth century. Central to the Progressive transformation, we argue, has been a critique of the Framers as antidemocratic figures whose separation of powers was useful only for protecting entrenched elites. While most commentators have focused on industrialization and communications as central to the changes wrought in the last century, we point out the importance of more specifically political trends, especially the felt need for a strong, nationally unifying president. The latter development was made possible and furthered by a decreasing concern with arbitrary and capricious rule, as Progressives emphasized democratic accountability instead of formal structures to prevent tyranny.

Chapter 6 sets out the governing characteristics of our new constitutional dispensation. The vast delegation by Congress of its power and authority to the president and the federal courts' increasing use of their decisions to issue policy directives to governmental organizations have produced a structure in which all branches share in the lawmaking power. This clear violation of constitutional separation of powers is called for under the new, partially formed constitutional morality. It undermines the rule of law while creating, depending upon, and fostering the rule of quasi-law. The various decrees of our presidents, whether termed executive orders, legislative signing statements, or waivers to provisions of various statutes, constitute orders lacking not just the pedigree of law, but also important, defining elements including predictability and consistency over time. When combined with judicial decisions lacking predictability, consistency, and legal pedigree, the result is a system dominated by judges and executive officers acting arbitrarily in pursuit of their own political ends even as they are shielded from effective political pressure. In practice as well as in theory, such a system lacks law and has a clear tendency toward further breakdown of the rules and procedures essential to limited, free government.

The conclusion emphasizes weaknesses of the new constitutional dispensation. In particular, it seems clear that the rule of quasi-law is not producing the promised society of individuals free to pursue their own goods in a system of justice and security. Instead, American society is, in essence, "clumping" in highly politicized fashion, with various interest groups defined by racial, ideological, and economic connections vying for governmental largesse. This is the very situation that has existed in various postcolonial nations for some decades. It does not end well, but in a vicious cycle of violence and poverty, as the institutions of civil society and governmental self-control break down. We can choose to continue on this path, or we can work to reestablish more natural relations. This second option would require, at the federal level, less of everything.

We insist throughout the book that centralized government can only do so much through law—far less than it currently attempts to accomplish. This is no call for uniform national libertarianism; far from it. What is required is a retrenchment of the federal government into a much smaller but more detailed and legalistic form that allows more actions to be taken by other institutions, be they states, localities, or associations within civil society. Progressives are correct that a vast national administrative state requires experts who act with discretion. If we want the rule of law we cannot have such a state. To shrink and tame the state requires not revolution but insistence that the federal government do only what it can do within the rule of law, and cede to lower levels of government or to civil society tasks not amenable to law.

We are not primarily concerned with providing any plan of action. What is most necessary is a rethinking of why we value the rule of law and how it demands a return to constitutional forms. Only a return to a pluralistic form of thinking can return to us power that is ruled by law. Were such a return to take place, there would be numerous struggles and policy differences. The tools to be used would be those in the Constitution that currently are ignored—principally the presidential veto, the lawmaking power (currently eschewed in favor of the unconstitutional power of delegation), and the power to impeach and remove from office those who violate their constitutional duties. The direction of reform would be toward clarity, adherence to forms and procedures, and abandonment of grand schemes of national greatness, uniformity, and efficiency in favor of administrative decentralization.

1

The Rule of Law

WHAT IS THE RULE OF LAW? Why is it of value? We seek to reestablish the importance of long-held, relatively simple answers to these questions: the rule of law is governance according to settled norms; it is valuable because it establishes predictable order, allowing for the pursuit of higher political ends as well as basic human flourishing. We argue for these answers because we are convinced they are true, and because these old truths, while not quite forgotten, have been overshadowed by ideological concerns destructive to law and the ends it by nature serves.

For over two hundred years debates have raged in the United States over what ends laws should serve and whether law should be subordinated or reshaped to better serve higher ends outside itself. In the process, the value of law and especially the virtue of law-abidingness have been called into question. Clearly not the highest of human goods, law-abidingness remains a virtue, particularly among rulers, that is necessary for social life. It restricts the use of force, especially among the powerful, and allows people to plan their activities in accordance with predictable rules, restrictions, and conduct on the part of their fellows.

Unfortunately, law-abidingness has been undermined severely by a general focus on abstract arguments concerning higher goods—especially justice, variously defined. We do not deny the importance of such concerns. But it seems clear that a widespread, narrow focus on them has led to a general decline in understanding of the importance of procedural norms—for example, that bad or unwise laws should be changed through legitimate, accepted means rather than simply or selectively ignored by subjects and/or rulers.

We approach our task through a critique of contemporary disagreements concerning the morality of law as a practice and an institution. It is important, in our view, to remember that laws are normative by nature in that they establish standards of conduct giving us reasons to deem some human actions worthy of sanction and blame. Recognizing this, we can see that laws, whether well or ill made, and whether aimed at good or bad ends, are concerned with, while not themselves constituting, morality. Laws are tools that, depending on how made, can well or ill serve lawmakers' ends. This does not mean that whatever the lawmaker wills is good. Rather, even modern positivists, along with their civic republican or communitarian critics and more traditional, natural law thinkers, all hold that social norms and customary procedures by nature shape the law and people's judgment of particular laws.

That said, and in opposition to much contemporary legal theory,[1] law is by nature limited in its capacity to direct and define virtue—including the virtue of justice. It is not the source of higher-order human goods. It must grow from and serve more concrete social ends, especially that humble form of justice by which courts vindicate the reasonable expectations of parties to particular disputes. Institutionalized as the rule of law, the normative standards we call laws are essential to social order and the possibility of a good life for persons and communities. Subjugated to particular, definitive ends, they may become tools of oppression, though, as we shall argue, the tool becomes less useful and more problematic as the ends become more pervasive and morally corrupt.

"A Government of Laws, Not of Men"

By the time John Adams included this phrase in the Massachusetts Constitution of 1780, its truth and meaning had been deeply embedded in Anglo-American tradition for centuries. The struggle to bring powerful figures under law had been bloody and hard fought. It had taken the form of armed rebellion on many occasions, not least important on the field at Runnymede in 1215, where the English barons won from King John his agreement to rules binding his actions—most especially that "[n]o freeman shall be taken or imprisoned, or disseized, or outlawed, or banished, or any ways destroyed, nor will we pass upon him, nor will we send upon him, unless by the lawful judgment of his peers, or by the law of the land."[2] From now on, Magna Carta declared, English monarchs would take action against their free subjects only as provided by law or procedures sanctioned by law and customary usage.

For many centuries, monarchs had presented themselves as the source of law. Claiming to be divine or semidivine, ancient rulers also claimed to create order out of chaos through their own will.[3] As creators of law, monarchs could not be bound by it. Indeed, monarchs could not be bound even by their promises, for they answered only to their own judgment of what was right. Thus, as late as the seventeenth and eighteenth centuries, the French king could renounce important public promises such as the Treaty of Nantes, which had granted toleration to French Protestants, and take back the charters he had granted (often at a high price) to municipalities guaranteeing them rights of self-government.[4] Any restraint on the king's power was an act of purely voluntary *self*-restraint, the argument went, and such a gift might be rescinded at will. Resistance was real and at times heated, but the theory of sovereignty was backed by force of arms.

In England, too, monarchs claimed to be above law. But, in England at least, monarchs slowly and haltingly were brought under law, as much through the growth of traditions of legal and political practice as through grand military contests. Monarchs in England were less able than their French counterparts to assert their wills, in part because they lacked sufficient independent revenue and standing armies. They were not able to overawe completely their more powerful subjects, and were in a variety of ways dependent on these subjects' loyalty. Thus, English monarchs over time came to be bound by a variety of legal processes restricting the means by which they could work to achieve their goals. If an English monarch wanted to strip a town's rights to self-government, for example, he or she had to initiate a legal proceeding and show wrongdoing or a lack of actual authority on the part of the town. And, as King James II found out, to act arbitrarily in these proceedings was to foment opposition among his own judges, even helping spawn rebellion.[5]

Other factors were involved as well—from the abiding power of the militia and baronial rights in England to the multiplicity of institutions and forms of law that continued to exercise power and authority there. Moreover, there were bloody conflicts and multiple instances of royal overreach in England as well as on the continent. But, in the hands of jurists such as Edward Coke, Magna Carta and the rule of law became an effective basis for resistance to arbitrary rule that survived civil war, suspensions of parliamentary power, and revolution itself. The eventual result was an odd and muted form of parliamentary supremacy; Parliament gained the power to make, alter, and remake the law, but still was bound to abide by it, especially as embodied in customs rooted in a common vision of the English constitution and the virtues demanded thereby.[6]

The Good of Order

In answering the question "What is the rule of law?" we have gone far toward answering its companion question, "Why is the rule of law valuable?" Even a cursory review of the relevant history demonstrates that rulers who are not bound by law may act in an arbitrary manner. Without the rule of law, those who are ruled live at the whim and caprice of a powerful person or group who may be virtuous and kind, but then again may not, and in any event will at times act hastily, irrationally, or out of narrow self-interest.

The rule of law limits the ability of willful rulers to impose their desires of the moment as commands to be followed by their subjects. It subordinates the will of particular rulers to settled forms and procedures, thereby providing citizens with knowledge of what they are required and forbidden to do. This knowledge enables people to predict official responses to their actions and plan their lives accordingly.[7]

In this light we may understand the reasoning of the Framers of the American Constitution, who sought a government of separated powers as a means of guarding against arbitrary rule. In *The Federalist*, Publius argues for the constitutional separation of powers by quoting Montesquieu: "When the legislative and executive powers are united in the same person or body . . . there can be no liberty because apprehension may arise lest *the same* monarch or senate should enact tyrannical laws, to *execute* them in a tyrannical manner." Further, if "the power of judging" were "joined with the legislative, the life and liberty of the subject would be exposed to arbitrary control, for the *judge* would then be *the legislator.* Were it joined to the executive power, the judge might behave with all the violence of *an oppressor.*" One who at once writes, interprets, and executes the law is above the law and will do as he or she wishes.[8]

Montesquieu (and following him Publius) saw the rule of law as a necessary condition for political liberty. Montesquieu stated that the liberty of the citizen is "a tranquility of mind arising from the opinion each person has of his safety," which can be found "only where there is no abuse of power." People ruled by a government with consolidated powers could never enjoy the "tranquility of mind" that is liberty because they would live under a constant apprehension of being subject to oppressive laws. Lacking stability and predictability in their lives, the people would be unable to plan with confidence; their fear of arbitrary treatment would immobilize them, leading them to seek order at all costs, whether through submission or revolution. Liberty cannot find root under such circumstances.

The rule of law alone is not sufficient to establish or maintain liberty. Rulers may promulgate oppressive laws.[9] But the rule of law remains necessary for liberty; it provides the first, fundamental social good—order—without which no decent, let alone free society can long exist.[10] Thomas Hobbes began his justification of an all-powerful sovereign in *Leviathan* with a dystopian vision of the state of nature as a war of all against all for a compelling rhetorical reason: he knew that people naturally recognize the hellish nature of a world with no order, in which one always must fear the actions of strangers or even of one's fellows. One need not accept Hobbes's portrayal of our natural state or his absolutist conclusions to see the necessity of order for any common life.

Even under absolute monarchs there may be a kind of order. It is in the ruler's own interest to give the subjects predictable rules. But a monarch (or legislature, or even people) that recognizes no superior will violate the rules out of passion, self-interest, or mere caprice, and the more this happens, the less predictability, order, and possibility for a decent life there will be in that society. The rule of law, on the other hand, provides a publicly known standard of conduct for rulers, binding them to act in a predictable manner.

The question arises at this stage whether the rule of law may not, under certain circumstances, actually undermine justice. That is, we must ask whether anarchy, or at least great conflict, may not be better than acceptance of a society ruled by bad law. But it is this overidentification of law with its content that has undermined our understanding and appreciation of the rule of law and its benefits. No legal system is perfect—either perfectly just or perfectly ordered. And any legal system, to the extent it is a system of law, will contain some element of justice and order.

At times citizens must face the question whether the system under which they live has sufficient justice to be worthy of their allegiance. Unfortunately, contemporary theories of law make this question more salient, common, and dangerous by stripping away people's understanding of the inherent, normative importance of the rule of law and by masking the moral element present in all legal systems, as well as the limits placed on the power of rulers to do evil by the very form of law. This is not an argument against resistance of any kind under any circumstances. It is, rather, an argument that resistance to arbitrary rule requires moves to strengthen law and legal procedures whenever possible, rather than moves to simply tear down what exists or replace one set of rulers or rules with another. This is especially true because those who claim to be seeking justice by rejecting or reshaping the law to accord with their own moral standards in effect place themselves and their supporters above the law, seizing, however benign the intent, arbitrary power.

Law's Morality

Modern theories of law begin with the drive to separate or emphasize the separation between law and morality. If law were merely another word for morality, legal positivists have pointed out, we would not need lawyers or judges. If law is mere morality written into specific rules, then it would seem not to require any specifically legal form of reasoning. It would mean, utilitarian philosopher Jeremy Bentham argued, that there is no *science* of law (and public policy making) that can improve the people's lives; there could be, then, only pointless battles over which theological vision is correct and how it can be imposed on the populace.[11]

The early positivist John Austin famously likened law to the command of an armed robber that one hand over one's money, or else. Each, Austin asserted, is a command backed by the threat of violence. Each is effective to the extent the threat is believed and so produces the result desired by the one who commands.[12] But few positivists would go so far in identifying law with power. H. L. A. Hart, for example, noted that the very term *command* includes more than the raw expression of power involved in an order or demand. A command's success depends on the recipients' possession of a habit of obedience and recognition of a hierarchy of authority; a system or rule of law, unlike a particular, isolated demand, is a sophisticated construct of an advanced society.[13] Thus positivism, in its moderate or "soft" form, recognizes the social (and, we will argue, moral) context of a system or rule of law.

Hart saw himself as breaking from the illusions of earlier, especially religion-based natural law theories by seeking merely to understand the nature and functions of law. He described law as a system of primary rules like that against murder and of secondary rules for introducing, modifying, or applying primary rules. Law's purpose? Like any "method of social control" law "consists primarily of general standards of conduct communicated to classes of persons, who are then expected to understand and conform to the rules without further official direction." To achieve its goal of social control, this system must consist of rules that "satisfy certain conditions: they must be intelligible and within the capacity of most to obey, and in general they must not be retrospective."[14] Predictability, for Hart, is a simple matter of efficacy; law cannot function as law without it, and law must function, or there will be chaos.

The need for predictability applies to the validity as well as the content of laws. People must know which commands to follow. Secondary rules—which Hart argued make up a "rule of recognition"—constitute criteria signaling which putative rules to treat as valid laws. Their effectiveness rests on general acceptance that, say, a presidential signature is necessary to make a bill passed by Congress into a law.[15]

The rule of recognition leaves ample room for immoral laws. Nonetheless, Hart argued, even immoral laws should be seen as providing justification for a person's actions. We should not, in Hart's view, formally, legally punish immoral acts, but only specifically illegal acts. Yet this prescription itself points to law's connection with morality: it is "a very precious principle of morality endorsed by most legal systems" that an act's legality is a crucial element in the determination whether to punish it.[16]

Perhaps counterintuitively, Hart had as a central goal maintenance of the superiority of moral over legal judgment. He made this prioritization

clear, for example, in stating that, once laws reach "a certain degree of iniquity" there is "a plain moral obligation to resist them and to withhold obedience."[17] He even welcomed the disintegration of some societies, particularly those "mainly devoted to the cruel persecution of a racial or religious
minority."[18] On Hart's view, the very "principles of legality" are to be
"valued so far only as they contribute to human happiness or other substantive moral aims of the law."[19]

Hart's moral imperative is clear: "[L]aw is not morality; do not let it
supplant morality." But what does this tell us about the moral status or
content of law itself? Despite Hart's concern to distinguish the two, it
remains the case that law and morality for him were intimately associated.
First, Hart recognized that justice is a relevant criterion to be used in eval-
uating laws; "natural justice" or procedural due process for Hart was a necessary means of achieving the legal imperative of treating like cases alike.[20]
Second, while the principles of legality are "compatible with very great
iniquity,"[21] still, "the normal generality of law is desirable not only for reasons of economy but because it will enable individuals to predict the future
and . . . this is a powerful contribution to human liberty and happiness."
Thus, while laws do not necessarily "reproduce . . . [the] demands of
morality,"[22] according to Hart there is "something in the very notion of law
consisting of general rules" that prevents us from treating it as lacking necessary contact with moral principles.[23]

Further, in Hart's schema the rule of law itself is a high, ordering value;
it should guide us in judging the value of particular laws. Rules that fail the
test of generality, for example violating natural justice, fail a test—they are
to be judged flawed because they undermine the legal system. Moreover,
the very existence of the rule of recognition, hence of the rule of law, for
Hart depends on judges recognizing and enforcing among themselves a
"common standard of correct judicial decision." Lacking such a standard
(and it would appear, though Hart never explicitly said so, a recognition by
judges of their moral duty to maintain it),[24] citizens would face "chaos"
amid the loss of consistent judicial orders.[25]

This does not mean that Hart's judges would eschew moral judgment.
He urged judges to use the considerable discretion afforded by the open
texture of law to serve policy ends he deemed just.[26] Where the law does
not dictate a particular outcome, Hart's judge should legislate according
to "his own beliefs and values."[27] We see, then, in Hart's soft positivism a

moral imperative behind the rule of law and moral duties assigned to legal elites.

Autonomy as the Morality of Law

Hart refused to put forward any specifically moral good as the rule of law's proper end. Rather, he argued, the rule of law should be seen as merely allowing a society to establish and maintain the minimum level of peace and stability necessary for members to pursue their own ends while living in common with their fellows. But Hart's demands of law are in fact extensive and normative. In criticizing the claim that some enactments of the Nazi regime were too unjust to be treated as law, Hart opined that, whereas the Germans had allowed positivist views of law to take on a "sinister character," in English history the view that "law is law" went along with the most enlightened "liberal attitudes." In the more enlightened, "truly liberal" English tradition, according to Hart, it was well known that laws ought to be obeyed only on account of such morality as they might possess.[28]

Far from rendering laws self-justifying, then, Hart's theory sets up a very high moral bar for law's legitimacy—though one rooted in a particular (English liberal) set of cultural habits and values. According to Hart, "[T]he use of legal coercion by any society calls for justification as something *prima facie* objectionable to be tolerated only for the sake of some countervailing good." Laws exert power; they not only punish those who violate them, but they also restrain those who obey them. This means that they inflict "a special form of suffering—often very acute—on those whose desires are frustrated by the fear of punishment." That is, Hart held a quintessentially liberal conception of the good as relatively unconstrained autonomy, with this good being dictated by the freedom-loving character of the (English liberal) person.[29]

Hart stated his moral convictions as mere observations, but the result is extremely close, at least, to an argument that human nature demands that law incorporate moral respect for human dignity. For example, Hart reflected that "so deeply embedded in modern man is the principle that *prima facie* human beings are entitled to be treated alike that almost universally where the laws do discriminate by reference to such matters as colour and race, lip-service at least is still widely paid to this principle."[30] In addition, the very separation of law from morality Hart so values is for him a product of social evolution, seemingly inevitable in its basic forms: "the social morality of societies which have reached the state where this can be distinguished from its law, always includes certain obligations and duties, requiring the sacrifice of private inclination or interest which is essential to the survival of any society, so long as men and the world in which they live retain some of their most familiar and obvious characteristics."[31]

Further, Hart argues, without basic rules, for example restricting free use of violence and requiring certain forms of fair dealing, "we should be doubtful of the description of the group as a society, and certain that it could not endure for long." The implication is clear to Hart, including that "in all communities there is a partial overlap in content between legal and moral obligation."[32]

Here Hart points to an important, permanent truth. Because they pre-scribe norms of conduct, laws by nature are concerned with judgments regarding what it is right and what it is wrong to do. We note the common distinction between an act that is *malum in se* (wrong in itself) and one that is merely *malum prohibitum* (wrong only because prohibited). But we would argue that the distinction is habitually overemphasized, including by Hart, and that this places far too many acts in the category of "wrong only because prohibited." We further would point out that the proliferation of actions only *malum prohibitum* is a serious problem for the rule of law.

Take, for example, the homely case of traffic ordinances. It often is said that speeding and even driving on a particular side of the street are acts only *malum prohibitum*. Were the law not there to tell us to drive only seventy miles per hour on the freeway, or to drive on the right-hand side of the street, the reasoning goes, we would be blameless to do otherwise. But such a view ignores or rather atomizes the inevitable social context of human action and so misconstrues the source and functioning of law. Since the demise of the energy-conservation-minded fifty-five-mile-per-hour speed limit, such rules are justified on grounds of public safety; they repre-sent and seek to concretize the legislature's judgment regarding the max-imum safe speed in a given area. To exceed the speed limit, then, is to drive at a speed that increases the chances of injury or death by a degree suffi-cient, in the legislature's judgment, to justify deterrence and punishment. Likewise, to drive on the left-hand side of the street, once a norm has been established otherwise, is to act wrongfully by needlessly and knowingly endangering oneself and others.

Of course, the legislature's judgment may be wrong, or influenced by inappropriate factors, and such circumstances lead to increased incidence of lawbreaking and decreased respect for law in general. These effects are especially problematic in the area of complex regulatory schemes. Regulations at least claim to be serving common ends worthy of support by the citizenry. To the extent the reasoning or ends sought are opaque or lacking, law becomes mere force, followed only when and to the extent necessary to avoid sanctions exceeding the savings realized from violation.[33] The more such regulations exist, the greater the diminution of habits of obedience rooted in general acceptance of the legitimacy of the rules and, ultimately, the regime. Metaphysics hardly are directly implicated in determinations of appropriate speed limits. Nonetheless, normative judgments are involved, and the more laws violate generally accepted, customary standards of what is just and in keeping with the common good (for example, necessary for reasonably safe streets), the greater the problem for law's legitimacy.

The need for laws to be seen as legitimate—in general accord with a society's basic underlying norms—is permanent. It reflects a fact of human nature, namely, that general consensus and cooperation is necessary for law-abidingness and simple order to survive over time. It is the basis for law's legitimacy that has changed over time. Eschewing previous grounding for law in religion or metaphysical understandings, custom, and tradition (we will return to these groundings later in this chapter), positivists look to reason itself as law's proper basis. But what form shall this reason take, and toward what goals is it to be aimed?

Liberal "Common Sense"

Hart recognized that law brings order, and that order is a positive good in all societies. Nonetheless, because Hart refused to posit a more concrete, substantive end, he claimed to maintain a separation between law and morality. That the life of individual choice and pursuit of self-chosen goods is a kind of good life, requiring specific social structures and both demanding and ruling out many kinds of activities, has been pointed out many times.[34]

As important, all such theories require that people act with a kind of virtue, such as, for example, emotional independence.[35] Apparently for Hart, not just Nazis but Germans more generally lacked the virtue necessary for liberty, giving legal positivism a "sinister quality" through their own vice. Moreover, the virtue necessary for liberalism cannot be merely individual; it requires social expression and social institutions, including some corresponding version of the rule of law.

To prioritize individual autonomy is to posit a common good and demand that society be structured for its promotion. We see this, for example, in modern family law, which has replaced the older conception of marriage as conferring a generally permanent status on all parties, encompassing a host of political, social, and economic rights, with a sub-contractual relationship among individuals. Modern marriage law allows either spouse to secure a unilateral divorce, prioritizing the autonomy of the departing spouse over concerns for social stability and the potential desire of the other spouse and any children for community and stability.[36]

Autonomy in the sense of self-actualization and self-definition is taken as a metaphysical highest good (or right), ordering other, lesser goods or rights. In the oft-quoted words of Justice Anthony Kennedy, "At the heart of liberty is the right to define one's own concept of existence, of meaning, of the universe, and of the mystery of human life."[37] We can and should, on this view, define and choose the nature and meaning of our own existence. And the Constitution must uphold this choice making by forbidding laws that might intrude thereon.[38] True or not, this presumption of the moral primacy of individual choice has led most modern theorists into a felt necessity to find a way to speak in terms of legal purpose without descending into the particulars of any specific moral theory. Most prominent among such attempts has been that of the philosopher John Rawls.

Rawls's most powerful contribution here is his notion of an "overlapping consensus" intended to maintain political order with moral diversity. It is an attempt to maintain a system in which "citizens, who remain deeply divided on religious, philosophical, and moral doctrines, can still maintain a just and stable democratic society." Rawls's theory was intended for liberal democratic societies, and such societies depend for their existence on maintenance of shared values. But the particular values of particular people vary, according to Rawls, and so democratic stability requires that people's deeper, more personal values be prevented from undermining the public consensus in favor of the liberal democratic regime.[39]

When important political issues are under discussion, according to Rawls, we all must use "public reason"—a thin, limited conception of the purposes of society and public life, in essence a lowest-common-denominator morality, wrapped up with a valuation of human equality and autonomy. Public discussions must be kept free from religious reasons and faith claims, as well as all systemic conceptions of the human good that cannot be explained in terms accessible to people holding different moral values.[40] Consensus, impossible to obtain where any important, constitutive beliefs are concerned, for Rawls nonetheless provides the sole legitimate basis for determinations of public policy and justice. Thus, the consensus must be a thin one, relating only to rather abstract goals, but also a very stringent one, ruling out forms of argument and expressions of belief in the political arena that go beyond a kind of "common sense" for a liberal democratic people.

Rawlsian public reason is a formalized version of values and assumptions that have lain deep within liberalism for some time; it sums up rather than serves as a source of liberal individualism.[41] In jurisprudence the influence of this form of reasoning is clear in Supreme Court decisions concerning "substantive due process." According to these decisions, laws, to be constitutional, must not be "arbitrary and capricious"; they must be supported by a "reasonable" legal justification. Moreover, these laws must protect our "fundamental rights." That is, constitutional laws are those that accomplish "reasonable" ends while imposing so little on individual moral choice that all rational citizens would say they are consistent with their own freedom and equality.[42]

It has been argued that the logic of substantive due process is "vacuous as a standard for devising any actual, concrete public order." Assuming the goodness of liberal democracy as defined and upheld in terms of mere overlapping consensus, the thin strictures of public reason cannot provide workable criteria by which to judge concrete burdens on individual liberty legitimate or illegitimate. "Any rational principle that *could* be forwarded as a valid *specific* limitation of autonomy" would be dismissed as a comprehensive, idiosyncratic view of what is good or bad. That is, any genuine reason sufficient to motivate any actual person would violate the demands of public reason.[43]

Nonetheless, overlapping consensus is, for Rawls, the fundamental good, the very raison d'être, of liberal democracy. And this means that to question the validity of public reason, with all its restrictions on public discourse, is to question the legitimacy of diversity, of a variety of viewpoints and lifestyles, and of liberal democracy itself. To question public reason, then, is impliedly to reject common sense as one pursues imposition of one's own narrow, irrational beliefs on others. One either accepts the consensus, with all its limitations on one's formulation and expression of the reasons for one's policy preferences, or one secedes, in essence, from full, legitimate participation in public life.

Public reason marginalizes critics by naming them would-be oppressors, lacking the virtue to lead autonomous lives and even lacking common sense, marking them out as extremists. But the theory itself is so self-referential as to be highly fragile in the face of genuine opposition. A public philosophy that demands we surrender our fundamental attachments, or at least give up reasoning in public by their lights, denies the importance of the very choices it promotes. Such a philosophy is at war with important and lasting human inclinations. It also seems to use law as a tool for policy ends outside itself. In this, liberal proceduralism serves as a prelude to a more robust, civic republican view of law as the servant of justice defined as pursuit of a "just" society.

The Civic Republican Critique and Program

Rawls's theories and the legal practices they justified spawned spirited debate during the latter part of the twentieth century. In particular, "civic republicans" (sometimes dubbed "communitarians" because of their insistence that persons find fulfillment only in communities) criticized Rawls for legitimizing a merely "procedural republic" treating people as individual monads lacking any substantive communal connections. The charge, made perhaps most powerfully by Michael Sandel, was that procedural neutrality undermines substantive discussion of the needs of actual, embedded (or "encumbered") selves in pursuing good lives. The result, on this view, is a morally vacuous state that empties law and political society of meaning and virtue.

Civic republicanism is a response to what might be termed the "creative destruction" of liberal proceduralism. Claiming to be morally neutral, proceduralism actually used law, conceived in positivist terms, to rearrange society, addressing injustices in public, private, and social life by reconstructing institutions and relationships to make them friendlier toward individual autonomy. Under the procedural republic (that is, during the decades-long reign of procedural liberalism—especially during the latter half of the twentieth century), judges abandoned their previous vocation of applying the law consistently so as to vindicate the reasonable expectations of the parties. Instead, these judges sought to "do" justice by maximizing individual autonomy, using law, or at least legal power, to build a more individualistic society. Civic republicans do not so much reject this practice as seek to make judges go farther; they would have judges demand justice of the parties, and of the wider society, by reinterpreting both law and society in a manner designed to bring forth civic virtue.

Sandel finds much to praise in Rawls's philosophy, understood in terms of egalitarian and solidarity-enhancing policy goals. In particular, he sees Rawlsian rejection of classical liberal economic arguments as fostering the civic virtue of solidarity.[44] But Sandel rejects Rawlsian public reason as incompatible with progress toward a truly just society: "To achieve a just society we have to reason together about the meaning of the good life, and to create a public culture hospitable to the disagreements that will inevitably arise." Sandel seeks to forge institutions, beliefs, and practices pushing us to argue over the justice of everything from financial bailouts to surrogate motherhood to same-sex marriage, and to determine, as a nation, how to shape society so as to pursue justice in our treatment of such issues. Justice, on Sandel's reading, is the crucial, architectonic social virtue; it "is not only about the right way to distribute things. It is also about the right way to value things."[45] Accordingly, Sandel seeks policy changes such as mandatory national service to cultivate concern for the common good and increased taxes to fund the building of museums and other "infrastructure of civic life."[46] At least as important, however, is his view of law as by nature a tool for teaching justice and restructuring society to both teach justice and itself become more just.

Rather than "civic republicanism" it might be more accurate to term Sandel's preferred mode of public life "juridical democracy." Sandel wants to bring an increasing number of issues and institutions before the bar of both public opinion and, more powerfully, the courts, to determine whether they are just. In this, as with its procedural republican predecessor, juridical democracy brings together rather than creates legal practices and latent opinions among our political elites; that is, Sandel already can point to a number of examples of how his preferred approach is being taken.

One case in point is that of Casey Martin, a golfer whose circulatory disorder makes walking significant distances painful and potentially harmful. Martin sought to become a professional golfer but was stymied by the fact that the Professional Golfers Association (PGA) did not allow the use of golf carts in top professional tournaments. As Sandel relates the story, Martin sued under the Americans with Disabilities Act (ADA), which "required reasonable accommodations for people with disabilities, provided the change did not 'fundamentally alter the nature' of the activity."[47] Martin won his suit,[48] though not many tournaments. What is noteworthy for our purposes is Sandel's, and the Supreme Court's, view of judges' role in such disputes.

Sandel criticizes Justice Antonin Scalia for objecting to the court's consideration of the question "Is someone riding around a golf course from shot to shot *really* a golfer?" Scalia in Sandel's view painted the question as both beneath the court's dignity and beyond its members' expertise. According to Sandel the golf cart case raises an essential, Aristotelian issue of justice; Martin's right to a golf cart depended on a court determination that "the essential nature of the activity in question" did not, in fact, require walking from shot to shot. The Aristotles in robes were to answer the question "Was walking the course essential to golf, or merely incidental?"[49]

One need not agree with Scalia that rules of games are inherently arbitrary to note the discretionary power exercised by a court deciding which rules are arbitrary and which are essential to a game. Martin's lawsuit did in some sense hinge on the "essence" of golf in that his right to use a golf cart over the objections of the organization in charge of meaningful tournaments depended on a finding that walking would not fundamentally alter the game. What is noteworthy is that the court chose to analyze on its own the ingredients making up the game of golf, weighing the importance of each in determining the game's "essence." Not the organization, not the members of the profession, and not the customary practice within the profession, but the court would decide. Indeed, on Sandel's view, those golfers insisting on the need for walking were attempting to portray the game as more physically demanding than it is so as to enhance their own honor at the expense of those, like Martin, who are capable of swinging a club, but not walking the course.[50]

Our point is this: Sandel is supporting the increasingly common practice by which judges determine for the public, as a whole and as members of various communities, what is just—not merely what is legal, or what is reasonable to expect given what the law requires, but what is "simply" just. Sandel demands that law be seen as a vehicle for justice, rather than as a normative tool for the settling of disputes. In this, civic republicans and their juridical democracy actually develop, rather than contradict, procedural liberalism. In both cases, law is seen as a tool for rearranging society to make it more just. But where Rawlsian, procedural liberalism posited the thin good of individual autonomy as the essence of justice, Sandel demands much more from judges.

Rejecting liberal tolerance as a highest good, Sandel instead demands that all people "engage" and debate the nature of justice or "the right thing to do" in all important areas of life. And the ultimate forum for such debates is the courts.[51] Courts become the final arbiters of the just in Sandel's democracy because they settle disputes not by (as in previous eras) accepting legal, customary, or professional definitions but by determining the nature of essential institutions and activities on their own. Intermediary institutions like the PGA receive no deference in determining the nature of the game, and the same goes for other institutions and most definitely for common social practice.

In a book written before the Supreme Court decision in *Obergefell v. Hodges*[52] requiring all states to issue marriage licenses to same-sex couples, Sandel applies the logic of the Casey Martin controversy to that issue. Here, too, he demands that judges determine the essence of a social institution (the family) and reshape law and social practice to fit and support their determination. Sandel praises a Massachusetts Supreme Court decision supporting same-sex marriage.[53] In that case the state Supreme Court examined rival explanations of marriage's essence to determine which was most plausible under current practice. The law's language, the drafters' intent, and the people's expectations as determined by public pronouncements and continuity of practice were subordinated as legal reasons to juridical democracy, in which courts exercise a logic of their own, bound only by their putatively philosophical understanding of essences.

This is no brief against same-sex unions. We have nothing to say here concerning the underlying issue itself.[54] Our concern is only to point out the conception of law and courts implicit in this decision, and Sandel's positive analysis thereof.

According to Sandel, the essential function of judges is to "argue rationally about the meaning and purpose of morally contested social institutions."[55] This preempts crucial questions concerning who should be determining the fundamental nature of a practice and who should determine the distribution of rights and responsibilities. It is unclear to us what special qualifications judges (or legal academics) have for engaging in philosophical analysis of social institutions or how privileging such analysis helps people, especially those without the money or sufficiently interesting disputes to attract elite support, in addressing the concrete problems of their lives. In addition, by forcing social issues into court, Sandel's preferred mode of juridical discourse takes them out of the hands of the public in their various communities, putting them within the power of a clerisy with values and attachments divorced from (even if "more progressive than") those of the people whose lives are to be reshaped and in whose name democratic governments exercise power.

The Nature of Law and Justice

It is ironic that Sandel places such emphasis on the determination of essences, given his open hostility toward the tradition of thought Aristotle did so much to shape, that of natural law. As Sandel puts it, "[W]ith the advent of modern science, nature ceased to be seen as a meaningful order. Instead, it came to be understood mechanistically, governed by laws of physics. To explain natural phenomena in terms of purposes, meanings, and ends was now considered naïve and anthropomorphic." Sandel here goes so far as to quote Winnie-the-Pooh, that innocent from children's stories, as the model of natural law thinking.[56]

Civic republicans and positivists both insist on the distinction between law and morality in significant measure to disassociate themselves from what many see as the discredited bases and implications of natural law. Natural law is rooted in assumptions about the nature of reality (in particular the view that "nature has a meaningful order") that some see as having been disproved by modern science.[57] At least as important, however, natural law is closely associated in the academic mind with religion, and Christianity in particular.

Natural law thinking, rooted in the philosophy of Aristotle and identified (too closely) with Christian thinkers like Thomas Aquinas, rests on the view that there is an abiding, objective order to reality, rendering some actions good or bad, just or unjust. On this view there are natural standards of excellence or virtue that all of us can recognize, provided we are raised with the habits necessary to think clearly and are careful to use these capacities as we ought.[58] People, being rational, are capable of recognizing (though not predestined to recognize) the structure of reality and, within limits, to guide their conduct in accordance with that structure. Law, also a product of reason, by nature is intended to help us move toward our good. Law serves its natural function, moving toward its proper end, when it furthers the common good, in particular by encouraging virtue and discouraging vice.[59]

The modern concern is that natural law's recognition of an objective, common good leads its adherents to insist that government dictate a specific code of conduct, punishing all deviations from that code. The result, for natural law's critics, is doubly wrong. The good sought is not necessarily good, and its pursuit necessarily entails violation of personal privacy as it demands strict religious observance, sexual morality, and the like.[60]

Like all substantive goals, natural law conceptions of the common good may lead to overbearing moral, political, and legal demands. But history provides a plethora of examples of tyranny, instituted for reasons ranging from personal power to ideological belief; the decline of any public role for religion—the traditional but not the only grounding of natural law—has not produced any clear, concomitant decline in instances of oppression and other forms of evil. Moreover, nothing in the natural law conception points to the necessity or even approval of any iron theocratic code demanding specific human conduct.

Opinions appear to differ widely on the question of whether law itself is moral. One might caricature the debate over law's morality as pitting the view that "an unjust law is no law at all"[61] against the view of law as power. Rather than dismissing imperfection as "not law," however, natural law, even in its most overtly religious formulation, recognizes a spectrum of just to unjust law as well as grounds for judgment regarding how citizens, lawmakers, and judges ought to treat orders given by their political leaders.

Natural law, even in its overtly Christian mode, is neither so rigid nor so confident in law's power to produce virtue as its critics seem to believe. Here we should look more closely at what Aquinas actually wrote about law and its relationship with justice. In addition to asserting that "an unjust law is no law at all," Aquinas quoted Augustine in stating, "[T]hat which is not just *seems to be* no law at all."[62] As Aquinas explained, "[T]he force of a law depends on the extent of its justice."[63] That is, law is not simply just or unjust, law or not law, but rather a human construct with more or less justice, hence more or less moral force. Thus, "every human law has just so much of the nature of law, as it is derived from the law of nature."[64] Law's nature is just, that is, in accord with the nature of our existence, but law's nature can be diluted by elements that are unjust because they are derived from improper assumptions or goals.

Even laws that are absolutely unjust still may bind a person's conscience, according to Aquinas, because each person has a duty to act in a just manner in regard to the social ends of a system of law. Disobedience may be illicit, should the possibility of scandal or tumult be too great.[65] Anarchy may be better than the rule of an irrational, murderous tyrant, but we have no right to throw our society into chaos out of a mere disagreement over what law may be best under given circumstances.

As not all "bad" laws should be ignored, so not all possible "good" laws should be promulgated. For example, Aquinas specifically rejected the notion that the state can or should outlaw prostitution. Such laws, Aquinas reasoned (citing Augustine), would succeed only in undermining other important relations and public goods through enforcement efforts and their unintended consequences.[66]

Thus, even in its overtly Christian form, natural law is not a rigid code demanding that human law force all human beings into a straitjacket of specific individual conduct. At its most basic level it is merely the understanding that law is a branch of ethics.[67] This means, to begin with, that there is room within natural law theory for much disagreement over what particular laws are necessary or beneficial to achieve the common good.[68] This is particularly true given the need for legislators to take into account a people's specific circumstances in determining its common good and how to achieve it. Most American jurisdictions today outlaw prostitution; it is easier to police against and is seen as more destructive on its own in our current circumstances than it was during previous eras. As important, judges generally do not, or at least should not, directly apply natural law to particular cases because that law does not provide a direct set of commands or policy goals. Natural law traditionally understood is to inform the decisions of lawmakers. As to judges, until recent decades natural law provided Anglo-American common law with a mode of reasoning rooted in philosophical precepts of "right reason" tied to recognition of certain basic, normative standards derived from the order of reality. The result was not a code aimed at any specific substantive goal, but rather an approach to judging that emphasized maintenance of long-standing norms rooted in historical practice and moral understandings deeply embedded in the broader culture.

Anglo-American Common Law

Early American colonies exhibited open hostility toward lawyers, treating them as mere promoters of destructive litigation.[69] Nevertheless, lawyers entered American public life fairly early on and were important for the practical reason that rules of legal procedure are unavoidably complex. They also were important, however, because law by nature is a system of both rules and customs, infused with moral assumptions and goals requiring broad education and a specific set of professional virtues to understand and apply.

Our courts combine a host of legal forms inherited from English traditions rooted in the medieval era, from royal law, to local law, to the law merchant, to canon law, to equity—the last of which was in theory the monarch's informed conscience.[70] Since American courts combined these forms within a single "common law" system, judges have looked to a variety of sources in determining how a specific case should be decided. Previous decisions, learned treatises, customary practice, and long-accepted maxims all have been used to help craft decisions vindicating the reasonable expectations of disputants. In particular, the dynamic between custom and maxim reflects the integration of historical expectations—rooted in circumstance and practice—with permanent principles stemming from the order of reality, or natural law; it is best understood as historically grounded normative reasoning.

Since the late nineteenth century, American law has been subjected to increasing codification—by which precedents and customs have been reduced to statutory language. Still, its assumptions remain those of common law. The "rules" of common law are not rules as one would find in a statute.

To illustrate, the "rule" requiring that someone suing for damages on a written contract show the presence of consideration (that the promise, say, to deliver shirts was paid for and not a mere gift, about which the disappointed recipient would have no cause to complain) has been with us for centuries. But for most of that time the "rule" requiring consideration never had been specifically laid down as a rule—it had been assumed in a variety of decisions, but never specifically stated in formulaic language.[71]

The common law is not promulgated like a statute; it grows up over time and remains in effect as long as and to the extent that it continues to be "received" or relied upon. The common law cannot be reduced to a system of rules because it "professes . . . to develop and apply principles that have never been committed to any authentic form of words."[72] Still, historically there has been great consistency in the common law, due to its lasting presence and the common understanding of justice as to an important degree resting on the reasonable expectations of the parties. A surprising or innovative decision is in an important sense unjust because it goes against the general expectations of the people. A surprising ruling lacks continuity with previous decisions, thereby undermining predictability, justice, and the rule of law.

Critics of the common law castigated it as a system by which judges "make" law through legal pronouncements based on their own prejudices. Austin famously gave readers the choice between seeing the common law as simple judicial imposition or the "childish fiction" that the common law was "a miraculous something made by nobody, existing . . . from eternity and merely declared from time to time by the judges."[73] Codification always has been spurred by the claim that it would restrict judicial discretion by binding judges to specific, written terms rather than supposedly vague statements subject to manipulation. Quite the contrary, however, common law reasoning bound judges—and the entire legal system—to the underlying cultural assumptions of society and law.

One can find common law's normative reasoning in a variety of maxims, such as "the common law does not favor self-help" or "one should not profit from one's own misdeeds." Again, never "handed down" as "law," such precepts have a long history and real-life implications in court; they may result in a person being convicted of assault when he was "only" trying to take back what was rightfully his, or in a grandson being prevented from collecting on the insurance policy covering the grandfather he murdered, even if there is no statute directing such an outcome.[74] Such maxims, fined and refined over centuries of legal decision making, are not iron directives but prudential guides to judicial conduct meant to embody natural, reasonable assumptions concerning the purpose of law and legal systems, thereby helping produce outcomes in keeping with common understandings and expectations.

Maxims have become objects of lawyerly scorn, particularly since Karl Llewellyn stitched together a table purporting to show a list of contradictory maxims on each side of a set of important questions of statutory construction.[75] The "contradictions" were, in fact, contrived through disingenuous choice and placement of examples. More important, the exercise merely demonstrates a central fact of legal reasoning: its principles are not embodied in simple, definitive rules, but instead must be found through the application of reason to experience in light of tradition.[76]

Lawyers and judges increasingly have rejected common law reasoning and especially its natural law bases. For some, the result has been an attempt to undermine legal maxims, but for most it has been a simple ignorance of these maxims and especially their normative context. The alternative for decades was legal positivism expressed through instrumentalist decisions and interpretations of programmatic statutes. But the results of this alternative mode, and their underlying premises, hardly have been value or norm free, and the civic republican model of legalism has reintroduced overtly moral criteria into legal decision making in a manner overtly hostile to the historical and practical groundings of the rule of law. What is inescapable is the intrinsically moral nature of legal reasoning and legal form.

Legal Virtue

Law, especially when viewed at the systemic level, as the rule of law, contains an irreducible, essential moral element. Law must have an internal, intrinsic virtue if it is to be coherent and serve its function. Unless laws are formed properly, they will not provide predictable order. Moreover, as we argue below, the pursuit of some goals (e.g., mass murder) is insusceptible to law. As important, conceptually, law exists on a spectrum. Laws that are ill formed, failing to provide predictable standards of conduct, and those imposing unjust constraints are corrupt or perverse. Such laws undermine the proper goal of law, which is the maintenance of social order through reasonable rules.[77]

Laws, properly so called, are characterized by a kind of internal virtue or morality.[78] This virtue is efficacious in that it enables laws to serve their ends; it is moral in the sense that it recognizes the dignity of the human person as subject only to rules that have been properly formed and enacted—itself a moral good.[79] And while this internal morality does not necessarily entail specific moral goals, on the whole it shapes law toward external morality as well. Law is, in an important sense, a tool for ends outside itself. But this tool is implicated by morality in that it must have its own internal virtue to serve properly its ends and the more general ends of the rule of law.

Lon Fuller was perhaps the most famous exponent of the view that a legal system, to be such in anything but name, must have an internal morality.[80] For Fuller the rule of law requires that laws be characterized by a set of virtues. But these virtues are distinct from the substantive criteria of morality many believe are embedded in natural law systems. Fuller thus distinguished between a natural law of institutions and procedures and a natural law of substantive aims.

Fuller summarized the procedural law of nature with a list of criteria meant to guide legislators in maintaining the rule of law. The list contains eight canons: rules must be general; they must be promulgated; typically, they must be prospective rather than retroactive; they must be clear; they should be structured so as not to require contradictory actions; they should be structured so as not to require actions that are impossible to perform; they must be relatively constant over time; and they should be structured to maintain congruence between the rules as declared and the rules as administered.[81]

Substantive natural law, on the other hand, sets criteria not necessary to and potentially undermining the rule of law. Such criteria, as Fuller represents them, "might include such diverse assertions as . . . no tax can be just that takes from the citizen more than the equivalent of what government renders to him [or that to] attempt to restrict the free sexual life of responsible adults is a violation of the principle of individual freedom."[82] These criteria (which are not, in fact, necessary components of or derivations from traditional natural law) aim at goods external to the law.

They concern goods toward which, on some views, the lawmaker should exert his or her efforts. They aim at the good of the people (imposing on them only tax rates commensurate with individualized governmental benefits or protecting autonomous choice in sexual conduct), not of the law itself.

The analytic power of Fuller's schema is shown, for example, in Hart's accepting the accuracy of his characterization of the inner morality of law, even while insisting that it is "compatible with very great iniquity."[83] Hart also seized on Fuller's internal/external morality distinction to deny the moral character of the legal enterprise. On Hart's view, Fuller's canons concern only the efficacy of law. According to Hart, the

> crucial objection to the designation of these principles of good legal craftsmanship as morality, in spite of the qualification "inner," is that it perpetrates a confusion between two notions that it is vital to hold apart: the notions of purposive activity and morality. Poisoning is no doubt a purposive activity, and reflections on its purpose may show that it has its internal principles. ("Avoid poisons however lethal if they cause the victim to vomit," or "Avoid poisons however lethal if their shape, color, or size is likely to attract notice.") But to call these principles of the poisoner's art "the morality of poisoning" would simply blur the distinction between the notion of efficiency for a purpose and those final judgments about activities and purposes with which morality in its various forms is concerned.[84]

In answering this charge we would emphasize that not every purposive action is equally valid, or capable of being described in terms of virtue. Hart himself used the term *virtue* to describe judges' best practices in interpreting laws so as to maintain legal principles—that is, of practical excellence in achieving an important, valuable end. Of course, Hart does not apply the term *virtue* in discussing judicial decisions aimed at undermining legal principles. This is in keeping with long-held views, notably Aristotle's, that "not every action or feeling admits of the mean [or virtue]. For the names of some automatically include baseness, e.g. spite, shamelessness, envy, and adultery, theft, murder . . . they themselves, not their excesses or deficiencies, are base."[85]

In part the distinction here concerns our willingness to use the word *good* to describe instrumental skills, competence at some useful function, and/or pursuits as elements of human flourishing. Alasdair MacIntyre asks readers to "[c]ontrast with 'good human being' and 'good shepherd' 'good thief'. Someone can be a good shepherd without being a good human being, but the goods of sheep farming are genuine goods. To be a good thief however is to be a bad human being. In calling someone a good thief we appraise her or his skills. But even if we judge, as we should, that it may be good to possess these skills, we are not at all committed to asserting that it is good to put them to the use to which the thief puts them."[86]

Perhaps the simplest way to untangle the problem with Hart's equation of good poisoning with good law is to point out that we would refer to an accomplished poisoner as cunning or skilled, but not moral or virtuous. One might respond that Aristotle and MacIntyre are making a moral judgment regarding ends being sought. But this is precisely our point. Legal systems are defined by their animating purposes—according to Hart provision of stability so as to enhance autonomous choice and according to Fuller the impartial resolution of disputes on the basis of authoritative precepts.[87] Fuller's point is that law's intrinsic purpose should be recognized as a moral good.

There is much disagreement concerning the nature and even existence of higher common goods, from ordered liberty to religious salvation, to substantive equality, to everlasting peace. Still, there remains an abiding consensus, obscured but not erased in contemporary debates, that the rule of law provides the moral good of order. Without order there can be no society, and hence no social order capable of providing the minimal rules even Hart deemed necessary for meaningful autonomous action. With order the society may be a bad one, but the rule of law will constrain the government's discretion in pursuing its bad aims, providing a modicum of stability and predictability.[88]

The efficacy of law in providing something more than stability is limited, for law by nature is an instrumental, not a final or ultimate good. Law may help a people achieve some (though far from all) of its ends, but only if properly formed. Law is the product of craft—of the concrete, practical virtue of concrete, fallible human beings.[89] As a builder becomes a good or a bad builder by building well or badly,[90] a lawmaker or judge becomes a good or bad lawmaker or law interpreter by developing good or bad habits in the crafting or interpretation of laws. Thus, Fuller noted that his canons are and should be implicit, resting on tacit assumptions rather than rulebook strictures, because good laws rest on sometimes almost instinctive readings of particular circumstances and requirements.[91] The virtue developed through good craftsmanship enables the craftsman to produce better buildings, laws, or interpretations. And those buildings, laws, or interpretations will, because they are better constructed (more just than unjust, more straight than crooked) perform their functions well.[92]

Aristotle saw law as by nature aimed at promoting virtue and suppressing vice, but in addition he recognized that laws fulfill their function better or worse according to how well they are crafted—according to the level of practical virtue used in their making.[93] On the other hand, as Fuller pointed out, at some point a system in which laws are crafted improperly will no longer function. People cannot, for example, obey secret rules, however noble the goals of those rules may be.[94]

Fuller emphasized the moral nature of the predicament faced by citizens of a state in which laws have been formulated in violation of his canons. For him, it was important to point out that people are not obliged to follow excessively ill-formed laws. Ill-formed, "inefficacious" laws fail to establish any rule citizens can know, predict, and follow, and "there can be no rational ground for asserting that a man can have a moral obligation to obey a legal rule that does not exist, or is kept secret from him, or that came into existence only after he had acted."[95] Of course, the issue of whether a particular regime's rules are binding must be addressed in the concrete, and in the context of the just/unjust spectrum on which laws and legal systems fall. But at some point variance from one or more canons will make the regime unlawful because it demands what is not possible (obedience to unknown rules) and so unjustly punishes acts that do not violate known standards of right conduct.

If the rulers fail in their essential "legal" task of establishing efficacious rules for the governance of human action, then the people cannot be expected to follow the resulting dictates, even if these dictates are called laws. Still, so long as governmental commands comport reasonably well with the internal morality of law, the people have a reason, and an obligation, to obey. This is true even if the people disagree with the policies furthered by those laws.[96] Thus, discussion of legal efficacy is moral by nature—it attaches moral authority to rules on account of their concordance with human reason and dignity—but the moral element is restricted to a zone defined by the intrinsic goal of law, namely order.

Evil Laws and Their Limitations

There may be nonlegal reasons for disobeying a law that is truly evil in its intent and/or practice. As Aristotle noted, a decent person, possessed of good character, will be more virtuous than a person whose justice derives solely from being a stickler for the letter of the law because decency may not be captured by the law. Indeed, it may be impossible for a rule to make for true decency in all circumstances, given the diversity of human experience.[97] Moreover, moral enormities, whether genocide in the literal sense or, for example, forcing religious groups to affirmatively violate central commandments of their faith,[98] cannot bind the conscience, even if instituted through well-crafted laws.

The fact that these moral concerns are extralegal limits, rather than eliminates, the moral element in law qua law. Law by nature aims at order, order cabins power, and evil demands that power be given free rein. It has been claimed that the formal requirements of law constitute no restraint on tyranny. On this view a government "can do as it wishes," pursuing bad and even specifically illegal ends so long as it simply changes the law to suit its needs before acting. On this view prevention of tyranny rests on some kind of list of "things that the government or sovereign could not do."[99] But there is significant historical evidence of the conflict between the internal morality of law and the use of law to achieve the most evil of ends.

The legal institution of slavery undermined specific constitutional protections in a manner that endangered the rights of all Americans. The battle over due process rights and their sacrifice by Fugitive Slave laws, which in the end could only be enforced by putting free African Americans at risk of simple kidnapping and being "returned" to slavery without the most basic legal procedures, was a significant cause of the Civil War.[100] Later, under the regime of segregation, it was seen that mere law could not keep African Americans in their subservient position, such that lynching—extralegal murders intended to instill sufficient terror to ensure obedience to unjust laws—were frequent.

Another example is provided by anti-Jewish laws enacted under the National Socialist regime. The Nuremberg laws (1935–1939) regulated Jewish activities in Germany, disenfranchising Jews and forbidding them from having marital relations with non-Jews. These Nazi laws were discriminatory and punitive, but had the form of law; thus their evil effects, while real and deplorable, had limits. Only after Kristallnacht did the Nazis aim specifically to exterminate the Jews, and they did so through nonlegal means. For example, the Star of David decree granted relevant functionaries authority to employ "additional police measures" and "more severe punishments" against Jews at their own discretion. Thus, the Nazis both aimed specifically at the most evil of ends (genocide) and abandoned the use of proper laws at the same time. A Nazi bureaucrat further noted that even the Nuremberg laws posed an impediment to extermination because they were "an annoying reminder that the continuing persecution was 'illegal.'"[101] Law by nature calls those in power to at least a minimal virtue; the call may be ignored, but then so is the law.

Certainly the Nuremberg laws were evil and worthy of resisting. But it is too easy to dismiss as unintended consequences of law the intrinsic qualities of law's internal morality. Internally moral laws provide order and deny to the state the terrorizing power of unpredictability. Explicit statements of abhorrent ends also tend to undermine the regime's legitimacy, putting the people on notice of the moral enormities it intends and making them face the reality of what is being done to their fellows. Moreover, those actually doing the injustice—for example murdering Jews or, in apartheid South Africa, torturing members of the African National Congress—operate more freely if they can do so without laws. Without laws, as one South African apartheid–era security official noted, "there are no lines drawn to mark where you cannot cross. So you can go very low—I mean very low—and it still doesn't hit you." Law constricts evil because people by nature hesitate to cross clear, normative lines even in the midst of committing evil acts.[102]

The Moral Limits of Law

Law by nature is a normative construct and a moral enterprise—both in its internal structure and as its aspiration or goal. Even laws aimed at bad ends, so long as they are characterized by most of the virtues of internal morality, restrict the practice of evil. Thus, those pursuing evil in the end will destroy or nullify the rule of law or fail in their endeavor. What, then, does this tell us of the moral limits of law? For example, it would seem to follow from law's moral nature that an ideal law is one that is perfectly crafted to achieve a perfect end. But can such a law exist? And if we attempt to promulgate and enforce it, would this require tyranny in the application? Moreover, have we not already argued that to reject as not truly law those laws that fail to meet perfectly demands for internal morality, let alone the service of external morality, would be to deny to ourselves the very real good guaranteed by the rule of law—order—and bring chaos?

Here it is necessary to remember that laws are rules. As we have sought to show, rules are not mere tools with no moral import; they are integral parts of the intrinsically moral pursuit of ordered social life. But morality cannot be reduced to rules. As the internal morality of law must in large measure remain a set of unwritten practices, so the proper goals of law often lie outside the scope of rules themselves. We cannot lay down rules that will succeed in forcing men and women to be good. The desired ends are too rooted in intricate and fragile patterns of conduct and social norms to be shaped successfully by the rather blunt instrument of statutory command.[103]

Some legal orders are better and some worse than others. But good, to say nothing of "best" societies are not primarily the product of law. Indeed, too much reliance on law may undermine essential elements of a good society.[104] Even the common law, which, being rooted in custom and the cultural assumptions of a people, is able to capture more of a society's conceptions of virtue and vice, can only take, preserve, and perhaps modestly improve traditions that by nature are imperfect and often include within themselves highly unjust practices. Moreover, while application of common law maxims and ameliorative statutes can fine and refine law to address abuses such as slavery, it is a long, uneven, and unsure process, rendering calls for more precipitous action both likely and understandable.

In part as a response to preexisting injustices, the United States has become much less of a common law country. In keeping with the demands of positivism, we increasingly depend upon statutes to directly command and forbid behavior. And these statutes increasingly are interpreted—as the Constitution itself is interpreted—according to liberal principles that demand maximum autonomy. The result has been a massive change in the assumptions underlying our legal system and, through this, our culture. Vindication of the reasonable expectations of the litigants has been displaced as the goal of adjudication by the promotion of a just society as defined by judges and legal academics.

Law today is seen not as a form of order allowing for justice but as a tool of social transformation. The result is what Bertrand de Jouvenel has termed "ambulatory law," that is, law that follows the will of the lawmakers and is aimed at molding society to be more just, as defined by those with power.[105] Even were lawmakers correct in their assumptions regarding what is just, however, law as power undermines law; it destroys the predictability and even the legitimacy of law by making it a battleground of ideology, deemed just or unjust according to the preferences or external morality of those who make it. Under such circumstances, law cannot inspire a habit of acceptance, which can be forfeited in extreme circumstances. Instead, law increasingly will rely for its efficacy on policy arguments (with which many may disagree) and force. Those who seek to use the state to achieve their ends may be willing to sacrifice order and predictability for efficient pursuit of their goals. Indeed, our argument rests on showing that this is precisely what has happened in the United States, particularly over the course of the twentieth century. But the end result is construction of political power that will not be controlled by law, or even by any particular group of "enlightened" experts for long.

While some (evil) ends will destroy the internal morality of law, we cannot use the tool of law to achieve perfect virtue, or freedom, or any other moral good. We can only do our best to develop practical lawmaking and interpreting virtues such that the laws we make will be efficacious in spelling out and enforcing duties in such a way as perhaps to encourage people to pursue virtue (or virtues, whether autonomy, tolerance, or even magnanimity) in the other institutions of social life. In this light the pursuit of the best regime purely through law, and in particular through better interpretation and application of existing laws, may be seen as undermining law's true function. This is true not because law is merely a mindless tool but because law is part of a network of understandings and goals that point outside itself. A good (or bad) regime also is a product of a particular kind of law—a constitution—that rests on lesser laws, customs, and cultural norms. It is to that constitutional form of law, to its nature and the limited good it can provide, that we next turn.

2

Constitutions

Ends, Means, and the Structure of Government

HAVING DEALT WITH THE NATURE and purpose of law, we now turn our attention to constitutions. A constitution is a kind of law in the sense that it often is a creature of legislative bodies that join with courts in arguing over its language and treat it as supplying reasons for and against certain actions. But what is this "law," precisely, and what is its purpose?

The term *constitution* comes from the Latin *constitutio*. Generally referring to an act settling or arranging something, in legal terms a *constitutio* was an important legal pronouncement issued by the Roman emperor. *Constitutio* included decrees with the force of law, decisions handed down in particular cases, and official, imperial answers to legal questions.[1]

Thus, a constitution, at its etymological root, is merely an especially important order coming from a high authority. Yet people think of a constitution as more foundational, more constitutive of a political unit than simply "an important law." Moreover, experience and common usage tell us that a constitution sets up a structure of government, defining the powers and jurisdictions of that government and its various parts. In modern times a constitution also establishes the unity and territorial claims of the nation-state, making it a claimant to the status of sovereign nation.[2]

This much, we think, is relatively uncontroversial. But it is far from the entire story. Constitutions are political as well as legal documents. It is, after all, a *government* that a constitution establishes. As such, political theory is directly relevant to constitutionalism in a limited but fundamental way: the manner in which one views the relationship between governmental actions and the wider society significantly affects how (and whether) constitutional provisions will function.

One may take an extremely instrumental view of the role of constitutions. H. L. A. Hart, for example, treated constitutions as simply an aspect of lawmaking. According to Hart, a society begins with only primary rules regulating people's behavior, but eventually moves on to needing certain second-order, constitutional rules. Second-order rules "specify the ways in which the primary rules may be conclusively ascertained, introduced, eliminated, varied, and the fact of their violation conclusively determined."[3] A constitution, on this view, is a set of rules for making, interpreting, and applying rules.

Louis Michael Seidman presents a seemingly disparate view of constitutional purpose. According to Seidman, constitutions exist as means by which to "command outcomes," that is, to take preconceived notions of what makes for "good" societies and turn them into political reality. Seidman writes in this regard, "[W]hat else would one possibly expect? Of course my choice of a constitution will be dictated by my hopes for the country to be governed by the constitution." Thus, constitutional issues, in Seidman's view, concern "what sort of country [he] should want to live in and . . . what sort of constitutional design would create such a country."[4] According to Seidman, constitutions can create the society desired by the designer, provided they are drafted with appropriate care. Moreover, Seidman argues, it is impossible for constitutional provisions *not* to shape, fundamentally, the character of a nation—its distribution of property, the nature of its political life, and the extent and character of its private sphere, as well as the legal rights and procedures to be respected by its citizens.[5]

Hart and Seidman appear to aim at very different ends. As we saw in Chapter 1, Hart's law in fact is intended to promote maximum protection of individual autonomy, including, as it does, a strong presumption against government action. One might consider here the distance between classical liberal, "procedural" law and more contemporary views of law's role in a just society. A classical liberal might argue that constitutions have three purposes: to establish a proper frame of government, to safeguard private rights, and to maintain and strengthen the unity of a state.[6] James Bryce, the nineteenth-century liberal who proffered this formulation, saw it as setting out only minimal constitutional functions, and also as a matter of common sense. But what are the private rights to be safeguarded? And what kind of government is "proper" to protect them? These are not morally neutral, commonsense choices.

Where Bryce would define rights largely in terms of the protection of property, Seidman, like Rawls, Sandel, and most constitutional lawyers today, would demand guarantees of "positive" rights to political participation, financial security, and government services. Each side, no doubt, sees itself as at odds with the other's vision of what constitutional government should provide, entail, and demand. But they share a crucial element, one we argue constitutes the single, defining, and destructive feature of liberal constitutionalism. That element is the belief that constitutions *command* the societies in which they exist—that they by their nature are political programs intended to shape the conduct of individuals, groups, and political actors to produce a society that has a specific character, whether it be deemed free, fair, or even oppressive.

A different conception of constitutionalism is rooted in historical practice and embodied in the United States Constitution as originally drafted and understood. According to that conception, a constitution properly does not command, but rather mediates among more primary social groups and institutions. Drafters of a mediating constitution would see it not as a fundamental guiding force according to whose elements society will be shaped, but rather as a suit of clothes made to fit a society that is already there, the integrity of which must be respected.[7] A mediating constitution seeks not to shape society from a grand original position, but to maintain peace, stability, and the rule of law within society so that the people and groups making up its way of life may flourish. A mediating constitution is concerned primarily with establishing a structure of government and binding those in positions of power to that structure; that is, it aims to establish and enforce the rule of law against the rulers.

The difference between mediating and commanding structures is not directly a matter of political program. The distinction does not rest on what norms one wishes a society to serve. The distinction rests, rather, on what role one believes a constitution can or should play in shaping that society— in Vincent Ostrom's terms, whether one sees administration as properly monarchical or democratic.[8]

Michael Oakeshott has distinguished between "telocratic" and "nomocratic" constitutions. Telocracy, for Oakeshott, is "the proper business of governing understood as the organization of the energies and activities of its subjects, and of the resources of its territory, for the achievement of a single, premeditated end."[9] In contrast, according to Oakeshott, nomocracy is "the belief that the proper office of government" is, first, "to be the custodian of a system of legal rights and duties in the enjoyment and observation of which the subjects of the government may pursue their own chosen ends and purposes while still remaining a single association," and, second, "to be the custodian of the interest of the association in relation to other similar associations."[10]

Oakeshott, like Hart, saw the state as a superficial construct, by nature only secondarily related to the life of a people. In such a vision, law serves as a background condition for more important acts and associations. Thus, it is civil association—the various voluntary organizations to which individual persons belong—that for Oakeshott provides the only public meaning for a people. And the nomocratic state exists to enable these associations to carry on their business undisturbed, principally through provision of laws regarding contracts, testamentary wills, and the like.[11]

Clearly, Oakeshott's nomocratic constitution embodies a libertarian vision of the state, in which the government intentionally restricts its actions to a minimal few, primarily associated with enabling private choice and conducting foreign policy.[12] There is a danger in Oakeshott's schema that constitutions will be seen as falling into the categories of nomocratic/libertarian (limited, law abiding, and good) and telocratic/social democratic (unlimited, expansive, and potentially totalitarian). Such a characterization would not be entirely unfair to Oakeshott, who at one point argued that "war is the paradigm case of a situation in which the variety of 'admitted goods' in a society is reduced, or almost reduced, to one; a 'state' at war is a paradigm case of *telocracy*. And it is not insignificant that the rhetoric of *telocratic* belief is always liberally sprinkled with military analogy."[13]

Historically, there is significant evidence for Oakeshott's concern with the connection between war and commanding constitutionalism. The early modern concentration of powers in European monarchies that produced the territorial nation-state and the absolutism that preceded late eighteenth-century revolution was rooted in the requirements for war. Recent scholarship has confirmed the views of Tocqueville and Bertrand de Jouvenel, among others, that the demands for new funds to produce arms and new powers to build mass armies brought administrative centralization, resistance, and a feedback cycle of political violence that damaged constitutionalism during the late medieval and early modern eras.[14] In the contemporary era, "wars" on poverty, drugs, and terror, for example, serve to concentrate governmental power and attention for particular ends.

Nevertheless, it is not possible for a constitution to be truly nomocratic or value neutral in the sense of taking no stand on substantive issues, any more than law itself can be morally neutral. Oakeshott's own political preferences are made clear in his argument that associations properly (that is, consistent with the rule of law) make substantive demands on their members only when there is freedom of entry and exit. Yet it is not the state alone that restricts this freedom.[15] The obligations of spouses and parents, for example, despite legal reforms in recent decades, are not pure matters of voluntary association—exit is not free or in many cases (as with children) even possible. To make such exit truly free would be to use the state to restructure (and arguably destroy) a fundamental association of every society. Moreover, Oakeshott implicitly recognized this fact when distinguishing legal authority from "mere advice." That is, he left room for the nexus of indirect legal sanctions and cultural demands that maintain, for most people most of the time, substantive links among family members.

The importance of social and cultural authority for law lies just below the surface in Oakeshott's schema: "For the believer in *nomocracy, how* a government acts is a more important consideration than *what* it does; while for the believer in *telocracy* it does not matter *how* a government acts so long as *what* it does promotes the chosen 'end' in view."[16] Here Oakeshott's view of the nature of the rule of law comes into play. According to Oakeshott, law, properly understood, can act on us only adverbially. It does not issue commands to do or not do, but rather gives rules for acting in a proper manner. Thus the state does not say, "You shall not kill," but rather, "You shall not kill murderously." There is common sense to this vision: self-defense killing, for example, remains killing, but it is not murder in the eyes of the law for the very good reason that it is neither morally nor socially worthy of blame. However, one should not lose sight of the fact that different societies will define different particular acts as murderous. Dueling provides one obvious example here, though honor killing perhaps puts the issue in more dramatic fashion.

Our point is that law must encompass customary understandings of the society in which it acts if its definitions are to be enforceable without requiring the reshaping of society.[17] And the same goes for constitutional as for criminal or any other form of law. One cannot escape cultural assumptions in law, including in constitutional law; one accepts them, seeks to improve them through efforts in the social and/or cultural sphere, or attempts to replace them with more or less principled commands from the center.

We would reference here Orestes Brownson, who observed,

> The constitution of the United States is twofold, written and unwritten, the constitution of the people and the constitution of the government . . . The written constitution is simply a law ordained by the nation or people instituting and organizing the government; the unwritten constitution is the real or actual constitution of the people as a state or sovereign community, and constituting them such or such a state. It is Providential, not made by the nation but born with it. The written constitution is made and ordained by the sovereign power, and presupposes that power as already existing and constituted.[18]

As with constitutional morality itself, one need not see the "Providential" unwritten constitution as somehow ordained by God to note its deep, constitutive nature. Americans did not come together in any mystical moment to form a social contract from scratch. Their communities grew (and changed) over time. And over time those communities saw reasons to come more closely together to form a tighter, more perfect union. Thus, the form of union they chose—their written constitution—by its nature depends for its character and its efficacy on the institutions, beliefs, and practices that preceded and helped produce it. Certainly in the case of the United States, where the "founding" of the nation took place over a period of over a decade—as the colonies became states that formed a confederacy, then chose to become a federal republic—the generative nature and role of culture and preexisting social and political unities seems relatively clear. Of course, a constitution's drafters may choose to reject the underlying, unwritten constitution (one thinks here of revolutionary France) but this sets the resulting government on a collision course with tradition, culture, and people.

A mediating constitution accepts the preexisting orders of society, in their broad outlines, and builds its structures upon this order. This does not mean that constitutional structures will not, for example, bring out the inherent injustice and constitutional incompatibilities of evil practices such as slavery. The internal contradictions of a people half slave and half free eventually will (and, of course, morally speaking should) force action. But a mediating constitution will enable and accommodate reform rather than attempt to dictate a specific, immediate solution at all costs. A mediating constitution will not have as its mission the reordering of society according to any preset principle or principles.[19]

All constitutions are implicated by morality in that they aim at providing order for a society and set forth certain ordering ideals—goals that are either rooted in the drive for mediating among accepted social orders (e.g., peace) or rooted in the drive to create a putatively better, more just social order. Of course, the danger for the mediating constitution is that it will tolerate injustice and perhaps even some types of evil. The danger for the commanding constitution is that its principles themselves may be evil, and also that these principles, even when not evil themselves, may justify evil means and make tyranny more likely and powerful by concentrating power in the political center.

As a general and structural form of law, a constitution grows from and supports more primary laws; it cannot replace them while remaining a constitution or upholding the rule of law. Our point is not that politics are separate from society, or that law is separate from politics, but that law and the higher law of the constitution are social constructs, that they are products of a people's culture, and that this dependence renders their capacity to bring productive change both highly limited and fraught with danger. To make our point we first turn to the historical development of constitutionalism and its relationship with the rule of law, before examining the rise of commanding constitutions and their consequences.

Origins: Roman and Higher Law

The Romans generally are credited with establishing the rule of law as a meaningful practical concept. In part this is a matter of intellectual development. As one study notes, in Roman hands "law became for the first time a thoroughly scientific subject, an elaborately articulated system of principles abstracted from the detailed rules which constitute the raw material of law."[20] For our purposes, however, it is more important to note the manner in which Rome's citizens developed the rule of law as a crucial underpinning

of constitutionalism and how the concepts and practices they institutionalized made possible meaningful constitutional government.

The Romans had a highly developed and complex constitution that was
of great interest to the framers of the American Constitution. But that constitution was not written down. Moreover, the influence of the Romans was
felt more greatly through their development of the rule of law and its formative role in later constitutionalism.

Roman law derived from three sources: statutes, edicts of the praetors
or magistrates, and the interpretations of jurists. The foundational, crucial
statute was the Twelve Tables, a set of behavioral and (legal) procedural
rules deeply rooted in long-standing custom, which the common citizens
had demanded be written down and published.[21] Always shown deference,
these rules provided a touchstone for legal developments well into the
Imperial period.

Praetors did not exercise direct power over the laws but rather over the
remedies available to litigants. That is, they could not pass laws or declare
them void but could craft means by which a wronged person might recover
against a wrongdoer under circumstances not contemplated by preexisting
law. For example, praetors determined that a debtor might be excused
from paying a debt even without receiving a formal release, as required by
the law, when the creditor had told the debtor not to pay. This result was
seen as the rational and just intent of the law. Rules and formulae like that
regarding debt forgiveness were set down in the praetor's edicts, which
were statements of how the law would be enforced during his (one-year)
term of office. Each praetor carried on the rules of the last holder of the
office, unless he specifically rejected some particular statement. The result
was development, over time, of refined rules of pleading and decision—in
effect a tradition of legal practice establishing rational, generally accepted
legal forms.[22]

Interpretations of the laws themselves in the Roman system did not
come from professional judges in formal opinions. Judges generally were
laymen who heard particular cases as a matter of public duty. These judges
depended heavily in their decisions on the interpretations of prominent
citizens who studied and commented on law, again as a public duty.[23] As
with edicts, so with interpretations, law developed through the application
of traditional rules to varied circumstances.

Roman law for the most part was not a codified system.[24] Like the later

English common law, it was rooted in custom and developed piecemeal, in accordance with habits of respect for and obedience to preexisting norms. This made law something higher than the will of any one judge or legislator. Law here was seen and treated as a normative structure with its own logic and purpose; its purpose was justice, taken as fit treatment, or what is owed to the parties, as determined by settled rules. Growing from this, for Roman citizens at least, was increased protection from arbitrary power. In Rome the law came to bind the rulers as well as the ruled. For example, as Jouvenel observed, in early Rome "the state, instead of using against the citizen any specific rights of police, had to bring an action against him, called the *actio popularis*"—a formal, legal action brought on behalf of the public interest.[25]

There is an obvious link between the view that law is independent of rulers and the view that it should bind those rulers. In Rome this link was recognized in particular by statesmen of the late Republican period whose thought was rooted explicitly in the natural law tradition. By the late Republic, thinkers like Marcus Tullius Cicero had expanded upon Aristotle's understanding of the role of law in achieving justice by taming passion through reason. Cicero understood law to include a demand that rulers enact laws that were themselves just, following the law of natural reason.[26]

According to Cicero, "[L]aw is neither an invention of man nor anything at all resembling the rules of day-to-day life; rather it is something eternal which governs the universe by the wisdom in which the orders and prohibitions are conceived." Particular human regulations, according to Cicero, are laws only by acquiescence; if they are to serve their proper purpose, they must instantiate the higher, natural law. For "[f]rom this law comes the nobility of that which the gods have given to mankind, which is in fact the reason and wisdom embodied in the man who has learnt to command what is good and prohibit what is bad."[27] Law, on this reading, is higher than any citizen, ruler, or even people. Inherent in the order of being, the natural law structures our lives and properly binds all of us to the demands of justice.

Natural law provides an objective standard of good and bad. In making this point we would reference an explanation provided by Montesquieu, who emphasized the sense in which natural law is rooted in recognition of the order of existence: "Before there were any laws made, there were intimations of justice . . . [T]o say that justice and injustice are only what is commanded or forbidden by positive laws is tantamount to saying that, until a circle had been traced, the radii were not all equal."[28] That there is a metaphysical element to natural law is as clear as it is off-putting to many. But one need not recognize a personal God in order to recognize in the very structure of law a source beyond the power of the state, or of the law-giver. In practical terms, as Jouvenel noted, if law is a creature of power then it cannot limit that power,[29] and if this were true there could be no lasting peace, order, or even human society—something our experience tells us simply is not true.

The descent of Rome into imperial tyranny, corruption, and dissolution was accompanied by a steep decline in the rule of law in European and Mediterranean cultures. But, caricatures of a vast Dark Age lasting until the Renaissance notwithstanding, the rule of law's fundamental elements were never entirely lost, either in ideal or in practice, and became part of a web of constitutionalism bringing significant amounts of freedom and stability to the Middle Ages. Long after constitutional documents ceased to be effective (after, for example, the Twelve Tables no longer served as the pattern for governmental conduct in Rome) the unwritten constitution of beliefs and practices regarding legal forms and decisions as well as the higher law carried on, if fitfully. And this unwritten constitution achieved resurgence as tradition as well as institutionalization sufficient to help shape public life for centuries to come.

Medieval Europe: The Constitution of the Realm

We have rehearsed the development of the rule of law and of higher law in Rome in order to show the dependence of constitutions on constitutionalism—on habits of respect for law and for rules limiting the power of rulers to make decrees according to their own will. It now is necessary to examine the vast Middle Ages to a very limited extent. Our purpose is to show that attempts to subject rulers to law are not strictly internal to the state and defined in code-like terms. In particular, they may come from customary, common law, and from habitual, tradition-grounded attachment to the dictates of the natural law.

It was during the Middle Ages that the term *constitution* took on something like its modern meaning. The medieval conception of a constitution was of the fundamental laws, procedures and customs of a realm, particularly though not exclusively as embodied in the institutional arrangements of a state.[30] Contemporary commentators tend to dismiss this form of constitution as less than law, or lump it together with other restraints on monarchs' power, such as coronation oaths, as vaguely "constitutional" but sub-legal because not formally enforceable in a court.[31] But many of these constraints were "law" in the sense that they were written down, and others were made binding by custom or common law. Moreover, we should not dismiss "merely" constitutional restraints on power. As shown by the example of Rome, unwritten practices are crucial to the development of a system of laws capable of binding the governors. Folkways, beliefs, and customs all are crucial to law, and customary practice will do more to limit power than any written constitution on its own.[32]

For example, in medieval France, customary constraints substantially limited monarchs' right to legislate, thereby restricting their ability to act arbitrarily. As late as the thirteenth century, the French king could only make law during or in preparation for war, and then only with reasonable cause, for the benefit of the commonweal, and not in violation of the law of God or morals.[33] Moreover, legitimate rule being based in consent,[34] it was crucial to find this consent, lacking any formal mechanism such as voting, in the practices of a people. Thus, the people were taken to consent to custom—no long stretch given the inherent rooting of custom itself in common, habitual practice—and, as such, custom also bound the monarch.[35]

Feudal rights and duties also limited monarchs' powers. These rights were rooted in property relationships whereby those lower in hierarchical status owed duties to the higher-ups in the form of servitudes on the land they occupied. They were hardly egalitarian or humanitarian, prominently including, as they did, possession of a gallows.[36] But these rights were highly differentiated, spread among a number of classes, and all held sacred.[37] Each group's rights determined its status. And this "whole bundle of legitimate interests and consecrated rights . . . had to be respected by all and could be opposed at need even to the sovereign himself." Such an assertion of rights could be made, for example, at any meeting of representatives of the various estates called by the monarch in his attempt to secure new tax monies.[38] The king was constitutionally bound to respect the existing state of the realm—the body of different rights held by different individuals and groups in different things.[39] In feudal terms the king was only first among equals; even his "royal prerogative" was only a set of rights "necessary to the fulfillment of his office" that were limited and did not entitle him to "alter the status of his subjects."[40] Custom, in its way, was king. And while this was not always and everywhere conducive to human flourishing, it did constitute a law binding rulers—in other words, constitutionalism.

Constitutionalism also developed through the competition and low-level conflict (we might say checks and balances today) of a multiplicity of authorities and legal jurisdictions. The pope won from the Holy Roman emperor the right to appoint his own bishops, securing for the Catholic Church powerful representatives in political as well as religious associations in various kingdoms. These representatives supported institutional checks such as interdicts and even excommunication of monarchs too seriously violating church (and other) rights.[41] In addition, the canon law of the Catholic Church, the law merchant, and royal, common law were only the most prominent forms of law, enforced in separate courts with overlapping powers and jurisdictions, that competed for power and fees from litigants by expanding and developing legal procedures and rights.[42] Constitutional documents like Magna Carta and various local charters[43] spelled out the lines of royal, church, and baronial jurisdiction while canon law delineated the institutional rights of popes, cardinals, and cathedral chapters.[44] And cities' charters not only defined their rights in relation to kings but also spelled out the rights and duties of mayors, councils, and other officers.[45]

Documents and commentaries, including the *Sachsenspiegel* in Germany and Bracton's work in England, institutionalized constitutional law by defining limits on and the location of jurisdictional competency, rules on selection of rulers, and the rights and duties of subjects.[46] The lines of jurisdiction were neither impermeable nor clear; they were less formal than would be the case with a fully codified constitution. The result was a loose system of perforated sovereignty and competing jurisdictions, fostering competition and conflict. Critically, this competition took place within an overarching consensus that each competitor had a duty to abide by the norms of legal process and pursuit of the common good. As in Rome, habits of respect for preexisting norms formed a conception of virtue in abiding by constraints, forging the elements of a constitutional morality. Thus, while there was much debate and even conflict over principle and policy, all parties had an interest in cooperation and compromise. And this, combined with competition for the loyalty and patronage of various groups, helped produce significant protections for the rights of individuals and groups—indeed, the formation of modern rights.[47]

The complicated nature of royal power during the medieval era can be summed up in Bracton's view that the king was under the law and yet had no superior.[48] In assessing this royal status, Brian Tierney has argued that the king was loosed from the laws in that, having no earthly superior, no one could enforce his obedience thereto, though it was his duty to maintain that obedience on his own.[49] There clearly was a call for such self-restraining virtue.[50] And this virtue may be seen as a precursor to constitutional morality in that it limited personal will and appetite in service to constitutional forms which were accepted as normative rules binding rulers. But overemphasis on personal virtue would cause us to overlook the broader, somewhat looser, but nonetheless real checks provided by medieval constitutionalism.

The medieval era's loose constitutionalism was bound together in significant degree by natural law. Now often dismissed as mere verbiage, there were real consequences for violating norms rooted in this generally accepted natural law vision. Coronation oaths, along with charters such as Magna Carta, and indeed custom itself, bound the king because his failure to abide by them was generally taken to be a violation of natural law, hence unjust.[51] King John attempted to evade adherence to Magna Carta by securing from the pope a declaration that the monarch's assent being gained through coercion rendered the "contract" invalid. But he and his successors often were forced to bow to the terms of the document, largely because it was seen by powerful barons as a restatement of preexisting, customary obligations.[52] It was taken to be a restatement of terms to which the king was bound by constitutional morality—something itself supported by a natural law–based moral consensus throughout Europe.

Even in the area of royal prerogative, the personal jurisdiction of the monarch within which he could act outside the law, natural law was deemed to cabin the sovereign will. Individual rights such as that to property could not be violated by the monarch except with proper cause and in the public interest.[53] Thus, Bracton's formulation reflected constraints on constitutional figures to abide by the limits of their office or jurisdiction.[54] Constitutional morality also gained significant power in medieval Europe from the ability of popes to declare null a monarch's actions contrary to natural law, thereby releasing subjects from their duty to obey them.[55] The declaration might or might not succeed in forcing changes in royal behavior. Popes themselves were far from all-powerful and often owed their election and continued power to particular royal patrons. But the system of multiple, conflicting authorities gave monarchs reason to pause before, and at times regret after, overreaching edicts and acts.

The multiplicity of competing authorities that characterized medieval constitutionalism often is seen as detrimental to the rule of law, and to good government in general. But, while there clearly was in such a system a potential for conflict, its fracturing of power provided protections against large-scale tyranny. Like the so-called gridlock of democracy Progressives found in the American Constitution's separation of powers, the medieval constitution protected existing expectations more than the desires of would-be saviors, consensus more than power.

The connection between medieval constitutionalism and the rights of individual persons and groups against the state made it the object of hostility from centralizing monarchs like Henry VIII in England and Louis XIV in France.[56] These rights stood in the way of monarchs' desire to make over their kingdoms in accordance with their own notions of what they should be. During the early modern era, monarchs were able to centralize power through standing armies and tax structures, both aimed at fighting and winning wars, and both setting in motion a series of clashes that stripped rights from their former rivals in the balanced constitutions of the Middle Ages; in so doing, these monarchs, now claiming a divine right to absolute power, were enabled to form and rule territorial nation-states.[57]

The character of medieval constitutionalism, mediating among primary groups, causes it to be more or less dismissed in most contemporary literature, when it is noted at all. Today's constitutional commentators and drafters look elsewhere for their models. Nonetheless, the model under which they write and act has deep historical roots. The misunderstanding of those roots and their natural products has grave consequences for constitutionalism, the rule of law, and the lives of peoples around the globe.

On Misunderstanding the Importance of Greece

The command model of constitutionalism stems in significant measure from a mistaken conception, or perhaps rejection, of the lessons to be derived from historical examples, particularly those provided by the Greeks. The best place to begin here is with a crucial term in Greek political thought: *politeía*. This term was used by Plato and Aristotle, among others in the ancient Greek world. Today *politeía* is generally translated as *constitution*.[58] Rarely has a mistranslation of a single term caused so much error and trouble. *Politeía* refers not to a constitution but to a regime—as Aristotle defined it, "a certain arrangement of those who inhabit the city."[59]

No doubt the overidentification of *politeía,* or regime, with constitution stems in part from Aristotle's careful and lengthy analysis of the particular rules of selection for office that establish rule by the one, the few, or the many—that is, rules to ensure who rules, what powers are distributed, and how.[60] But Aristotle was not merely laying out a structure of government and secondary rules. The regime was not merely some collection of laws, but an arrangement of social beings. Thus, Aristotle went so far as to declare that "the governing body *is* the regime."[61] The individual person and the community, the citizen and the city, were one and the same; the arrangement of those citizens made the regime what it was.

Here mistranslation of another term, *polis* as *city-state*, exacerbates misunderstanding of the distinction between constitution and regime. Giovanni Sartori points out, "[T]he Greek *polis* was by no means the citystate that we are accustomed to call it—for it was not, in any sense, a 'state.' The *polis* was a citycommunity, a *koinonía*. Thucydides said it in three words: *ándres gar polis*—it is the men that are the polis. It is very revealing that *politeía* meant, in one, citizenship and the structure (form) of the *polis.*"[62]

As Aristotle noted, the fundamental principle of a regime—be it virtue, wealth, or freedom—determined the distribution of prerogatives.[63] And, in the interest of shaping the people so as to maximize virtue, protect wealth, or maintain the rule of the many, all arrangements were liable to regulation. Such regulations encompassed all of life, from the supply and consumption of food (e.g., common messes), to the freedom or slavery of the workers, to the classification of citizens into particular groups eligible to vote or hold office (or not) according to criteria ranging from the status of one's parents, to wealth, to geographical placement. The regime in the ancient Greek city was, then, an all-encompassing power structure defining and ruling life, with no escape into any putatively private sphere.

Rather than showing the necessarily comprehensive character of constitutions, however, the expansive understanding of the regime in the ancient Greek city shows that it is inaccurate to equate the Greek *politeía* with a modern constitution—or even to see the one as an embryonic form of the other. Sartori's reference to the polis as a "citycommunity" rather than a "citystate" highlights the chasm separating ancient Greek life from the politics of the modern and contemporary worlds. The state in any meaningful sense came about only with the externalization of political forms—that is, their institutionalization as structures outside the community, acting upon it through political mechanisms. Such mechanisms might be described in a document called a constitution, but that document would not describe all of society. Where today one sees calls for political structures that better shape communities, the community in ancient Greece made up—actually constituted—the political as well as social, religious, and "private" spheres.[64]

In part, the extreme unity of the Greek polis was simply a matter of scale. That cities with populations measured in the thousands would instantiate a way of life different from nations with populations measured in the millions should come as no surprise. Aristotle differentiated nation from city, noting the lack of commonality of experience and knowledge in Babylon, as opposed to Greek communities.[65] Nations seem to partake of the nature of an alliance, for Aristotle. They lack the commonality, face-to-face relationships, and most especially the character of a partnership in pursuit of a good life lived in common, being instead agreements to prevent injustice and conflict between more fundamental groups such as cities or tribes.[66]

Scale was not the only factor enforcing unity in Greek polities. Tribal relations, the persistent threat of famine, and the very real possibility of extermination by a city's neighbors forged ties too strong for most contemporary academics to grasp. As Sartori notes, "[N]ot only were the ancient cities very small, but the citizens lived symbiotically with their city, being tied to it, as it were, by a common destiny of life and death . . . The compact community [was] unified by a converging religious, moral, and political *ethos* that was the *polis*."[67]

We are not arguing that the ancient Greeks were somehow of a different species from people today, nor that they shared none of the concerns common in modern and contemporary life. But the meaning and import of crucial political terms were seen in a radically different light from today, owing at least in part to the radically different form of life intrinsic to small communities engaged in a constant struggle for survival and domination. To take a well-known example, freedom for ancient Greeks referred not to the autonomy of the individual to do as he wished but rather the freedom or independence of the city from domination by any other political entity.[68]

As to the individual person, whether slave or free, he (and, of course, in this context the male pronoun is exclusive, indicating the subordinate status of women) was a creature of the community. He often was a distrusted creature, liable to being banished from his home, not as a punishment for any misdeed but rather as a precautionary measure to prevent any one citizen from being too much better than the others, hence posing a danger to the commonality of the regime. In such a regime, the individual citizen's only protection against punishment, or preventive banishment, was wise exercise of his share of the sovereignty.[69] Only by defending himself in the assembly and by presenting himself in the streets and especially on the field of battle as a loyal citizen could the individual protect his interests. This was quite by intention; the Greeks demanded that citizens put the city's interests before their own as a means of combating the factional strife so prevalent. But it created severe tensions and pressures.

A good citizen tended to be a poor individual; having devoted himself to the polis, giving his blood and toil in war, and his time and mental efforts in times of peace to the administration of public affairs, he had little left over for tending to his own affairs. The result, often, was in fact a worsening of factional conflict as the demands of public office led those holding it to see it as the only means of tending to their own needs. Corruption and class warfare ensued as groups, defined in particular by their possession or lack of wealth, fought over political office and its power to distribute and redistribute offices, honors, and rewards.[70]

It was this conflict, the result of extremely high stakes in a political sphere that was in essence the only active sphere of life,[71] that the drafters of the American Constitution sought to avoid. In the well-known words of Publius from *Federalist* 9, "It is impossible to read the history of the petty republics of Greece and Italy, without feeling sensations of horror and disgust at the distractions with which they were continually agitated, and at the rapid succession of revolutions, by which they were kept perpetually vibrating between the extremes of tyranny and anarchy."[72] Publius in fact blames the governance of these ancient cities for perverting the directions in which the talents and endowments of these extraordinary people might have been directed. He also blames the experience of the ancient polis for giving modern tyrants verbal ammunition with which to attack republican government and the very idea of civil liberty; for, if republican government were truly destructive of peace and liberty more generally understood, it would have to be abandoned by all possessing good will.[73]

Too often overlooked, Publius's point is basic but important: order is required for freedom to be possible, let alone meaningful. As Sartori remarks, "[W]hen the chips are down, what we ask of political freedom is protection."[74] Whether acting alone or in a group, whether pursuing higher ends or merely our self-interest, we cannot live decent, let alone free lives if we are in fear that someone will do us harm. And, while the city, state, or nation may protect us from neighbors and strangers, we also need protection from political authorities who may seek our harm. "How can we obtain it?" Sartori asks. "In the final analysis, from the time of Solon to the present day, the solution has been sought in obeying laws and not masters. As Cicero eloquently phrased it . . . we are servants of the laws in order that we might be free . . . The problem of political freedom always lands at the search for *rules* that do curb power."[75]

After pointing to the dangers of Greek politics, Publius introduces his defense of republican government by discussing improvements in "the science of politics." He specifically references separation of powers, checks and balances, judges holding office during good behavior, and representation of the people in the legislature by deputies of their own choosing.[76] These rules for ruling, ensconced in the constitutional document, were intended to subject the governors to the rule of law—to limit their powers and actions so as to protect the people from tyranny.[77]

Such mechanisms were not unknown to the ancient world. Again, Aristotle expended much effort analyzing various plans for the distribution of offices and the encouragement of particular people to seek such offices (for example, fining the rich for not participating, or paying the poor for attending assemblies, trials, and the like). Moreover, both Greek and Italian cities had arrangements dividing powers between and among various offices, whether assemblies or kings.

What was missing, or at least highly fragile, in the ancient Greek world, as Aristotle recognized, was the rule of law itself, that is, respect for rules among those in positions of power. Aristotle highly praised the rule of law, which subjects citizens to reason rather than the beastly desires of rulers. In addition, however, the well-blended regime in particular must defend the law, because violations multiply and undermine this regime, which is dependent on law for its survival.[78] But Aristotle had little confidence in the staying power of the rule of law in the Greek polis; various groups would pursue their own advantage at the cost of law-abidingness, most laws were only good in the limited sense of serving the rulers' particular interests, and, overall, more was to be expected of a prudent concern for the well-being of those not allowed into the centers of power.[79]

The rule of law was the hard-fought product of centuries of legal and political development. It was beyond the reach of the prideful Greeks, and fragile and slow to develop among the prideful Romans and their successors, in large part because the stakes of power were so high. Constant threats of famine and conquest for the community, and poverty or banishment for the citizens, made political power an essential tool for well-being and even survival. Corruption and high-level conflict followed, undermining stability and the rule of law.

The rule of law gained increasing traction during the Middle Ages, despite many obstacles, and maintained a presence even in the midst of royal claims to absolute authority, particularly in Britain, where these royal claims had the hardest time gaining unquestioned sway. The British constitutional tradition in turn helped form constitutionalism in the United States. But it is not to that tradition we now turn, for it is not to that tradition that most constitutional lawyers today look in forming their criticisms, interpretations, and even new constitutions. Their lodestar is found across the channel, in a very different mood and time, in France.

The French Revolution: Goals, Means, and Results

Greek "constitutions" failed in their most basic task of applying the rule of law to rulers. But what mechanism can enforce a constitution? It has been observed that, once a community opts for a higher law constitutional system, the problem becomes one of how to guarantee that higher law's "normative integrity and supremacy." The contemporary view is that the constitution protects its commanding role by establishing a judicial mechanism providing neutral assessments regarding "the legality of all other legal norms with reference to the constitution."[80] Second-order rules require a second-order court, it is said, to enforce them, including against the rulers.

But most systems of judicial constitutional review, throughout history, have been decidedly ineffective. Constitutional review (or enforcement) can be effective only when and to the extent that important constitutional disputes are actually brought to the reviewing authority on a regular basis, the judges actually give reasons for their rulings, and the rulings themselves are given some precedential effect.[81] And this will happen only if there is an actual, active, and authoritative constitutional morality sufficiently strong to compel obedience among most political actors most of the time. To simply assert that the court is the one with this power is to invite conflict that the court, having neither purse nor sword, is bound to lose.

One may ask, then, why or how constitutions can succeed in cabining power—why those with power would abide by constitutional rules that interfere with achievement of their policy goals.[82] The problem would seem all the more acute where the rulers have been vested by the constitution itself with the responsibility of constituting a just, equal, and prosperous society. Yet this is precisely what is expected of constitutions today.

The best-known example of a commanding constitution, indeed the very model of modern, commanding constitutions, is that of revolutionary France. Often depicted as liberating a nation from the dead hand of the past, the French Revolution was an attempt to make the world, or at least the nation and those neighboring countries it eventually conquered, anew. It was rooted in faith in the abstract faculty of reason as the only necessary guide to human conduct. As Tocqueville pointed out, the Revolution actually carried on political trends begun under the Old Regime. But the revolutionaries used those structures to reshape their society, with results well worth contemplation by students of constitutionalism.

It is, of course, wrong to assert that it was a specific constitution in France that, for example, abolished feudalism and made members of the clergy employees of the state. Many of the "constitutional" acts of the French Revolution were undertaken by the preconstitutional National Assembly, attempting to act as a largely self-appointed, all-powerful legislature.[83] But much was in fact included in the three constitutions instituted beginning in 1791 and ending with the rise of Napoleon Bonaparte in 1799.

The most famous, and at six years the longest lasting, of the revolutionary constitutions was that of June 24, 1793—or "year one" as the revolutionaries styled it. This constitution guaranteed "equality, liberty, security, property, public debt, freedom of worship, public schooling, public relief, unrestricted freedom of the press, the right to assemble in groups, and the enjoyment of all the rights of man." These rights were to be secured and protected by a national assembly reliant on popular sovereignty, decrees of which were to be carried out by separate executive, administrative, and judicial bodies.[84]

The 1793 constitution referenced the rights of man. Those rights have been seen as motivating the French Revolution (and many of its successors) through the Declaration of the Rights of Man and of the Citizen, adopted by the National Assembly in 1789. This declaration was intended as a reminder to "all members of the Social body" of their rights and duties "in order that the acts of the legislative power, as well as those of the executive power, may be compared at any moment with the objects and purposes of all political institutions and may thus be more respected, and, lastly, in order that the grievances of the citizens, based hereafter upon simple and incontestable principles, shall tend to the maintenance of the constitution and redound to the happiness of all."[85]

In keeping with its nature as a declaration of the rights, not just of man but of man "and of the Citizen," this declaration emphasized the nation as the locus of sovereignty and font of authority and justice. By its terms, the natural rights of man include liberty, property, security, and resistance to oppression. At the same time, all distinctions, by its terms, must be founded only on the general good, and "no body or individual may exercise any authority which does not proceed directly from the nation."[86]

The Declaration of the Rights of Man espoused the rule of law and the separation of powers to foster respect for rights. But it also declared that law is "the expression of the general will."[87] And who embodies the general will? Even Rousseau, from whom the notion was derived, limited operation of his social contract to small communities akin to Swiss cantons.[88] But French constitutions attempted to answer that question by emphasizing the role of the national legislature. The question also was answered by individual rulers, including Robespierre, who saw its embodiment in themselves. Thus Robespierre in 1793 asked, "[W]hat do we care for devices devised to balance the authority of tyrants? It is tyranny that must be extirpated: the aim of the people should be, not to find in the quarrels of their masters short breathing-spaces for themselves, but to make their own right arms the guarantee of their rights."[89] Thus, once "the people" were in power, there was no need to separate, let alone check, that power. In particular, judges would no longer be allowed to stand in the way of revolutionary justice; they would be elected, their elections overturned, their positions threatened, and their authority subjugated to decrees from the Assembly so that enemies of the Revolution might be executed with little or no judicial process.[90]

Estimates of the number of people executed by the French revolutionary regime during the Terror range in the tens of thousands. This number fails to include murders perpetrated by rioters, representatives of the regime acting in the provinces, less than fully official groups of revolutionaries, opposing sides in the various civil uprisings, and anyone outside the narrow time frame of 1793–1794.[91] But it is most important here to note that the semijudicial murders of the Directorate, which have set a pattern for "constitutionalism" in the revolutionary mode, were not the product of chaos or of a few bad men, but rather the natural consequence of an extreme concentration of power and authority at the political center.

The various legislatures of the French Revolution exercised greater power than the king ever had held, in part because, taken as an expression of the general will, their actions were seen as by nature legitimate—certainly by the legislators themselves.[92] Barriers to the exercise of centralized power were destroyed by a centralized administration that could eliminate opposition rooted in geography, class, custom, and religion. These makeweights the king, despite the increasing centralization of power since the sixteenth century, had dared not attack.[93] It was not just that the old aristocracy was all but extirpated, or even that the Church, hitherto a major landholder and jurisdictional check on the central power, had ceased to exist as a corporate group, its members becoming employees of the state. Regional assemblies were eviscerated. Local law was eliminated, its jurisdiction and tribunals subordinated to or subsumed in the center. Estates were confiscated and split up. The very provinces were all but erased in favor of departments of the central state. Of course, there was resistance, but it was put down with merciless zeal. Then Napoleon not only ended, but in ideological terms brought to fruition, French revolutionary constitutionalism: "The Revolution is closed; its principles are fixed in my person.

The government in being is the representative of the sovereign people. There can be no opposition to the sovereign."[94]

Clearly, most of today's academics would be in favor of upholding constitutional provisions of which they approve—including protections for independent courts following procedures barring summary executions. Seidman, for example, argues that Americans should "give up" on the Constitution, but still asserts that we should retain rights he deems fundamental.[95] The question is how such adherence is to be achieved. We submit that it cannot be achieved when those in positions of political authority are empowered and obligated by their higher law to restructure, in fundamental terms, their societies. The general will concentrates power and expectations in the center, such that constitutional checks on power come to seem illegitimate roadblocks to progress. Such roadblocks will not stand, given their weakened and degraded state, against those claiming to represent the general will.

One might respond to such an analysis by stating that law is by nature power, such that constitutions by nature are needed principally to direct that power, for good or ill. If a constitution is by nature a roadmap for society, encompassing and institutionalizing its goals, then we would seem able to choose only between progress and reaction. We would seem to be faced with the choice between enshrining and enforcing "good" values (such as equality and autonomy), or enshrining and enforcing "bad" values (such as traditional moral norms). The only other choice would seem to be a badly designed constitution that fails in its task of efficiently structuring power to good ends, instead producing gridlock and inaction. But what happens, in fact, when constitutions command?

Commanding Constitutionalism and Its Failures

A constitution "formalizes" a nation. It makes clear the nation's status as a sovereign state. It also sets up the nation's structure of government and basic procedures for the operation of governmental machinery, particularly as to the promulgation of laws. In addition, contemporary academic standards demand that constitutions fit within a rather narrow set of parameters. Absolutist constitutions exist, formally vesting absolute authority in a single person or group (one might mention here the constitution of Saudi

Arabia). Also with us, in theory, is British-style legislative supremacy, though, particularly since the institutionalization of a British supreme court, it arguably is no longer effective even in Great Britain. But the "higher law constitution," complete with extensive lists of rights, essentially owns the field of proper constitutionalism, at least in principle.[96]

A higher law constitution is one in which the constitution itself is taken to be a law higher than the particular statutes enacted by the lawmaking body, such that constitutional rules are binding on the rulers. Such a regime, it is assumed, also requires a body—generally a constitutional or supreme court—tasked with policing the other governing officers to keep them within the bounds of the constitution. This constitutional court is of particular importance, in contemporary terms, as enforcer of the other central characteristic of contemporary higher law constitutions, namely a charter of rights. Of the 116 constitutions written since 1985 (not all of them still in existence), every one of the 106 on which there is reliable information contains a charter of rights—101 providing for rights review by a constitutional court.[97]

One may choose to see in this dominance of formalized, codified constitutions, constitutional courts, and especially of constitutional rights in contemporary governmental formation a progressive trend toward good, free government. Indeed, we can speak of a number of moments of hope directly tied to spurts of constitution drafting. The end of Western colonialism in Africa after World War II, the end of Soviet occupation of numerous countries in Eastern Europe and parts of Asia, and the so-called Arab spring beginning after 2010 were only the most famous and widespread such occasions. The hope among many, particularly among Western observers, was that the revolutions would replace tyrannical governments and "backward" societies with democratic states that would produce economic development and egalitarian social justice.

But how has constitution making fared in "emerging democracies"? We submit that the record should give pause to those proposing that written constitutions be used to remake societies in this progressive mold. Constitutions enshrining rights have become the norm, but actual respect for human rights—indeed, constitutions that function in the more basic sense of providing stability, peace, order, and protection against political violence—remain all too difficult to establish and maintain.

The percentage of countries ranked as "free" by the civil libertarian

Freedom House has increased from 29 to 45 over the last three decades.[98] But progress has hardly been steady, let alone explosive.[99] Freedom House notes particular concerns regarding corruption and dangers to liberties in the Ukraine, Hungary, South Africa, and Turkey. Moreover, the broad categories of "free," "partly free," and "not free" obscure substantial abuses and worsening conditions in countries maintaining their status within a given category, and especially within those nations already deemed not free. Especially in sub-Saharan Africa, countries already suffering under autocratic regimes have experienced significant crackdowns, particularly in the area of freedom of association and respect for the rule of law.[100] Perhaps most important, these ratings include those nations of the Atlantic world that have had well-established, relatively free constitutional governments for many years. Subtracting the twenty-four nations of Western Europe, along with the United States, Canada, and Australia (to go no further), reduces the percentage of "free" countries in the remaining world to thirty-six—little over one-third.

It seems at least questionable whether the structures of contemporary constitutionalism can produce the results desired by their proponents. Constitutions in recent decades have emphasized the duties of the state to provide goods for the people ranging from medical care to "equitable development," along with more traditional individual and political rights. Meanwhile, political violence remains endemic and ordered liberty uncommon.

For example, Ethiopia's constitution, adopted in 1995, in Articles 43 and 44 guarantees people the right to a clean and healthy environment, to improved living standards, and to "sustainable development." Yet a 2011 BBC investigation found in the southern region of Ethiopia "villages where whole communities are starving, having allegedly been denied basic food, seed and fertilizer for failing to support [the now late] Prime Minister Meles Zenawi." Also evidenced were "mass detentions, [and] the widespread use of torture and extra-judicial killings by Ethiopian government forces."[101]

The Constitution of Uganda commits the government to providing equitable development, food security, medical services, and gender balancing, among other rights. But this is at the same time that the regime practices summary suppression of media outlets and nongovernmental organizations deemed too critical of the regime and is persistently accused of employing torture through its antiterrorism organization.[102] Examples could be multiplied many times over—from Eastern Europe to the many regions of Asia, to Latin America and the Middle East.

It is little wonder, given the huge gap between constitutional promise and political reality, that civil wars, coups, and coup attempts are sadly common; between 1960 and 2001 there were eighty-two successful coups in Africa, and another sixteen between 2000 and 2012.[103] Of course, Africa is not alone in suffering political instability and violence. As one scholar notes, "Since 1950, in Africa, Central and South America, and Asia, one finds over one hundred examples. In some countries, the military coup d'etat remains a constant threat. Between 1997 and 2006, there were at least twenty-five coup attempts in these areas and at least fourteen were successful."[104] And this does not include the massive bloodshed of civil wars in Rwanda, Kosovo, Sudan, and Congo-Kinshasa, to name only a few.

It would be easy for constitutional lawyers in particular to dismiss such tragedies as "not our fault" because they are rooted in the failure of regimes to live up to the promises of their constitutions, and the world has long known the cynicism of sham constitutions. But it is both self-serving and simplistic to dismiss the gap between promise and performance as the result of powerful bad actors. Indeed, the question must be asked: "Is it possible for a regime, particularly in areas of the world lacking in material wealth, to live up to the constitutional promises currently deemed essential to constitutional government?"

The 1998 constitution of Sudan puts the issue in stark terms: "The State shall give due regard to social justice and mutual aid in order to build the basic components of the society, to provide the highest standard of good living for every citizen, and to distribute national income in a just manner to prevent serious disparity in incomes, civil strife, exploitation of the enfeebled and to care for the aged and disabled."[105] The Sudanese state here is given the responsibility (and the right) to command the good society for its citizens—constructing the components of that society, establishing a high standard of living, distributing income "fairly," and caring for those not able to care for themselves. Would that it had at least commanded its own forces to stop committing genocide in its Darfur region.

Social democratic goals hardly are unique to sub-Saharan Africa. What is more, the poor performance of such constitutions has produced the hypothesis, supported by significant evidence, that "less repressive regimes have less-enumerated rights," that is, that freer governments tend not to spell out in great detail the rights of the people, in part because they have not taken on the responsibility of providing happiness for those people.[106] Whatever one makes of current economic crises in long-standing liberal democratic nations, the question arises whether states in less wealthy regions possibly can perform on the all-encompassing promises that seem demanded of them. Such pressures seem extreme, given the scarcity of economic resources in developing countries in particular. To constitutionalize—that is, to make a higher law duty—a state's responsibility for establishing and maintaining a fundamentally new, just, and prosperous economic, political, and social order, while expecting in addition respect for individual and political rights seems, frankly, a recipe for disaster.

The argument has been made that the central roadblock to development has been ethnic attachment that prevents sufficient loyalty to the state and its mechanisms. But far more damaging has been placement of the state at the center of power and especially of high expectations, with control over economic goods in nations where scarcity is the norm and starvation a persistent threat; such conditions make the state a center of conflict among those who must compete in a zero-sum game on behalf of their families and neighbors. The result is a state that is not capable of remaining above the fray of interest politics, instead becoming the battleground itself.[107] Positive rights sometimes are termed "aspirational" to denote the inability and even unwillingness of the state to put them into effect. One should not be surprised that such dissembling fails to save the state's legitimacy when it fails to produce on its stated goals.

Nations of limited resources and often recent establishment have been called upon to command, through their constitutions, the empowerment of people, freeing them from oppression, poverty, and the bonds of custom, to make them into members of a cosmopolitan, egalitarian, and relatively affluent society, complete with guaranteed provision of numerous public, government services, all in combination with respect for individual and political rights. The idea was that placing the goals of just development into the higher law of the constitution would make them into central aspirations and spur the nascent states to appropriate action. The result has been dashed hopes and political violence.

Constitutional Models

What does this cursory review tell us about the nature of constitutions? It is clear that constitutions provide roadmaps for the governing structure of a regime. But this roadmap need not be in writing, and need not be fully formalized. More important to a constitution's reality, that is, its empirical existence, is its practical ability to bind rulers' conduct. Thus, constitutions, like law more generally, are by nature concerned with establishing the rule of law, of preventing arbitrary action by winning adherence to their terms.

The contrasting experiences of the ancient Greeks (and the revolutionary French) and medieval Europeans show that constitutions may, but need not, be concerned primarily with settling ideological principles and empowering those with political power to shape society in accord with those principles. A constitution also may be seen primarily as a means of hedging in political power so as to protect more fundamental associations, institutions, and customs. But this dichotomy of negative versus positive constitutionalism does not fully capture the range of constitutional forms.

To begin with, the language of "negative" and "positive" constitutionalism shares the flaw of the positive/negative rights dichotomy; it bespeaks a clarity of distinction that is more apparent than real. A government intent on protecting the "negative" rights of individuals to be free from various forms of discrimination and limits on their autonomy may find itself regulating or even denying "positive" rights of full participation in various associations so as to vindicate a principle of negative liberty. Such is the case with various organizations that have sought to exclude African Americans, or women, or homosexuals, or non-Christians from membership or from leadership positions. Thus in the name of nondiscrimination or "negative liberty," a commanding constitution may demand a reordering of fundamental institutions. We note in passing the call by some legal theorists for legal action against the Catholic Church for refusing to anoint female priests.[108] A "positive" commanding constitution would simply be one that made a different choice as to which type of rights to champion—for example, establishing a particular ideology or religion and using law to make people "free" as it defines that term.

Alternatively, the government may see its job as mediating between the various groups within which individual persons may act, thus binding itself from interfering either with the rights of persons or with the rights of the groups they form. On these terms a "negative" constitution does not seek to reorder a society to maximize individual autonomy, virtue, or any other final value. It thus also would be a "positive" constitution in that it would allow other associations and institutions freer rein to act independently, exerting their own power in society and over their members. It would make no sense to deny, for example, that the medieval Church exercised great control over members of its clergy or that the status of the nobility allowed its members to exercise power over "their" peasants. This same principle would lie behind the refusal to penalize nongovernmental associations for discriminatory policies.

The crucial, substantive difference between forms of constitutionalism has to do with the nature of the relationship between the political state and other associations. A commanding constitution seeks to order and reorder society in keeping with a specific set of principles, such as justice, equality, and/or autonomy. A mediating constitution, on the other hand, is drawn so as to exist in equilibrium (and perhaps tension or balance, but not command) with other primary institutions and associations; it presumes and seeks to maintain a polycentric distribution of power growing from organic communities.

Not everything depends on the distinction between commanding and mediating constitutions. Nevertheless, it is important to note the significant difference between the commanding and mediating approaches to constitutionalism. Among the implications of these differing modes is the proclivity for common or customary law methods in societies with a mediating constitution, versus an attachment to statutory law alone in societies with a commanding constitution.[109] As important, mediating constitutions will put greater emphasis on political decision making that goes through "a multistage and multifiltered process"; such indirect decision making offers precautions and restraints disfavored under commanding constitutions. Perhaps most crucial, however, is the favoring, in mediating constitutions, of modes of decision making intended to produce consensus rather than democratic action. Where commanding constitutions would avoid gridlock, mediating constitutions would avoid undue haste and the possibility of rash, factional action—Jouvenel's ambulatory law. Ambulatory law being the mere will of the majority or its legislature, custom and natural law will be cast aside as impediments to progress. Once this happens, Jouvenel observes,

The despot whom a political wave carries to Power can twist into the most fantastic shapes what had already lost all certainty of form. Immutable verities being things of the past, he can now impose his own—intellectual monstrosities resembling those creatures of nightmare with the head taken from one animal and the limbs from another. By setting up a kind of vicious "alimentary circle" he is enabled to feed the people on ideas which they return to him in the guise of general will. This general will is the breeding grounds of laws which are ever more divorced not only from the divine but also from the human intelligence . . . Law has lost its soul and become jungle.[110]

We do not expect most of our readers to share Jouvenel's nightmare vision of the commanding constitution in practice. Rather, our point is to show the fears that lie behind the skepticism toward "democratic" political action evinced in mediating constitutions and, in particular, the prime example of such a constitution in modern times: the United States Constitution of 1787. It is to that constitution we now turn.

3

The Framers' Constitution

THE UNITED STATES CONSTITUTION established structures intended to serve limited political purposes, with domestic legislation principally aimed at "regulation of . . . various and interfering interests."[1] It also, of course, aimed to maintain the rule of law, both for the people and for those who would hold positions of power in the government. The new government would mediate among rather than reshape or dominate preexisting interests and institutions in the interest of peace, stability, and ordered liberty.

We begin here by showing the Framers' view of the limited purposes of the Constitution, particularly in light of their concern that the new government fit the character of the American people and of their preexisting governments. This requires laying out, in summary fashion, general assumptions at the time of the founding regarding republicanism and federalism, as well as the specific character of the federal government as one of limited, enumerated powers. We then turn to the means chosen by the Framers to bind the federal government to its proper ends within the limits set by the rule of law. The constitutional means thus chosen were the relatively familiar ones of a separation and restrictive enumeration of powers, maintained by checks and balances, and a distinctly limited judicial power to uphold the law of the land. We conclude this chapter with an outline of the nonmechanical means necessary for the constitutional structure to work, namely, constitutional morality.

Clothes and the Wearer

In a letter to the Marquis de Lafayette, Alexander Hamilton agreed with Montesquieu, that prominent source of constitutional wisdom to the founding generation, "that a nation's form of government ought to be fitted to it as a suit of clothes is fitted to its wearer." And Hamilton recognized the implications of this statement, continuing, "consequently . . . what may be good at Philadelphia may be bad at Paris and ridiculous at Petersburgh."[2] Such a comment, particularly when emanating from Hamilton, the great nationalist, might be taken to mean only that this founder understood some peoples to be capable of sustaining some forms of government while others were not. And that interpretation would be accurate, as far as it goes. But Hamilton's recognition of the need for governments to fit the nature of the people raises the question of what kind of government was deemed fit for Americans at the time of the drafting and adoption of the American Constitution.

Delegates to the Philadelphia Convention were not creating a new government, ex nihilo. They sought not to form a new nation, but rather "a more perfect union." They had to craft a constitutional framework suited to the character of the people if it was to have any chance of achieving ratification, let alone establishing a government that would last. The new constitution would mediate among rather than usurp or destroy preexisting institutions, abiding by rather than replacing preexisting beliefs and practices.

Focusing on *The Federalist* as our guide, it seems clear that the Constitution's Framers saw the character of Americans as both republican and localist. To begin with, rule by consent of the governed had become both habitual and legitimate as a matter of faith with the American colonists long before independence. Only republican government would fit the character, or "genius," of the people.[3] And the long history of Americans living in isolated communities within independently governed colonies possessing their own constitutions, laws, and customs meant that any new, federal constitution would have to be constructed upon, rather than replacing, preexisting political entities.

Republicanism

Numerous historians and political scientists have charged the drafters of the Philadelphia Constitution with a hostility toward majority rule.[4] Indeed, the Constitution as a whole has been painted as a kind of plot by which aristocratic forces sought (with great success) to cabin and minimize the more revolutionary, democratic impulses of the American people, as found in writings such as the Declaration of Independence.[5] We would do well, however, to remember just what kind of government that Declaration stated was the natural right of man, namely, government by consent.

In the oft-quoted second paragraph of the Declaration, we are told of "certain unalienable Rights" with which we are endowed by our Creator, including "Life, Liberty and the pursuit of Happiness." The Declaration continues, stating that "to secure these rights, Governments are instituted among Men, deriving their just powers from the consent of the governed."[6] We are not entering here into the various debates concerning the precise nature of natural rights.[7] Rather, we note the fundamental element on which the Declaration insists for the protection of rights, namely, governments "deriving their just powers from the consent of the governed." This is no absolute demand for majority rule on all things at all times. It is, rather, an inclusive statement of the rightful origins of governmental powers in the people.

The scope of the demand for "consent" is hardly universal. To begin with, not even consent can justify tyranny. As Publius put it in *Federalist* 10, a central goal of the American Constitution was "to secure the public good and private rights against the danger of [majority factions], and at the same time to preserve the spirit and form of popular government."[8] Liberty, requiring peace of mind and the rule of law, remained the chief goal of government, though one to be achieved, if possible, through republican means.

And what are republican means? What, indeed, is a republic? The definition of republican government (as opposed, of course, to modern "civic republicanism") begins with its differentiation from monarchy, not with calls for direct democracy. As the Framers recognized, republican government means rule dependent upon the consent of the governed; it does not mean—cannot mean if it is to last—direct rule by popular majorities. On this point Publius, the great defender of the Philadelphia Constitution, had no need to prevaricate. Democracy was an unstable, unworkable form of government, even in the small polities of ancient Greece.[9] It was to be avoided.

To be sure, rule by the consent of the governed was absolutely crucial in America, where republicanism was the order of the day, and where it had been practiced for many decades, as the colonies had governed themselves in a republican fashion even as they sought to remain loyal subjects within the British Empire. Such republicanism-within-monarchy had been an essential element of colonial life. Colonial governing documents attest to the prevalence of local powers of self-government that were structured in a republican fashion, ranging from town meetings to representative assemblies exercising control over the vast majority of local issues, and even of judges active within the colonies.[10] Violation of these norms of republican self-government by new British policies had served as a major cause of the American Revolution.[11]

As to the new constitution, Publius notes in *Federalist* 39 that every branch of the new government would conform to the genuine principles of republican government because it would be one "which derives all its powers directly or indirectly from the great body of the people, and is administered by persons holding their offices during pleasure for a limited period, or during good behavior."[12] Essential, then, to republican government, according to Publius, is that the officeholders be appointed, directly or indirectly, by the people, and be reliant on the people for any continuation in office. Obviously, "the people" was defined much more narrowly (free males possessing varied amounts of property) than we today would deem just. But this definition was in important ways a live issue in this and succeeding eras.[13]

Antifederalists were no more sensitive to the calls of democratic justice for slaves and other disenfranchised Americans than were federalists. Antifederalists were, however, convinced that "the legislature of a free country should be so formed as to have a competent knowledge of its constituents, and enjoy their confidence. To produce these essential requisites, the representation ought to be fair, equal, and sufficiently numerous, to possess the same interests, feelings, opinions, and views, which the people themselves would possess, were they all assembled."[14]

As one group of antifederalists argued, the small size of the houses of Congress in relation to the population meant that "men of the most elevated rank in life will alone be chosen. The other orders in the society, such as farmers, traders, and mechanics, who all ought to have a component number of their best informed men in the legislature, will be totally unrepresented."[15] Antifederalists considered the extent of representation in the proposed constitution insufficient to produce the necessary mix of interests and opinions in the legislature.

Federalists and antifederalists alike were committed to a representative form of republican government with a franchise of limited extent (though in historical terms rather broad), designed to maintain ordered liberty. The great fear of the antifederalists was that the national Congress would assume for itself the rights and powers of the states, render itself permanent, and constitute itself a new aristocracy able to deny the rights of the people. Antifederalists proposed a set of amendments to the Constitution, including ones regarding taxation, control of the militia, and control over elections. They also consistently argued for a set of traditional and common law rights protecting states, communities, and individual persons from federal powers.[16] In sum, they argued for increased protection of ordered liberty in the face of federal republican majorities.

The implications of Americans' republican character for constitutional design go beyond the election of officeholders. If the genius of the American people demands republican government, and the good of government is ordered liberty, then the Constitution of the United States must have as a primary goal the reconciliation of these two potentially conflicting goods. Publius argues that such a reconciliation would be accomplished under the new constitution due to its application within an extended republic.

As often has been noted, a chief innovation of the political theory of *The Federalist* is its taking what antifederalists deemed an absolute bar to republican government—extensive territory and a multiplicity of interests—and arguing that it is, in fact, an essential basis for just, long-term republican liberty. The primary danger to ordered liberty under republican government, Publius points out, is faction, defined as "a number of citizens, whether amounting to a minority or majority of the whole, who are united and actuated by some common impulse of passion, or of interest, adverse to the rights of other citizens, or to the permanent and aggregate interests of the community."[17] A republican government is capable of preventing minority factions from causing great damage because it is ruled by the principle of popular sovereignty. But majority factions within a republic could be deadly because there would be no way to keep them from pursuing their ends at the expense of the public good and of the rights of minorities.

It is here that Publius emphasizes the benefits of an extended republic. Because homogeneity is impossible to achieve in a free government, greater diversity of interests is to be preferred to lesser; in this way majority factions generally will be prevented from ever forming. The variety of interests represented in a large and diverse republic by nature precludes frequent coalescence of passion and interest among a majority of the people.

The structure of the Constitution, in particular its representative form and the relatively large number of citizens represented by each legislator, would further weaken factions in their pursuit of political power. A relatively small legislature could not possibly mirror all the variety of interests within an extended republic, precluding that form of republicanism advocated by antifederalists. In Publius's view, however, the Constitution would provide better protections for liberty than could any mirroring representation. The process of representation within the large districts provided for in the Constitution would produce a filtering effect, in which "fit characters" distinct and relatively distant from the specific passions and interests of those they represent would be elected.[18]

While the multiplicity of interests in an extended republic would not create any Olympian group of purely public-interested statesmen, it would produce a divergence of interests among the representatives and, more important, a distance between representatives and their constituents' interests sufficient to allow for dispassionate consideration of the merits and demerits of proposed legislation. Perhaps most important, there would be a significant number of truly disinterested representatives—that is, representatives simply lacking any connection with a particular issue or interest, be it financial, ideological, or professional—on any given issue. These disinterested representatives would be able to act as arbiters between factions, seeking the public interest and checking any "schemes of oppression."[19]

The plural structure of society and the filtering effect of representation would, then, produce a government in which factions would almost always be minority factions. They would have to sell their ideas to a significant group of representatives who would have a certain amount of virtue (being fit characters) and, perhaps more important, simply would not have any dog in the fight, so to speak. Thus, while sustained majorities in any republican government must eventually get their way, even if that way undermines ordered liberty, in an extensive representative republic, disinterested mediating groups would hold sway on the vast majority of issues and be able to prevent republican government from becoming oppressive.

Federalism and Localism

Self-evidently, the new constitution would not leave the states in the dominant position they had held under the Articles of Confederation, with full, independent power to regulate their own affairs, the affairs of their citizens, trade with other states, and even their decision whether (or not) to pay into the common treasury. But the new constitution would remain in large measure a federal one, as that term has come to be understood. It would mix elements of state self-mastery with elements of national power and cooperation between levels of government.

As Publius argues in *Federalist* 39, the new constitution would be federal in its foundations in that its ratification would be performed not by the American people as a whole but by the people of each state, acting as sovereigns of their particular realms. The new government would be national to the extent that it was empowered to act directly on the citizens of the various states, rather than through the operations of the states themselves. But the actual powers of the federal government would be distinctly limited, encompassing only specific, enumerated powers, leaving the bulk of power and authority at the state level. And, while the federal representatives would have a role to play in deciding upon any constitutional amendments, the states also would have a necessary role in such decisions, rendering them both national and federal.[20]

The Constitutional Convention grew from the determination to address specific problems with the Articles of Confederation—predominantly those relating to trade, taxes, and foreign relations. Addressing these problems required a new mechanism of government with new powers that, in certain instances, would act on people as individuals rather than through their states. But the new government would have to act within the context of a people attached from both habit and belief to the preexisting societies and governments of their states and localities.

The Constitution is built upon a series of compromises intended to recognize the primary importance and maintain a central status and integrity for the states within a new form of union. The famous "Great Compromise" produced a two-house legislature in which population would be represented in the lower house and state interests secured (through appointment of senators by state legislatures) in the upper. Even the notorious "three-fifths rule," by which slaves were to be counted as three-fifths of a person for federal voting purposes, had as a key motive the maintenance of state interests within the national government.

The Constitution took shape as a mechanism intended to regulate relations (that is, mediate) among states and between the general government and other nations. It built upon a set of preexisting structures in the states and the localities with origins and traditions rooted deep in American history. As Donald Lutz has pointed out, local self-government was integral to the first "founding" of America by the English colonists in the seventeenth century. Design for local government was left to the settlers, provided local laws did not contradict those in England. When added to the colonies' distance from a mother country preoccupied by its own civil war, this constitutional latitude fostered predominantly local self-government. The isolation of communities in a hostile environment often characterized by physical dangers put a premium on cooperation, which was maximized through regular and inclusive meetings. Lutz notes, "Town or colony meetings were often a regular event before any foundation document was written and approved."[21]

Of course, foundation documents were, in fact, written and approved—one of them near the very beginning of permanent English settlement in the New World. The Mayflower Compact famously brought together settlers of Plymouth Colony to "covenant and combine [themselves] together into a civil Body Politick, for [their] better Ordering and Preservation" and the glory and honor of God and king. This "combination" necessarily implied common governance, such that the signers committed themselves to obey the future acts of their "Body Politick," stating that they would "enact, constitute, and frame, such just and equal Laws, Ordinances, Acts, Constitutions, and Officers, from time to time, as shall be thought most meet and convenient for the general Good of the Colony."[22]

Such tight-knit, local communalism went hand-in-hand with a federal view of governance, in which responsibilities were greatest at the most local level and ceded upward to larger, more general governing bodies only where the interests served clearly were more general and where their

pursuit at this more general level was consistent with the continued flourishing of more natural, local communities. During the American Revolution,
this localism played out in the colonists' claims that the natural and historical form of a free society was federal. This presumption continued its
dominance after the Revolution. Thus, in 1788, for example, "The Impartial
Examiner" argued that each of the states constituted its own separate
society; each state had its own unique interests, needs, and circumstances,
rendering any common scheme of rule or even taxation unjust on account
of its incapacity to fit local needs.[23]

This is not to say that there were no attempts to alter more radically the
American form of government, or to transfer more comprehensive powers
to the center. Perhaps the clearest attempt to "nationalize" the United
States at the Constitutional Convention was Madison's idea, put forward in
the Virginia Plan, for a power in the national legislature to "negative" or
veto state legislation.[24] It failed utterly to gain the delegates' support.

Deliberations at the Constitutional Convention took place within a
definite understanding of the limits of legitimate, acceptable change—
limits with their roots in the (whether grudging or happy) recognition of
a preexisting set of political, social, and cultural realities. The Framers'
Constitution retained a structure in which most important powers and the
focus of governance remained in the states. It did not meld the various
states into a new, unitary government with full, sovereign governing powers.
Rather, it set up a mechanism exercising specific, enumerated powers with
the limited intention of providing a respectable common front in dealing
with other countries and the basic apparatus of free trade among the more
organic, fundamental member states.[25]

Decades later, in commenting on "the complex nature of the Constitution of the United States," Tocqueville still found the federal structure of
governance intact. He argued that the Constitution "consists of two distinct
social structures, connected, and, as it were, encased one within the other;
two governments, completely separate and almost independent, the one
fulfilling the ordinary duties and responding to the daily and indefinite
calls of a community, the other circumscribed within certain limits and
only exercising an exceptional authority over the general interests of the
country."[26]

Here Tocqueville referred not just to the relatively new, formal federal
Constitution—nor even to the formal constitutions of the states. These

"two governments" fulfilled duties and responded to calls rooted in the unwritten constitution of the people, organized in its various communities and making up the "two distinct social structures" of nation and state. Within the constitution of the realm of the United States, the federal government played a limited role covering exceptional events and circumstances.

It remains true that the Constitution was designed to play an essential role in governing the United States. As a mediating constitution it includes key provisions aimed at maintaining internal peace, good relations, and, in particular, the ability of citizens and commerce to traverse state boundaries. Thus, in Article I, Section 10, the Constitution bars states from a number of activities (e.g., entering into treaties, imposing revenue-producing duties on imports, impairing obligations of contract, or keeping troops or ships of war in peacetime) that would put a state at odds, commercially or militarily, with other states or the union. Thus, also in Article I, Section 10, the Constitution bars states from a number of actions (e.g., passing an ex post facto law or bill of attainder that in essence enacts a legal judgment against a particular person or persons) undermining the liberties and legal character of the United States. Along these lines, the Constitution specifically guarantees, in Article IV, Section 4, a republican form of government to each state.

And Article IV includes a number of provisions protecting citizens of one state in their dealings with and in other states. The Full Faith and Credit Clause requires, most fundamentally, that each state recognize the judgments of courts in other states when they have decided on the merits of a case. Thus, a citizen winning a lawsuit in one state need not retry the case in other states in order to collect from a defendant who has moved there. Article IV also guarantees every citizen protection of his or her "privileges and immunities" when in another state. As one early Supreme Court opinion put it, these privileges and immunities include "protection by the Government; the enjoyment of life and liberty . . . the right of a citizen of one State to pass through, or to reside in any other State, for purposes of trade, agriculture, professional pursuits, or otherwise; to claim the benefits of the writ of habeas corpus; to institute and maintain actions of any kind in the courts of the State; to take, hold and dispose of property, either real or personal; and an exemption from higher taxes or impositions than are paid by the other citizens of the State."[27]

Finally, in Article IV we find provisions requiring states to assist in returning fugitives, including fugitive slaves, to the state from which they have escaped.

That interpretation of these provisions would spawn significant debate among states, and between a variety of states and the national government, is not surprising. Perhaps most tragic, persistent attempts to enforce fugitive slave acts, in general terms permitted and even required by the Constitution, can be seen as a substantial cause of the Civil War. Ever-more draconian laws, showing ever-more contempt for due process rights of African Americans, whether enslaved or freed, endangered the rights of all Americans and produced substantial resistance from courts and state governments as well as American citizens and communities, precipitating vigorous questioning, even in Northern areas, of the supremacy of federal law and court decisions in relation to slavery.[28] This tragic episode within a tragic section of American history shows not the nationalist character of the Constitution but rather the dangers to its federal character from overreaching by any one party or section seeking to defend its own interests.

Americans no longer are accustomed to thinking of their government as composed of "twenty-four [or fifty] small sovereign nations, whose agglomeration constitutes the body of the Union." We no longer think of the national government as "the exception" and the state governments as "the rule."[29] Thus it appears clear that our unwritten constitution has changed. Nonetheless, the federal Constitution was designed as a partial, mediating structure, intended to be part of a more complex federal structure. American states came first in time, first in importance, and first in generative power. That is, the states, as full-fledged governing entities, provided the limited motive force, and their peoples provided the limited legitimate authority accorded to the center, whose tasks focused upon mediating between the more local and fundamental social and governmental units.

Limited Government

The well-known failures of the Articles of Confederation, under which interstate trade wars, economic dislocation, international humiliation, and domestic unrest all proliferated, prompted and shaped the drive for constitutional change. Almost as important as these problems, however, (as shown by the nearly successful opposition of the antifederalists) was Americans' abiding fear of an overpowering, arbitrary central government. Supporters of the new constitution argued that its federal nature constituted a fundamental protection against any such danger. As James Wilson argued in his State House speech, where state governments might be seen as by nature invested with every power not specifically excepted by the people in forming them, the new, federal constitution was an artificial construct under which only those powers specifically granted might legitimately be exercised.[30]

We begin here by summarizing those powers specifically granted the national government, particularly as set forth in Article I, Section 8, dealing with Congress. These include the power to tax, pay debts, and provide for the common defense and general welfare; to borrow money; "to regulate commerce with foreign nations, and among the several states, and with the Indian tribes"; to set uniform laws regarding naturalization, bankruptcy, monetary values, weights and measures; "to establish post offices and post roads"; to award patents; to declare war; to raise, support, and regulate national armed forces; and to exert substantial control over the militia.

These are significant powers, over the proper definitions of which much of our constitutional history has been fought.[31] In particular, the power to regulate commerce has grown over time. This power began as a limited one aimed at preventing state actors from interfering with cross-border transactions—to maintain free trade among the states.[32] Such a power necessarily implicates activities such as transportation that naturally cross state lines, but interstate commerce went no further.[33] Increasingly after the Civil War, the Supreme Court rejected this understanding, particularly as embodied in the distinction between commerce (trade) and manufacturing (making things, including goods that might serve as inputs to other goods assembled in other states). Over time, the commerce power came to encompass all aspects of economic and even social and private life having any significant effect on "commerce"—now defined to encompass the health of the economy as a whole.[34]

But for decades after the Constitution's ratification, commerce and other enumerated powers were recognized as being distinctly limited. There was no general, national power to legislate. Legitimate national legislation was rooted in specific, limited grants of power. Flexibility in the application of these powers was provided by another grant made in Article I, Section 8, namely, the power "to make all laws which shall be necessary and proper for carrying into execution the foregoing powers, and all other powers vested by this Constitution in the government of the United States, or in any department or officer thereof." But this provision's inclusion in Section 8, without any special emphasis or systemic interpretive authority, makes clear its purpose as that of providing only incidental powers to carry out those specifically enumerated in the document, rather than granting any new, separate powers.[35] Moreover, as Richard Epstein has shown, a reasoned interpretation of the Necessary and Proper Clause demands that governmental actions be both necessary *and* proper, and places actions within its purview somewhere along the limited spectrum between "appropriate" and "indispensable." That is, the clause only authorizes actions taken in furtherance of specifically enumerated powers that are more than merely appropriate for carrying out such power, though they need not be absolutely necessary.[36]

We are not arguing that the Constitution is some kind of libertarian document decreeing a particular, uniform structure for society.[37] Rather, it was written as a mediating constitution, granting particular powers for particular purposes and placing limits on those powers, even as it placed certain restrictions on state powers in order to maintain the overall structure of dual government. In this light, inclusion of specific limits on federal power in Article I, Section 9 and specific limits on state powers in Article I, Section 10 shows the intrinsic purpose of the Constitution to serve as a frame of government, specifically assigning and limiting powers among its constituent parts so as to fit the national government within the constitution of the realm.

Finally, the addition of the Tenth Amendment, however often dismissed as redundant by recent courts, emphasizes its mediating structure. The Tenth Amendment states that "the powers not delegated to the United States by the Constitution, nor prohibited by it to the States, are reserved to the States respectively, or to the people." In so doing it makes clear that the Constitution was not intended as a general grant of power to the federal government. Far from "redundant," such a provision dictates that particular grants of power be read in a relatively narrow fashion. In this way the Constitution would be effective in its sphere while respecting the integrity of the states and preventing them from becoming merely the interstitial residuum of a general power held by the national government. This would mean that, as noted in *Federalist* 33, a congressional act beyond its enumerated powers is a "usurpation" that deserves to be treated as such.[38]

The Constitution was drafted as a limited grant of power for specific purposes, intended to protect a preexisting set of institutions, habits, and arrangements while securing greater stability, freedom of internal trade, and capacity in dealings with other countries.[39] But how was this structure to be maintained? The answer is to be found largely in the structure itself. Understanding this structure requires understanding some of the less often noted though fundamental goods it was intended to provide, namely, the prevention of oppression and, primarily, the rule of law.

Oppression, Tyranny, and the Rule of Law

We already have encountered one form of oppression against which Publius argues the Constitution would provide protections: the depredations of faction. The circumstance of an extended republic, combined with a system of representation that filtered out much natural self-interest, would, for the most part, prevent majority factions from forming and enacting oppressive legislation. In addition to the problem of factious majorities, however, Publius recognizes another form of oppression that must be addressed: oppression of the people by the governors. As he notes in *Federalist* 51, it is necessary to both guard "one part of the society against the injustice of the other part" and to guard "the society against the oppression of its rulers."[40]

Factions are portions of the people. Thus, their factional legislation would institute injustice to be perpetrated upon one part of the society by the other. What, then, is the oppression of the people by the rulers? How is it to be defined? *Federalist* 47 provides the classic, if often misunderstood, statement: "The accumulation of all powers, legislative, executive, and judiciary, in the same hands, whether of one, a few, or many, and whether hereditary, self-appointed, or elective, may justly be pronounced the very definition of tyranny."[41]

It is important to keep in mind that Publius here portrays tyranny as a state of affairs, or form of regime, rather than one or more bad acts. That is, it is the fact of a combination of powers that makes for tyranny, not the particular acts that might result. This is not to say that the particular bad, oppressive acts, say, of a factious majority are unimportant. It is, rather, to recognize the primary source of such bad acts in the loss of the rule of law.

We already have noted Publius's citing of Montesquieu in pointing out that a union of the legislative and executive powers would mean that "there can be no liberty, because apprehensions may arise lest *the same* monarch or senate should *enact* tyrannical laws to *execute* them in a tyrannical manner." Further, should the judicial power be "joined with the legislative, the life and liberty of the subject would be exposed to arbitrary control, for *the judge* would then be *the legislator.*" And, should judicial and executive powers be combined, "the judge might behave with all the violence of an oppressor."[42]

Montesquieu's emphasis is on the actions of particular governmental officials exercising combined powers, and the effects of such actions on the peace of mind necessary for liberty. Yet particular oppressive acts need not destroy liberty. One bad law may harm particular persons and undermine the common good, but in and of itself one bad law (usually) will not an utterly oppressive regime make. The more general problem Montesquieu describes is one of regime change. That is, should executive, legislative, and judicial powers be combined, with one branch exercising all the powers of one or more others, the regime itself would become a tyranny—that is, a society ruled by a person or group operating outside the law.

We can see in Publius's arguments (and Montesquieu's fears) a commonality between the problem of faction and the need for a separation of powers. The principal danger posed by factions is that a particular self-interested group will achieve a majority in the legislature. A majority faction will not need to appeal to any disinterested section of the legislature and thus will be able to act as judge in its own cause—that is, it will be above the law. Any group in the society—creditors, or mechanics, or any other organized alliance—if it secures a majority of legislators to its cause, in effect will act for its own interests, without the need to justify itself to the "bar" of public, or at least congressional, opinion.[43]

In much the same way, a president who has achieved control over the lawmaking process will be in a position to act arbitrarily. He or she will be able to both enact and execute laws, without needing to justify his or her actions before the legislature. Should a political leader also achieve mastery of the judicial function, Montesquieu argues, "all would be lost." Montesquieu references the republics of Italy in his time, in which "the body of the magistracy as executor of the laws, retains all the power it has given itself as legislator. It can plunder the state by using its general wills; and, as it also has the power of judging, it can destroy each citizen by using its particular wills."[44]

In these Italian republics, according to Montesquieu, the magistrates had freed themselves from the bonds of law. By taking unto themselves the executive and judicial as well as the legislative powers, they had acquired the ability to act in an arbitrary fashion. Whether through statutory pronouncement, administrative or police action, or through decisions in the courts, they acted as they wished, rather than as demanded by any laws they were bound to obey. The result, Montesquieu argues, was a system as despotic as any found anywhere within his ken, regardless of whether it began as a republic, a monarchy, or a despotism. Any form of rule lacking the primacy of law is, whatever its formal name, tyranny. It cannot support or countenance liberty, for "every private citizen" must live with the knowledge that he may be ruined at any time by the decisions of the rulers.[45]

Scott Gordon has corrected the fundamental historical inaccuracy of Montesquieu's characterization of Venice in particular. Yet his correction underscores Montesquieu's point. Venice gained a reputation for brutal governance through a combination of significant, though limited, abuses of power by its security forces in times of political unrest, a general hostility to this powerful city-state among its rivals, and a fundamental misunderstanding of its governing structure. Far from a totalitarian despotism, the regime in Venice was one of proliferating checks and balances among a variety of institutions with overlapping powers, structures, and terms of office. There was no grand sovereign. Indeed, Gordon argues, "'Sovereignty' is a concept that is inapplicable to a political system that, like the Venetian one, is an equilibrium of plural centers of power."[46] Venetian government was characterized by a variation of the separated powers Montesquieu espoused as necessary for ordered liberty. But Montesquieu failed to recognize this fact, probably due to faulty information, the dearth of examples of such regimes in his time, and the sheer complexity of the Venetian model. He failed to recognize the source of law in Venice and so came to believe that there was none.

Maintenance of the rule of law was central to Publius's under-standing of the Constitution, and the separation of powers in particular. For example, he praises functional separation as a means of preventing legislators from exempting themselves from their own laws. Legislators would be disinclined to pass oppressive laws if they (and their families and friends) would be subject to them. And legislators would remain under the laws so long as they did not assume for themselves the executive and/or judicial power. A merger of legislative and executive powers, for instance, could result in the legislature passing unjust or oppressive laws and then executing them in a partial manner to exclude members of the legislature and their families and friends from its provisions (as with, for example, congressional exclusions from provisions of various labor laws and the Patient Protection and Affordable Care Act—Obamacare). As Publius observes in *Federalist* 57, with an effective separation between the branches, the legislators "can make no law which will not have its full oper-ation on themselves and their friends, as on the great mass of the society." This fact alone, he holds, helps to ensure that they will not pass "oppressive measures."[47]

Of course, legislators might be willing to subject themselves to oppres-sive laws. And rulers with arbitrary power might exercise it with wisdom and enlightened concern for the common good. Finally, despite the sepa-ration of powers and despite the filtering effect and other outgrowths of an extended republic, a faction might succeed in instituting an oppressive law from which it would exempt its members and their favored constituents. But these last would be extraordinary circumstances requiring the people to act with vigilance and spirit—qualities without which no republic can survive when facing great troubles.[48]

Origins and Purposes of the Constitution's Separation of Powers

The connection between the separation of powers and the rule of law was no mere bit of sophistry from the mind of Publius. That separation of powers had taken hold in the colonies is attested to by the fact that after independence eleven of the thirteen states in their new constitutions pro-vided for precisely this formal structure.[49] Of the six states that prefaced their constitutions with a statement or declaration of rights, four expressly called for separation of the three branches of government. For example, the first article in the body of the Georgia Constitution of 1777 provides that "the legislative, executive, and judiciary departments shall be separate and distinct, so that neither exercise the powers properly belonging to the other."[50] The Massachusetts Constitution, authored by John Adams, added to its provision for the separation of powers a clear statement of its purpose, "to the end it may be a government of laws and not of men."[51]

But none of the states embraced what might be considered a model constitutional separation of powers. As Publius painstakingly shows in *Federalist* 47, the state constitutions could be faulted for blending governmental powers. And, perhaps worse, they lacked any effective means of maintaining the separation that did exist, relying for this purpose primarily on officeholders obeying "parchment barriers." As a result, these states had little success in maintaining the separation of powers called for in their constitutions, with the legislatures eventually dominating the other branches, even assuming some of their primary functions.

As Jefferson remarks in his *Notes on the State of Virginia*, "[A]ll the powers of government, legislative, executive, and judiciary, result to the legislative body." This concentration he regarded as "precisely the definition of despotic government" since "one hundred and seventy-three despots" can be "as oppressive as one." In Virginia, he noted, the legislature had *"decided rights* which should have been left to *judiciary controversy"* and its *"direction of the executive, during the whole time of their session, is becoming habitual and familiar."*[52]

These experiences at the state level provide the backdrop for a fuller understanding of deliberations surrounding separation of powers in the Philadelphia Convention. A useful case in point is the debate over the Council of Revision. The Virginia Plan provided not only for a separation of powers, but also for a Council of Revision that would empower "the Executive and a convenient number of the National Judiciary" to veto measures passed by the legislature.[53] Leaving to one side the full details regarding proposed powers of the Council, what is striking is the persistence of its supporters (primarily Madison and James Wilson) and the arguments against its adoption that ultimately prevailed.

After initial rejection of the Council of Revision, it was reintroduced some six weeks later to be rejected again and then reintroduced in modified form a month later for its final and decisive rejection—8–3, with each state voting as a unit. Why this persistence, we may ask, in light of the fact that, as its opponents were quick to point out, it authorized the merger or blending of two departments in seeming violation of the separation principle? Madison provided the answer by way of supporting its reconsideration: "Experience in all the states," he observed, "had evinced a powerful tendency in the Legislature to absorb all the power into its vortex. This was the real source of danger to the American constitutions; & suggested the necessity of giving every defensive authority to other departments that was consistent with republican principles."[54]

Wilson, in a last-ditch effort to gain approval of a modified Council veto power, pointed out that, while tyranny was most commonly associated with a "formidable" executive, "where the executive is not formidable" tyranny should appropriately be linked with the legislature." He agreed with the thrust of Madison's reasoning in arguing that "the joint weight of the two departments [executive and judicial] was necessary to balance the single weight of the Legislature."[55] What seems clear, then, is that those who supported a Council of Revision did so in light of the states' experiences; they sought to protect the two weaker branches from legislative aggrandizement in an effort to preserve the separation of powers.

The objections to the Council were weighty. John Dickinson at an early stage set forth the most basic, namely, that review of legislation by the executive and members of the judiciary "involved an improper mixture of powers." Specific objections took the form of pointing out that judging "the policy of public measures" was "foreign" to the judicial function; that judges "ought to be able to expound the law as it should come before them, free from the bias of having participated in its formation," and, similarly, that judges "in exercising the function of expositors might be influenced by the part they had taken . . . in framing the laws." There was fear, too, that judges' participation in "legislative business" might lead to party divisions in the judiciary.[56]

Interesting in this aspect of the deliberations is that both those for and those against the Council of Revision subscribed to the principle of separation of powers. While there were obvious differences over how best to maintain a separation, all agreed that, as Nathaniel Gorham put it in the final debate on this issue, "a check on the legislature is necessary."[57] And, from almost the outset of the deliberations, there was agreement that the executive should possess a veto power, with the major point of disagreement centering on what proportion of both chambers would be necessary to override the veto.

The debate over the manner of electing the president also illustrates the Convention's agreement on the need for a separation of powers and the ways in which its provision intruded upon other highly cherished goals. The Virginia Plan, in accordance with prevailing practice at the state level, provided for election of the executive by the combined chambers of the legislature. The Convention initially accepted this mode of election, but added a proviso that would make the executive "ineligible a second time." Slightly over a month later, the delegates reaffirmed election by the national legislature, but also by a narrow vote eliminated the provision barring reeligibility. A major reason for this reversal centered on Gouverneur Morris's view that "ineligibility . . . tended to destroy the great motive to good behavior, the hope of being rewarded by a re-appointment. It was saying to him, make hay while the sun shines."[58]

The possible ramifications of this decision were almost immediately voiced. There were those who felt that the terms of office should be shortened if reeligibility were allowed. This was to some extent countered by the radical motion that the president serve "during good behavior" on grounds that reeligibility would "keep him [the president] dependent forever on the Legislature" and that "the independence of the Executive [was] equally essential with that of the Legislature." While the motion apparently did not have widespread support, Madison, among others, argued that it should be seriously considered, pointing out that the "Executive could not be independent of the Legislature, if dependent on the pleasure of that branch for reappointment." Invoking the authority of Montesquieu, Madison warned of the consequences of the union of two branches, namely, "tyrannical laws . . . that may be executed in a tyrannical manner."[59]

Madison eventually framed the essential issue in the following terms: the preservation of republican government "required some expedient for the purpose" of restraining the legislature, but "in devising it . . . the genuine principle of that [republican] form . . . [must] be kept in view." It would seem that Wilson had this in mind when he proposed a method of election designed to provide for reeligibility without the drawbacks cited by Madison, namely, that the "Executive be elected for 6 years, by a small number, not more than 15 of the Natl. Legislature, to be drawn from it, not by ballot, but by lot and who should retire immediately and make the election without separating."[60] This proposal never received serious consideration.

In late July, the Convention came back to its original position, namely, election of the executive for a seven-year term by the national legislature with no reeligibility. This decision, as we know, did not settle the matter; the Convention finally fixed upon election by the Electoral College. But the debate and deliberation over the manner of electing the executive are sufficient to explain why election by the Electoral College was gratifying to most of the delegates; it assured executive independence from the legislature while allowing for reeligibility.

Enforcing Separation of Powers: Checks and Balances

As the deliberations of the Philadelphia Convention unmistakably show, the legislature was considered the branch most in need of restraint if the constitutional separation of powers was to be maintained. In *Federalist* 48, for instance, Publius issues a stern warning: "[I]n a representative republic," in which executive powers are "carefully limited, both in extent and duration," and where the representative "assembly . . . inspired by a supposed influence over the people" and possessing "an intrepid confidence in its own strength; which is sufficiently numerous to fuel all the passions which actuate a multitude, yet not so numerous as to be incapable of pursuing objects of its passions, by means which reason prescribes; it is against the enterprising ambition of this department, that the people ought to indulge all their jealousy, and exhaust all their precautions."[61] Publius makes essentially the same point in discussing the president's power of veto when he writes of the "tendency . . . almost irresistible" on the part of the legislature to "absorb" the prerogatives of the other branches. "The representatives of the people, in a popular assembly," he continues, "seem sometimes to fancy, that they are the people themselves, and betray strong symptoms of impatience and disgust at the least sign of opposition from any other quarter."[62]

The conviction, reinforced by the behavior of the state legislatures, that Congress would be the aggressor in its relations with the executive and judiciary, plays a significant role in shaping Publius's answer to the question of how to maintain the necessary constitutional separation. Will, he asks, "parchment barriers"—marking out "with precision, the boundaries" of each department—serve to contain "the encroaching spirit of power?" Such barriers, he answers, have "been greatly overrated" by the drafters of state constitutions; they have not served to prevent the "legislative department" from "everywhere extending the sphere of its activity and drawing all power into its impetuous vortex."[63]

Can appeals to the people when there is an evident breach of the constitutional separation keep the branches in their proper orbits? Again, for various reasons, Publius is wary of this proposal. Such appeals, suggesting defects in the Constitution, in a number of ways would undermine popular confidence in and support for it; they would arouse the "public passions" thereby "disturbing the public tranquility." "But the greatest objection of all" to these appeals is that they would not preserve the constitutional separation; given the number, influence, connections, and prestige of the legislators—the most likely instigators of a transgression—the people would most likely side with them. Even if this were not the case, Publius observes, the popular resolution would not "turn on the true merits of the question," but instead upon partisan considerations. This, he concludes, would mean that "passions," not "reason" would carry the day.[64]

Finally, Publius considers whether provision for review of alleged transgressions at fixed intervals by a specified agency, such as that provided for by Pennsylvania with its "council of censors," empowered to review the actions of the branches, might serve to preserve the separation. Once again, he finds multiple reasons to reject this solution. If the transgressions occur close to the time of appeals, passions will again dominate; if they be distant from the time of appeal, they may already have taken root and "could not be extirpated" or they may have achieved their "mischievous effects"; or the institution reviewing the allegations would most likely consist of individuals who had participated in the actions under review. Additionally, he remarks, the "distant prospect of public censure" would scarcely serve as an effective deterrent, particularly against the encroachments of a numerous assembly.[65]

What, then, is Publius's solution? Its general contours are set forth at the outset of *Federalist* 51, where Publius writes that since these "exterior provisions" are "inadequate," the "only answer" resides in "so contriving the interior structure of the government, as that its several constituent parts may, by their mutual relations, be the means of keeping each other in their proper places." In this vein, he holds that the "great security" against the concentration of powers comes down to providing "those who administer each department, the necessary constitutional means, and personal motives, to resist encroachments of the others."[66] The "constitutional means" are those designed to weaken the stronger department, the legislature, and strengthen the weaker departments, the executive and judiciary.[67] The fact that, as he puts it, "in republican government, the legislative authority predominates," requires that it be weakened by dividing it "into different branches; and to render them, by different modes of election, and different principles of action, as little connected with each other, as the nature of their common functions, and their dependence on society, will admit."[68]

On the other hand, following this weaken/strengthen formula, Publius argues that the presidency should be "fortified" against potential assaults by the legislature. This fortification came in the form of a qualified veto, one that would require a two-thirds vote in both chambers to override. In keeping with the doctrine of separation of powers, the primary purpose to be served by this veto, as Publius takes pains to note in *Federalist* 73, is to enable the executive to repel encroachments by the legislature on executive powers; its secondary use relates to securing good government and neutralizing the excesses of popular government by blocking the passage of "bad laws, through haste, inadvertence, or design."[69]

Publius's remarks concerning the presidential veto, though brief, again reveal his concern over legislative encroachment. He acknowledges, for instance, that "at first view," "an absolute negative" would appear to be the "natural defence with which the executive should be armed." Indeed, the absolute negative would have been in keeping with Montesquieu's teachings. But, reflecting concerns raised in the Constitutional Convention, he points out that such a veto power might not be "altogether safe, nor alone sufficient." "On ordinary occasions, it might not be exerted with the requisite firmness; and on extraordinary occasions, it might be perfidiously abused."[70] Yet he appears to regard this lack of an absolute veto as something of a shortcoming when he refers to it as a "defect." In any event, he believes this defect can be overcome; he envisions the distinct possibility that a bond might develop between the Senate and the executive, presumably because they must cooperate in important functions and duties such as executive and judicial appointments and treaty making. Such a bonding would go a long way toward assuring that presidential vetoes would not be overridden. But, again, the fact that Publius would favor such an alliance indicates the degree to which he feared legislative aggrandizement.

Returning to the key ingredients of Publius's solution, we can readily perceive that the constitutional means he sets forth would be for naught if officeholders lacked the "personal motives" to employ them. What good, for instance, is the veto power if the executive fails to wield it when necessary to protect his constitutional authority? Thus, the second pillar of Publius's solution is connecting "the interest of the man," that is, the officeholder, "with the constitutional rights of the place." "Ambition," he insists, "must be made to counteract ambition."[71]

Publius later acknowledges that it is the "defect of better motives"— the dearth of persons who reliably show restraint or voluntarily obey written injunctions—that leads him to endorse a "policy" that relies on "supplying . . . opposite and rival interests."[72] The constitutional means, therefore, are a necessary but not a sufficient condition for maintaining the constitutionally prescribed division of powers. Without the appropriate personal motives, without the interest of the officeholder attaching to the "constitutional rights of the place," they will not serve their purpose.

Ultimately, then, the American system of separation of powers rests on the Framers' understanding of human motivation, particularly that of officeholders. Publius does not dwell on this understanding. His account does not inform us how officeholders are to be given the requisite "personal interest," how, in this context, "ambition" will be "made to counteract ambition," or how "opposite and rival interests" are going to be supplied. He simply assumes that the creation of institutions with different powers and functions would by itself be enough to provide individuals with motivations sufficient to preserve the separation. In today's vernacular, he assumes that politicians would "defend their turf."

Courts and the (Limited) Protections of the Law of the Land

Amidst the rough-and-tumble of politicians defending their turf, it might be supposed that the Supreme Court would play a major role as a kind of neutral, paternal arbiter, preventing tyranny from a position above the fray. And it is true that courts have a role to play in maintaining the structure of the Framers' Constitution. But it is a distinctly limited role, rooted in a limited view of the legitimacy and power of courts to interpret and apply the Constitution. That role primarily is to protect the people from laws violating the express provisions of the Constitution; only secondarily and in limited fashion are the courts conceived of as affecting the actions of other branches of government.

The source of the Supreme Court's authority to police the Constitution's structural boundaries can be found in the idea of judicial review. That review, or rather something akin to it, was not novel at the time of the Constitution's drafting. As Publius points out in *Federalist* 78, the very logic of constitutionalism demands a hierarchy of laws, with the fundamental law supreme: "[E]very act of a delegated authority, contrary to the tenor of the commission under which it is exercised, is void. No legislative act, therefore, contrary to the Constitution, can be valid. To deny this, would be to affirm, that the deputy is greater than his principal; that the servant is above his master; that the representatives of the people are superior to the people themselves; that men acting by virtue of powers, may do not only what their powers do not authorize, but what they forbid."[73]

The question, as Publius presents it, is not whether the Constitution—the legal act commissioning the people's representatives—is to be upheld in opposition to any clearly contrary act of those it commissions. The question concerns who, or rather what branch of government, is by nature best suited to determine the requirements of that Constitution and use them in judging lesser laws valid or invalid. Only specific, precise wording would indicate an intention to leave this power with Congress, which in exercising it would be judging in its own cause. Lacking such specific language, "it is far more rational to suppose, that the courts were designed to be an intermediate body between the people and the legislature, in order, among other things, to keep the latter within the limits assigned to their authority."[74]

Publius thus sees the Supreme Court playing a defensive role, protecting the people from governmental acts transgressing the fundamental law of the Constitution. The American Constitution is a limited one, that is, "one which contains certain specified exceptions to the legislative authority; such, for instance, as that it shall pass no bills of attainder, no *ex post facto* laws, and the like." And such limitations "can be preserved in practice no other way than through the medium of courts of justice, whose duty it must be to declare all acts contrary to the manifest tenor of the Constitution void. Without this, all the reservations of particular rights or privileges would amount to nothing."[75]

The Bill of Rights would add to the list of limitations on the powers of the federal government. But it would do nothing to alter the means by which the Supreme Court would protect the people from governmental acts violating the Constitution, namely, interpretation of the laws. Publius observes, "A constitution is, in fact, and must be regarded by the judges, as a fundamental law. It therefore belongs to them to ascertain its meaning, as well as the meaning of any particular act proceeding from the legislative body. If there should happen to be an irreconcilable variance between the two, that which has the superior obligation and validity ought, of course, to be preferred; or, in other words, the Constitution ought to be preferred to the statute, the intention of the people to the intention of their agents."[76]

Thus stated, the Supreme Court seems to have been granted an awesome power, to "say what the law is" in the Constitution and in the acts of Congress, and then settle any conflicts between them by siding with the Constitution. But this power can be overstated. To begin with, we should keep in mind Publius's following statement—that this power supposes no "superiority of the judicial to the legislative power. It only supposes that the power of the people is superior to both; and that where the will of the legislature, declared in its statutes, stands in opposition to that of the people, declared in the Constitution, the judges ought to be governed by the latter rather than the former. They ought to regulate their decisions by the fundamental laws, rather than by those which are not fundamental."

Publius's phrasing is important here. Judges should "be governed by" the Constitution. They should "regulate their decisions" according to the Constitution. That is, judges have a duty to uphold the laws and apply them—consistently favoring the superior to a conflicting inferior law—in any case or controversy coming before them. Publius thus emphasizes the relatively passive nature of courts in waiting to have cases brought to them, and then merely deciding them according to the hierarchy of relevant laws.

This is not to say that Publius is unaware of the dangers of judicial power. But, he adds,

[I]t can be of no weight to say that the courts, on the pretense of a repugnancy, may substitute their own pleasure to the constitutional intentions of the legislature. This might as well happen in the case of two contradictory statutes; or it might as well happen in every adjudication upon any single statute. The courts must declare the sense of the law; and if they should be disposed to exercise WILL instead of JUDGMENT, the consequence would equally be the substitution of their pleasure to that of the legislative body. The observation, if it prove anything, would prove that there ought to be no judges distinct from that body.[77]

Publius points here to the ever-present danger of judges acting arbitrarily—that is, according to their own conception of what is right, just, or advantageous rather than according to the judgment of their superior (the people) made concrete in law. Particular laws represent the will of the representatives of the people. They are rules of conduct formalized according to the procedures required by the Constitution, which is the fundamental expression of the people's direct, authoritative will. And the derivative laws, products of the derivative will, are to be judged in their form, content, and intent according to the rules laid down in the fundamental law. Thus, courts behave properly only when acting under the law, seeking to find and apply their judgment to something they have no right to create through their own will.

Central to understanding the Framers' Constitution is recognizing that, for the Framers, the judicial function—including as applied to the Constitution—is, in fact, judicial. That is, as Philip Hamburger has argued, judicial review of congressional legislation was not some radical new political power developed at or after the time of the Revolution. It was, instead, a part of a long-standing Anglo-American tradition according to which judges did their duty by deciding cases in such a manner as to uphold the law of the land.[78]

Refusing to be guided by laws going against the "manifest tenor" of a superior law was in itself a centuries-old recognition of judicial duty, of the normative "obligation of law in conscience."[79] Judges in the Anglo-American tradition long had invalidated acts of the monarch by upholding the claims of subjects when those claims were opposed by decrees or other royal acts that conflicted with the manifest tenor of the British constitution.[80] And, while it was true that courts could not hold acts of the legislature unconstitutional, this fact was rooted in circumstances specific to the "high court" of Parliament. That body served as the chief and highest expositor of the common law. Particularly given that Britain's was an unwritten constitution, Parliament held the role of highest constitutional interpreter, even being termed the "supreme court." And this left lower courts without the authority to question Parliament's decisions regarding its own powers.[81]

In America, judges were not bound to defer to legislatures as chief expositors of the law. American legislatures simply did not hold that office. Indeed, acts of colonial legislatures were seen as mere subordinate corporate rules. What is more, the colonies were governed by a common law undergirded and cabined by formative statutes, written charters, and, after the Revolution, written constitutions. These fundamental laws were both superior to regular legislative acts and amenable to judicial interpretation. While state constitution drafters did not feel the need to mention the generally accepted understanding that unconstitutional laws were unlawful, the federal Constitution was explicitly enacted by the preamble's declaration, "We the People . . . do ordain and establish this Constitution for the United States of America." In addition, the Supremacy Clause of Article VI declared the Constitution to be the law of the land, supreme over state laws and state judges.[82]

Thus, American judges could hold acts of their legislatures void as against the law of the land. Courts often lacked the independence to act according to their judicial duty during the colonial era. But such actions against legislation were far from unknown. As Hamburger reports, the number and geographical spread of decisions holding governmental acts unconstitutional as violating higher law "suggest how profoundly these ideals [of law and judicial duty] were a part of the logic and culture of Anglo-American law."[83]

Judges had an important constitutional role to play. But the role was that of judges, not grand arbiters of constitutional meaning. Conflicts between statutes and the Constitution were treated essentially the same as those between different statutes.[84] To the extent that courts refused to uphold laws on account of their being at variance with the Constitution, they did so in the process of deciding legal issues brought before them. Such issues were not to be decided as matters of political philosophy. As recognized well into the twentieth century, there was no general, abstract power of judicial review in the Framers' Constitution.[85] True, constitutional as well as statutory and common law meanings often are arrived at through the use of interpretive methods, structural arguments, and doctrines developed over time. But these methods, like common law maxims, served as tools and background understandings for deciding specific controversies. They were not philosophical designs intended to make laws cohere to any particular vision of the just or the good.[86]

Publius addresses courts exclusively as adjudicators. Courts' authority extends so far as to give the final word on the law as written, but only within their own, judicial sphere. Such is implicit in *The Federalist,* and made explicit by long practice and by numerous sources during the early republic.[87] Thomas Jefferson put the argument in its strongest terms in explaining his decision to cease prosecutions under the Alien and Sedition Acts. Abigail Adams had criticized Jefferson for ending prosecutions under that law; he had done so on the grounds that the law, despite being properly promulgated and upheld by the Supreme Court, was in his own opinion unconstitutional.

In a letter to Adams, Jefferson rejected the view that such determinations were up to the courts: "The opinion which gives to the judges the right to decide what laws are constitutional, and what are not, not only for themselves in their own sphere of action, but for the legislature and executive also, in their spheres, would make the judiciary a despotic branch."[88] Instead, Jefferson later argued, "[T]he Constitution has erected no such single tribunal, knowing that to whatever hands confided, with the corruptions of time and party; its members would become despots. It has more wisely made all the departments co-equal and co-sovereign within themselves."[89]

Along these lines, James Madison wrote that "as the Legislative, Executive, and Judicial departments of the United States are coordinate, and each equally bound to support the Constitution, it follows that each must, in the exercise of its functions, be guided by the text of the Constitution according to its own interpretation of it; and consequently; that in the event of irreconcilable interpretations, the prevalence of the one or the other department must depend on the nature of the case, as receiving its final decision from the one or the other, and passing from that decision into effect, without involving the functions of any other."[90]

Each branch must determine (and be allowed to determine) its constitutional duties for itself. As Jefferson pointed out, the courts have no legitimate power to order Congress to fulfill duties such as paying judges or funding the militia, or to order the president to appoint judges or issue military commissions.[91] Each branch must be recognized as sovereign within its own sphere, lest one of them usurp the powers of one or more of the other and so become, in effect, an arbitrary tyrant.

The Supreme Court helped maintain the governmental structure by exercising its own "sphere sovereignty." For example, courts in the early republic would balk at being saddled with the nonjudicial task of determining who might be eligible for veterans' disability payments, particularly when such decisions might be overturned by executive branch officers.[92] And, in *Marbury v. Madison,* the Supreme Court denied that it had the power to hear a case the Constitution reserved for first hearing in a lower court, even when this meant refusing compliance with a statute.[93] The court thus refused to cooperate with executive or legislative acts that would have blurred functional lines among branches.

This is not to say that the Supreme Court would have no influence beyond the narrow confines of its intrabranch decisions. But, according to Madison, that influence would have to be indirect, based on its reputation as "the surest expositor of the Constitution, as well in questions within its cognizance concerning the boundaries between the several departments of the Government as in those between the Union and its members."[94] The least dangerous branch was not suited to demanding more.[95] Indeed, the Framers had taken special care to provide for its independence out of fear that it would fall under the control of Congress.

Judicial review, then, was not some grand creation of judges in the early republic, let alone the sole creation of Chief Justice Marshall in the supposedly seminal decision in *Marbury v. Madison.* Rather, it is a grand name attached to the more prosaic traditional practice by which judges decide cases. The phrase "judicial duty" better captures this practice because it highlights the significant constraints on a judge properly acting as such. As Publius notes, courts must use judgment, not will. And this is no small, easy task. Judges require both institutional protections and virtues of personal restraint; they must be free from both the will of external forces, such as the crown and legislature, and from their own internal will, desires, and intellectual pride in order to do their duty.[96]

Judges also require the support of their profession if they are to maintain their capacity for restraint. Thus, for example, investiture ceremonies, of which the law retains the barest shadow, once served to exert social pressures and make clear professional expectations that helped judges place themselves within a wider tradition of judicial duty under law, as well as duty to their God.[97] It is easy for observers today to dismiss the motivations and comforts provided by professional standards and even (perhaps especially) religion in support of judicial duty. But such clearly were considered important in the early republic.

Hamburger relates the story of Rhode Island Supreme Court Justice Thomas Tillinghast, who, after holding a state statute ineffective as contradicting the law of the land, was not reappointed. Explaining his decision, Tillinghast said that, despite the inevitable damage to his career, he had "felt himself perfectly independent, while moving in the circle of his duty." Moreover, "however he might be affected for the honour of the State, he was wholly indifferent about any consequences that might possibly respect himself." Why so? Because his opinion had "resulted from mature reflection, and the clearest conviction," and "he was happy in the persuasion that his conduct met the approbation of his God!"[98]

The Framers' Constitutional Morality

Tillinghast's religious moorings clearly gave him comfort and helped motivate his actions. But his sense of duty was not tied directly to any theological vision. Rather, it was an aspect of constitutional morality. He sacrificed his career for the honor of his state. Having exercised judgment ("mature reflection") rather than will, he to his own mind had lived up to the requirements of his vocation; he had done his judicial duty.[99]

Judicial duty was a crucial aspect of constitutional morality. By conquering their own will and limiting themselves to the exercise of independent judgment, Tillinghast and other judges upheld the norms of their profession and supported the Constitution. Of course, not only judges had duties to their profession and the Constitution their professions served. The code of conduct required by the American Constitution differed in significant ways in its particulars according to the particular position of particular persons. The duty of a judge was different from that of a legislator or administrative officer because their roles, powers, and duties differed. But each was bound to act in support of both his profession and the constitutional structure as a whole, seeking the common good within the confines of that structure.

Publius states the fear critics of the Constitution had concerning the powers of the Supreme Court: "The power of construing the laws according to the *spirit* of the Constitution, will enable that court to mould them into whatever shape it may think proper; especially as its decisions will not be in any manner subject to the revision or correction of the legislative body." Publius answers this charge in several parts: first, the Constitution includes no express words empowering the courts to interpret laws according to its "spirit"; second, the possibility of impeachment will keep in check any design on the part of judges to mold laws into their own preferred shapes; third, and most important for our purposes, such pursuits would violate the logic of constitutionalism and hence any proper conception of judicial duty. As we saw in our discussion of judicial review, the activity of judging in America was defined in large measure by the exercise of judgment and not will. And this established judicial restraint as well as independent judgment as standards of excellence and virtue.

Auxiliary precautions like susceptibility to impeachment were part of the constitutional program to maintain the Constitution and, with it, the rule of law. But of even greater importance was personal discipline rooted in conceptions of duty. Virtue was necessary for all those in positions of public trust. As Publius notes, "Republican government presupposes the existence" of human qualities worthy of esteem "in a higher degree than any other form."[100]

The Constitution was a mechanism filled with "auxiliary precautions" meant to supplement mere "parchment barriers" dependent on the virtues of mere mortals. That said, no mechanism can eliminate the need for virtue.[101] Like criminal laws, auxiliary precautions can only do their job, only produce obedience to general standards, if those general standards are followed without the need for enforcement by the vast majority of the people the vast majority of the time.

Some elements of the constitutional morality would flow, more or less automatically, from human nature as modified by constitutional structure. Such was the case with the imperative that political actors protect their own turf, thereby helping uphold the separation of powers. Other elements required the development of virtue—of habits pointing beyond immediate self-interest. These included restraint on the part of all political actors, a concern among the voters to choose fit characters for their representatives, and the willingness of those representatives to stand, when not involved directly or through the interests of their constituents, as neutral arbiters. Whatever their station, all participants in the political process had a duty to act uncorrupted by outside influences (beginning, of course, with bribery) in judging what course of action would be most in accord with their duty.

The proper course of action would be constrained by the powers of the office. Thus, a president might not seek the public good by simply legislating according to his own will, just as a legislator would not be acting virtuously by seeking to overstep or unduly restrict proper bounds settled by constitutional structure. While private interest and the force of counteracting ambition often would prevent such overreaching (and, perhaps, even lack of appropriate reaching, or defense of one's institution), there would be times when such checks and balances might not be enough. Again, no structure can eliminate the need for virtue. Moreover, where the people were called on to exercise the limited constitutional morality involved in choosing officers who could be trusted to act for the public good within the confines of the Constitution, political actors would have real power, and presumably a desire for more, greater power, if only in order to do more good. A restraining virtue, akin to simple law-abidingness but more demanding, would be required if the Constitution were to last in anything but name.

Whence would come such virtue? Not from the government, for the Constitution was of the limited, mediating variety, resting on recognition of the separate natures of government and society. Rather, the people would have to be brought up, in their families, churches, and local associations, to recognize and value the rule of law (especially as embodied in the Constitution) and the character traits necessary to maintain it.

One key support for the constitutional morality was a culture in which the desire for honor was deeply rooted. To take one famous example, George Washington studiously cultivated for himself the image of a modern Cincinnatus, leaving his farm to serve his country, then returning to private life, first from the military, then from the presidency, with his duty done. He forged this image out of a desire for honor difficult for observers today to understand. A brief passage from a letter Washington wrote to a congregation of admirers congratulating him on his election may help illustrate the mindset active at the time: "To be approved by the praise-worthy is a wish as natural to becoming ambition as its consequence is flattering to our self-love—I am, indeed, much indebted to the favorable sentiments which you entertain towards me, and it will be my study to deserve them."[102] The "becoming" ambition—the honorable search for honorable fame—that Washington praised was a personal virtue he exercised and one that he held up as necessary for public virtue. One need not see this conception as the height of virtue to recognize its utility in maintaining constitutional structures in the face of other, more materialistic ambitions. It could, indeed, motivate behavior intended to solidify a reputation for deserving praise.

In the same light we might consider the importance of oath taking in early America—going forward until quite recently and going back well into the medieval era and beyond. Aside from the religious terrors accompanying oath breaking for religious believers, we should not overlook the high price to one's honor one would pay for breaking a public oath. Oath-breaking monarchs courted armed rebellion; lesser figures courted derision, ostracism, or worse.

Adherence to the constitutional morality also rested on an understanding of the normative implications of the Constitution itself. Constitutional morality is a secondary, derivative morality. Only if the Constitution is seen as somehow good can upholding it be deemed good. Only if there is an internal morality to the Constitution's law can constitutional morality make sense. The Constitution, if it is to be followed, must be authoritative. And this requires acceptance on the part of representatives, judges, and executive officers, along with the people, of the importance of the Constitution's formal structures and procedures. Only with such recognition can restraint in the approach to and use of these procedures be seen as a positive good, particularly when they stand in the way of one's substantive goals.

Constitutional morality required seeing the Constitution as a limited but necessary fundamental law, requiring restraint and judgment for its continued survival. It required a common understanding and valuation of the Constitution as a frame of government establishing mediating procedures, intended to secure limited goals prioritizing maintenance of the rule of law and limited government over efficiency and the provision of positive goods. It required acceptance that the machinery of checks and balances, intended to protect the separation of powers, were not flawed because they produced gridlock; they were functioning properly to the extent they prevented precipitous action in favor of reasoned deliberation and consensus building. It required that the Constitution itself be valued for what it was intended to be by its Framers.

Another Constitution would, if it were to succeed, beget a different constitutional morality. But what would happen if the constitutional morality itself changed over time? Clearly there were multiple changes in American law and society during the century following adoption of the Framers' Constitution. But it is our contention that the Framers' constitutional morality itself was changed in large measure by those who were ideologically opposed to it, whose response to perceived changes in economic, social, political, and other forms of reality was to seek fundamental change in the conduct of political actors, severing them from the Constitution's internal morality.

There would be changes and challenges for the Framers' Constitution throughout its lifespan. There would be the development of parties under Andrew Jackson and challenges to separation of powers from the exigencies involved in fighting a bloody civil war. After that war would come adoption of the Fourteenth Amendment, intended to correct some of the injustices of slavery and establish a more stable, coherent, and just political order by extending to Americans of whatever race rights of due process, equal protection, and the various privileges and immunities of national citizenship.

A number of recent authors, not to mention justices of the Supreme Court, have looked to that amendment as demanding a fundamentally new constitutional structure.[103] But, as we analyze the arc of constitutional change in America, we must not forget that those demands did not take shape until well into the twentieth century, and were only made possible with the advent of a new theory of government. In the following two chapters we turn to this new theory regarding the purposes of the national government, of the limitations of the Constitution in the service of these purposes, and the need for a new constitutional morality to transform the practice of government.

4

Progressives and
Administrative Governance

O UR GOAL IN THIS CHAPTER is to show how the Framers' constitutional morality was undermined by a newer vision of the purpose of constitutional government. The Constitution operates very differently today than it did prior to the era of the New Deal. Changes in the manner in which our nation is governed were not the result of some conspiracy, democratic revolution, or natural growth in our form of government. Changes in the unwritten constitution of the people, in particular their habits and beliefs concerning the nature and purposes of the federal government, both helped produce and were in part produced by a changed view among those serving in government and those in positions to influence public servants regarding the Constitution and the duties of public officers serving thereunder. We trace developments in this area through discussion of the literature on public administration during its early, most fecund and influential stage, the era of Progressivism.

The meaning of the Constitution was contested from before its ratification, as it has been contested ever since. The nature and demands of constitutional morality also have been contested at critical times in American history. Conflicts over the extent of executive, federal, and judicial authority were frequent, heated, and important. In the very early republic, for example, the Bank of the United States was chartered, the charter allowed to lapse, and a second charter vetoed amid debate over whether the bank was "necessary and proper" for carrying out the federal government's fiscal responsibilities.[1] Internal improvements were planned, undertaken, and limited according to various parties' opinions of the proper limits of federal power within the states.[2] The list could be extended almost beyond measure.

Yet well after the Civil War, the United States remained a federal republic characterized by administrative and political decentralization with limited, enumerated powers being exercised from the center. For over one hundred years, both the Framers' Constitution and its corresponding constitutional morality formed a coherent whole regarding the importance of structure, process, and separate, limited governmental functions. This is no longer the case. Indeed, it would be an understatement of grand proportions to say that lawmaking in the United States today differs from that envisioned by the Framers. To a degree alarming to many, lawmaking powers in effect have been delegated by Congress to the president or, more exactly, to the bureaucracy. Clearly, however, this state of affairs did not occur suddenly, at one point in time, or even over a well-defined period of time. Realization of the new dispensation of American constitutionalism had to be piecemeal for, if it had been presented as a package for an up or down vote, say, a hundred years ago, it would have been rejected outright as being too revolutionary, even contrary to the basic principles of the Constitution. We say this not to charge that the demise of the original constitutional morality was the result of some grand conspiracy, but merely to point out that the transformation took place over the course of decades and was propelled by ideas and developments, often at odds with one another, that have identifiable sources, characters, and implications.

The rise of the administrative state generally is seen as both inevitable and laudable given the requirements of a modern industrial and postindustrial society committed to an egalitarian distribution of life chances. The story is familiar. The demands of economic efficiency (encouraged by individual greed and/or collective demands for better and cheaper consumer goods) spurred the growth of large-scale industrial organizations, bringing the limited liability corporation to new heights of size and power and spawning the era of large trusts, through which often-unscrupulous investors might gain control over numerous corporations and potentially develop monopoly power in a given area of economic activity. Frightened by the growth of enterprises seemingly beyond the control of consumers, workers, and the democratic process (not to mention various elites), leaders in both political parties began looking toward "progressive" changes in the administration of government, founding the first independent agencies intended to bring unbiased expertise to bear on the problems of excess power and industrial organization. Slow to begin, the process of state-building accelerated as the disaster of the Great Depression became apparent. The administration of Franklin Roosevelt, over the objections of putatively laissez-faire Supreme Court justices and political opponents, institutionalized the basic elements of an administrative state—from industrial regulations to old-age pensions.[3]

Since the founding of the administrative state there has been debate among the political parties over the pace at which it should grow and how fully it should be integrated to provide maximum security to the less powerful and well off. Here debates over the proper form and level of social benefits and issues of race and sex become particularly salient. But there has been little question of dismantling the state Roosevelt built—or the one Johnson entrenched and Obama worked to complete.

We would not quarrel with the basic outlines of this narrative, save to emphasize the importance of developments significantly prior to the New Deal. But, whatever the political, economic, or even socioideological motivations behind the growth of our administrative state, that state was instituted in a particular way and had particular consequences for our constitutional morality, and with it the rule of law. Here we outline the changes in constitutional, political, and especially administrative theory that made possible the changes in political conduct leading to the demise of the original constitutional morality.

If we look to Dwight Waldo's classic, *The Administrative State*,[4] we can identify some of the more important practical and theoretical concerns relating to the role of the bureaucracy in a republican constitutional order that have produced the new dispensation. His work leads us to appreciate the role of administrative theory in providing both an impetus and a justification for the gradual transformation of the role and function of Congress and the presidency. Most, but not all, of these theories are connected to reform movements intended to expand the role of government—principally the national government—and to improve the operations of government in the execution of its expanded powers. At the same time, these theories, mindful of the republican or democratic character of the American system, sought, albeit in varying degrees, to provide some form of popular control over the operations of the executive branch. By all accounts, the

Progressives, who emerged as a powerful political and intellectual force by the early part of the twentieth century, were crucial in bringing about and justifying these reforms and alterations in relations between Congress and the executive arm.[5]

Much has been written concerning the Progressive movement, particularly its political ideology and goals. Opposed to the rise of (immigrant) machine politics, Progressives championed more direct, democratic rule by the people through various electoral, legal, and constitutional reforms. Direct election of senators, women's suffrage, split-ticket voting, and referenda are among the most famous Progressive reforms aimed at clean, efficient, and more democratic government. As we shall argue, these reforms were not universally aimed at increasing the direct power of majorities. They were, however, aimed at eliminating the formalistic barriers to direct, efficient governance included in our original constitutional structure and central to its constitutional morality.

Certain principles and ideas have played a crucial role in structuring Progressive reforms in a fashion that conscientiously seeks to accord attention to democratic principles. Perhaps the most critical among these during the early Progressive era was the notion that policy formation—that is, the decision to pursue a given policy—can be separated from policy execution—that is, actions involved in carrying out or implementing the policy decision. While, as we shall see, the idea of a separation of politics and administration eventually gave way to an emphasis on their practical inseparability, the very idea of a separation between the two paved the way for development of the major elements of modern administrative theory.

Progressives assumed that some form of democratic input would be required in deciding what should be done. But they also assumed that an independent administrative apparatus was necessary to provide considerable latitude for the introduction of expertise and the pursuit of efficiency in implementing policy free from democratic controls. This separationism even spawned a kind of science of administration, still very much with us, aimed at securing effective and efficient policy implementation isolated from politics. Concomitant with this development, another principle inherent to the division of the political and administrative realm emerged and soon came to be regarded as axiomatic, namely, that democratic accountability requires centralization of authority.[6]

Centralization, with its corollary principle, unity of command, has lent enormous theoretical support to those who have sought, with considerable success, to transform the presidency into the predominant branch in our constitutional order. Principled commitment to centralization and unity as necessary for sufficient democratic accountability allowed Progressives to argue that the president should assume two roles that unified the political/ administrative functions. First, the president became overseer of the administrative apparatus, making sure that it faithfully, efficiently, and honestly executed policy. Second, eventually, the president took on the role of spokesperson for the people in articulating the policy ends to be pursued.

While at the outset these principles and ideas were tailored to constitutional processes and institutions, the reverse has been true of many more recent reforms. There developed over time—and rather early, in historical terms—a strong body of opinion according to which the realization of efficient and accountable government required substantial constitutional overhaul or even abandonment. The chief shortcoming in the original constitutional design, from this perspective, was the separation of powers. In reformist eyes, the separation of powers served not only to diffuse responsibility but also to allow for interference in the administration of policies at the cost of effectiveness and efficiency. Advocates of centralization have reason to be pleased. Congress has become increasingly amenable to its own reduced authority, placing ever-increasing discretionary power in the bureaucracy, seemingly unmindful of its increasingly diminished role compared with that of the presidency.

The following survey of reformist theories is not intended to be comprehensive. Its purpose is to identify values and circumstances that have contributed to centralization and to the bureaucracy's success in taking on its now-substantial role in making and enforcing laws. A major objective here is to analyze aspects of these theories focusing on democratic accountability and the concern (more or less acute at differing points) that the processes of policy formation and execution allow for popular input or control.

It may seem odd to begin, as we do, with the British philosopher John Stuart Mill and his views on the proper role of the legislative body.[7] We do so because Mill's work provides an overview of later American thought. This is not say that American Progressives consciously borrowed from Mill. This is not the case. However, Mill provides a comprehensive discussion of the major concerns and problems that preoccupied the Progressives and formed the political vision that undermined the Framers' constitutional morality. In addition, we examine the writings of Woodrow Wilson, Herbert Croly, Franklin Goodnow, and Pendleton Herring. The first three are acknowledged as among the most significant contributors to Progressive thought, expressing ideas well within the confines of Progressivism's broader values. While Herring wrote in the early stages of the New Deal era, by all evidences he shared the Progressive vision. His perspective on and treatment of the issues raised in early Progressive thought are particularly interesting because he dealt with these issues at a time when the national government was undertaking Progressive programs on a massive scale. Finally, it should be remarked that the following survey touches upon the major concerns evident in virtually all the Progressive reformist writings, concerns that are very much with us today.

John Stuart Mill and Representative Government

In his *Considerations on Representative Government,* published in 1861, Mill marks out the "proper functions" of a representative assembly. While he grants that "it is essential to representative government that the practical supremacy in the state should reside in the representatives of the people," he also contends that "it is an open question what actual functions, what precise part in the machinery of government, shall be directly and personally discharged by the representative body." Mill telegraphs the broad outline of his answer almost immediately by maintaining that "the essence of republican government" is preserved so long as the representative assembly retains "control of everything in the last resort." That is, the tenets of republicanism mandate that the policies and directions that government undertakes *ultimately* have the approval of the legislature: "[T]here is a radical distinction between controlling the business of government, and actually doing it."[8]

Having drawn this distinction, Mill has much to say about the proper division of responsibilities between political and administrative agencies. For starters, "numerous representative bodies ought not administer." Such bodies, he observes, are inherently unsuited to the tasks of administration. "Even a select board, composed of few members, and these specially conversant with the business to be done, is always an inferior instrument to some one individual" who could direct and control the others. Nor is a numerous representative assembly suited "to dictate in detail to those who have the charge of administration." Why so? Because "every branch of public administration is a skilled business" and possesses "its own peculiar principles and traditional rules, many of them not even known" save by those few who have had firsthand experience with them. These rules and principles, which Mill insists are vitally important for effective administration, are beyond the ken of legislators; only an individual with a thorough understanding of these "modes of action . . . is capable of judging" when they should be ignored or altered. Such an understanding, on Mill's showing, is not easily acquired, requiring both knowledge and judgment "almost as rarely found in those not bred to it, as the capacity to reform the law in those who have not professionally studied it." "All of these difficulties," he maintains, "are sure to be ignored by a representative assembly which attempts to decide on special acts of administration."[9]

Mill is not content merely to point out why it would be imprudent for the assembly to meddle in administrative affairs. He goes on to express doubts that representative assemblies can be trusted to refrain from impinging upon the administrative domain. Even in the absence of an "interested motive to intervene," the assembly will make "light of," and perhaps even resent, the very idea that administrators might "have a judgment better worth attending to than its own." When interested motives exist, even if only within a few members, the danger of meddling is very real, because others, even a majority, "cannot keep their minds vigilant or their judgments discerning in matters they know nothing about." Moreover, while those in charge of offices may suffer for their mistakes, representatives are not held to account for their transgressions: "An assembly never personally experiences the inconveniences of its bad measures, until they have reached the dimension of national evils," whereas "ministers and administrators see them approaching, and have to bear all the annoyance and trouble of attempting to ward them off."[10]

Largely for these reasons, Mill sees the assembly's "proper duty" relating "to matters of administration . . . [as] to take care that the persons who have to decide them shall be the proper persons." Unfortunately, "numerous bodies never regard special qualifications at all." Why not? As Mill sees it, "[T]here is scarcely any act respecting which the conscience of an average man is less sensitive; scarcely any case in which less consideration is paid to qualifications" and this because people neither know nor care about "the difference in qualifications between one person and another." Thus, "party connexion or private jobbing" are most important for gaining appointment, "the worst appointments" being those "made for the sake of gaining support or disarming opposition in the representative body."[11]

Even "merit" appointments are problematic. Often, Mill writes, "the merit may be of the most opposite description to that required" for the office at issue. In other cases, "the appointment may fall to those with a reputation, often quite undeserved, for *general* ability" or "for no better reason than" personal popularity.[12]

How, then, should the legislature maintain its proper authority? "It is enough," according to Mill, "that it virtually decides who shall be prime minister, or who shall be the two or three individuals from whom the prime minister shall be chosen." The appointment of lesser ministers then becomes the responsibility of the prime minister, with the understanding, as Mill puts it, that these lesser ministers have "the undivided moral responsibility of appointing fit persons to the other offices of administration which are not permanent." With this process, in his opinion, "things seem to be on as good a footing as they can be."[13]

Mill does not stop here in setting forth what he regards as prudent limitations on the powers and functions of representative bodies. Indeed, in a statement that might astonish some unfamiliar with his views, he writes that it is increasingly "acknowledged [by whom he does not say] . . . that a numerous assembly is as little fitted for the direct business of legislation as for that of administration." "Making laws," he holds, is an "intellectual" undertaking that requires "experienced and exercised minds . . . trained to the task through long and laborious study."[14]

Experience and expertise are needed for wise legislating primarily because laws need to be coherent in two fundamental senses: they should "be framed with the most accurate and long-sighted perception of [their] effect on all the other provisions," and they should form a "consistent whole with the previously existing laws." But "it is impossible," he contends, "that these conditions should be in any degree fulfilled when laws are voted clause by clause in a miscellaneous assembly." By way of proving his point, Mill turns his attention to Parliament, whose "legislative machinery" has proved increasingly incapable of meeting these conditions. For lack of time, comprehensive legislation "hangs over from session to session," and, even when it is considered, essential clauses are "omitted" or amendments introduced, usually by individuals with so little knowledge of the subject at hand that the amendments render the legislation internally inconsistent.[15]

Even comprehensive measures drawn up by highly qualified individuals are eviscerated, according to Mill, "because the House of Commons will not forgo the precious privilege of tinkering it with their clumsy hands." Nor, he states, are those charged with the responsibility of "explaining and defending" a measure and "its various provisions" normally those "from whose mind they emanated." Consequently, "their defense rests upon" those who must cram "for all . . . arguments but those which are perfectly obvious," who are unaware of the "full strength" of their "case" or the "best reasons to support it," and who are "wholly incapable of meeting unforeseen objections."[16] In short, the ignorance, interests, and arrogance of the members of a numerous assembly render it incapable of producing coherent and consistent legislation.

If, Mill surmises, a "majority of the House of Commons" were to contemplate these matters, "it would soon be recognized" that "the only task to which a representative assembly can possibly be competent, is not that of doing the work, but of causing it to be done; of determining to whom or to what sort of people it shall be confided, and giving or withholding the national sanction to what is performed." Accordingly, Mill proposes a "Council of Legislation" or "Legislative Commission," "a small body, not exceeding in number the members of a Cabinet . . . having for its appointed office to make the laws." Its members would be "appointed by the Crown" for a period of five years, with provision for reappointment.[17]

Mill makes clear that no proposal from his council can have the force and effect of law until it is approved by Parliament. But he would empower the council to propose legislation to Parliament for consideration, in effect making it, not Parliament, the potential initiator of policy. In fact, given the low esteem in which he holds representative bodies, there is good reason to believe that he felt the bulk of legislation would be initiated by the council. At the same time, Mill grants that either house of Parliament might "exercise its initiative, by referring any subject to the Commission, with directions to prepare a law." Indeed, once this system is set in motion, Mill envisions that "private members of the House" would seek permission from their chamber to avail themselves of the services of the council since this would "likely . . . facilitate the passing of their measures through the two Houses." The council, for its part, would be obliged to comply with Parliament's wishes, "unless" its members "preferred to resign their office." While Parliament could, under Mill's scheme, send a measure back to the council for revision, none of the measures submitted by the council would be subject to amendment by either chamber. Save for those measures remitted to the council for revision, Parliament would only have the option of voting them up or down.[18]

Mill believes his "arrangements" would render government "fit for a high state of civilization." The representative assembly would no longer try to perform tasks for which it is incompetent, "legislation would assume its proper place as a work of skilled labour and special study and experience," and the "liberty of the nation" "would be fully preserved" since the "law would be assented to by its elected representatives." But these are by no means all the benefits he envisions from his reforms. Shedding the legislative function would allow the legislature to do what it can do best, namely, oversee the activities of government. The legislature would keep watch over and control the administration, investigating complaints about its operations, publicizing "its acts," and censuring those who abuse "their trust" or seem out of step with the "deliberate sense of the nation."[19]

The assembly, as Mill envisions it, would be both "the nation's Committee on Grievance, and its Congress of opinions." In this vein, he writes, "I know not how a representative assembly can more usefully employ itself than in talk." Accordingly, Mill wants the assembly to be a place in which "every interest and shade of opinion in the country can have its cause even passionately pleaded," where interests are obliged to listen to one another, and where there is vigorous and productive give and take. The representatives must come to realize "that they are not a selection of the greatest political minds in the country," but rather "when properly constituted, a fair sample of every grade of intellect among the people which is at all entitled to a voice in public affairs."[20] Thus, the assembly is the institution through which the people's will can be known and through which the people can exercise control over government.

Mill concludes this chapter by remarking that the only way in which "popular control" can be combined with the requisite experience and expertise (requisites he holds are "growing ever more important as human affairs increase in scale and in complexity") is by "disjoining the office of control and criticism from the actual conduct of affairs" in the manner he has set forth.[21]

Mill on Good Government

Another major dimension of Mill's thought as presented in *Representative Government* is highly relevant for understanding twentieth- and twenty-first-century developments in our system. To see this aspect of his teachings requires that we examine his broader theory, while keeping his views on the need for curtailing the function of the assembly in mind. Here we begin by noting Mill's criteria for "good government." These views are unexceptional and roughly correspond with classical teachings.

The most important "element" a government must "possess," according to Mill, is a tendency to promote "the virtue and intelligence of the people themselves." Indeed, "the first question in respect to any political institutions is, how far they tend to foster in the members of the community the various desirable qualities, moral and intellectual." Mill concludes: "We may consider, then, as one criterion of a government, the degree in which it tends to increase the sum of good qualities in the people, collectively and individually." We note that Mill is not merely recommending this tendency to improve the people as one moral goal, but positing it as a necessary element of government qua government. A government must improve the people for the sake of its own efficacy, for the "good qualities" of the people "supply the moving force which works the machinery."[22]

Mill's second criterion is related to the first: a government is to be judged on the extent to which it "organize[s] the moral, intellectual, and active worth already existing, so as to operate with the greatest effect on public affairs." To a great extent, his treatment of the functions of representative assemblies can rightly be viewed as recommendations in keeping with this need to establish arrangements taking full advantage of existing "moral, intellectual, and active worth." It is significant that this existing worth is largely to be found in the "Council of Legislation," not in the representative body. This fact is highlighted in Mill's chapter dealing with the "infirmities and dangers" to which representative governments are prone. Here he points out virtues of governments "in the hands of governors by profession" or, as he puts it this time around, the "bureaucracy."[23]

Mill even compares "representative democracy" with "bureaucracy" and concludes that "it must be acknowledged that a bureaucratic government has, in some important respects, greatly the advantage" in terms of qualities necessary for good government. Assembly and bureaucracy are two separate entities, with bureaucracy alone possessing existing worth. Government must "attain as many of the qualities of the one as are consistent with the other" and "secure, as far as they can be made compatible, the great advantage of the conduct of affairs by skilled persons, bred to it as an intellectual profession, along with that of the general control vested in, and seriously exercised by, bodies representative of the entire people."[24]

Mill recognizes that good government requires infusing worthy qualities into the representative assembly. One of the two "positive evils and dangers of representative government" he identifies is the "general ignorance and incapacity, or, to speak more moderately, insufficient mental qualifications, in the [assembly]." Alleviating this condition would not be easy because "a democracy has enough to do in providing itself with an amount of mental competency sufficient for its own proper work, that of superintendence and check." But Mill is clear that the assembly's "mental incapacity" must be addressed, or all manner of serious abuses and wrongdoings will ensue: corruption and incompetence will be tolerated, if not encouraged; "abuses of trust" will be overlooked and even rationalized; laws will be ignored; "good laws" will be "abrogate[d], while bad laws are enacte[d]"; and, among the other evils, "selfish . . . capricious and impulsive . . . shortsighted . . . ignorant and prejudiced" policies will be "countenance[d]."[25]

Later in his work, Mill urges measures clearly designed to overcome the danger of "insufficient mental qualifications." Two of these measures, a literacy test and plural voting for university constituencies, are relatively insignificant. A third measure, to which Mill devotes considerable attention in his chapter on the "representation of minorities," requires more consideration. The Hare system of voting was an early form of proportional representation intended to secure legislative seats for minority parties. To achieve its end, the Hare system would award seats in accordance with the percentage of the total vote in each district and then allocate votes beyond the minimum necessary to win a given seat in a manner aimed at assuring small-party representation. Mill would rely on the Hare system not only to raise the intellectual level of the representative body, but also, and perhaps more importantly, to overcome "the danger of its being under the influence of interests not identical with the general welfare of the community."[26] In counteracting this second infirmity, minority representation also would, on Mill's showing, substantially elevate the moral character of the assembly.

Mill observes that an evil afflicting all governments—monarchies, aristocracies, and even democracies—is that the interests of the rulers often run counter to the general welfare or long-term interests of the whole. Such contrary interests are "sinister" and their effects can be devastating, but overcoming them is next to impossible. "What it is the man's interest to do or refrain from," Mill writes, "depends less on any outward circumstances, than upon what sort of man he is." To know, then, "what is practically a man's interest" depends on "what sort of man he is," and this, in turn, requires that "you . . . know the cast of his habitual feelings and thoughts." While, for instance, "a person who cares for other people, for his country, or for mankind," is usually "a happier man than one who does not," it is virtually impossible to convince "a man who cares for nothing but his own case, or his pocket" of this. "It is like preaching to the worm who crawls on the ground, how much better it would be for him if he were an eagle."[27]

Assemblies inevitably contain rulers whose selfish dispositions are "called forth and fostered by the possession of power." And power brings forth an individual's "disposition to prefer" his "selfish interests to those which he shares with other people, and his immediate and direct interests to those which are indirect and remote." Mill fears that such partiality will produce legislation "for the immediate benefit of the dominant class." Such legislation must be thwarted.[28]

To solve the problem of partiality (which appears eerily akin to the problem of factions noted by Publius) Mill seeks to ensure that "no class, and no combination of classes, likely to combine, should be able to exercise a preponderant influence in the government." This, he thinks, can be achieved if those with sinister interests balance each other out so that "those who are governed by higher considerations" will hold a critical "balance." Within the representative body "there ought always to be such a balance preserved among personal interests, as may render any one of them dependent for its successes, on carrying with it at least a large proportion of those who act on higher motives, and more comprehensive and distant views."[29]

Again, there are strong parallels between Mill and Publius concerning the dangers of interested political actors. But, whereas Publius relies on a combination of the plurality of interested representatives produced by an extended republic and the intrinsic virtues of a significant number of representatives who would remain disinterested on any given issue, Mill looks especially to minority voting through the Hare system. Mill's strong attachment to the Hare system is due largely to the fact that, in his judgment, it would open the way for the election of representatives who would act on the basis of "higher motives"—representatives who could be counted on to secure this needed "balance" within the representative assembly.

Hare's electoral system, according to Mill, would "afford the best security for the intellectual qualifications desirable in the representatives." It would allow "the minority of instructed minds scattered through the local constituencies [to] unite to return a number, proportional to their own numbers, of the very ablest men the country contains." This party of the wise eventually would force the major parties to offer up abler, more worthy candidates. While Hare representatives would only be a minority within the assembly, Mill argues that "as a moral power they would count for much, in virtue of their knowledge, and of the influence it would give them over the rest." Adoption of the Hare plan would, he insists, go far beyond simply arresting "the tendency of representative government . . . towards collective mediocrity"; it would provide an "occasional Pericles," as well as an "habitual group of superior and guiding minds."[30]

Mill, then, is forthright in setting out his convictions concerning the proper relationship between the administrative and political branches. First, the functions of the representative assembly must be narrowed; to entrust representative bodies with drafting or formulating legislation will have highly undesirable consequences. Second, the administrative branch is naturally superior to the legislature in intelligence and virtue, and should be accorded wide latitude in the policy-formation process. It seems clear that Mill saw these experts as possessing many of the same attributes as his party of the wise. Finally, he links education, intelligence, and knowledge with a higher morality; the "instructed minority" has a greater capacity to act on the basis of higher motives than the majority and their representatives. These convictions and their treatment in Mill provide a useful framework for understanding the twists and turns we find in Progressive thought in America, though, where Mill is up front on these matters, in the

American context they often are unarticulated premises underlying reform proposals.

Bureaucracy in a Democracy: Foundations of Progressive Thought

Although Mill was not a direct source of Progressive thought, it is important to note the great influence of another British writer, Walter Bagehot, on Woodrow Wilson in particular. Bagehot, a younger contemporary of Mill's, famously criticized the American Constitution for not having a single center of sovereign authority. Agreeing on the need for such an authority, Wilson proceeded to find it, first in Congress and later in the president. It was this fixation upon sovereignty, taken directly from Bagehot, that guided Wilson in his rejection of the Framers' vision of separation of powers and the very idea of overlapping jurisdictions in favor of a top-down, monarchical system of public administration.[31]

Wilson's 1887 essay, "The Study of Administration," often has been seen as the foundational work on public administration theory in the United States. Wilson's major concern here is to point up why Americans should develop a "science of administration" and the difficulties of doing so within the confines of popular government and constitutional allocation of powers. In this endeavor, he takes care to note that the United States is behind European nations (though not England) and that "American writers have hitherto taken no very important part in the advancement of this science." In explaining this state of affairs, he advances a concern shared by virtually all Progressive theorists who are to follow him: "The poisonous atmosphere of city government, the crooked secrets of state administration, the confusion, sinecurism, and corruption ever and again discovered in the bureaux at Washington forbid us to believe that any clear conceptions of what constitutes good administration are as yet very widely current in the United States." In sum, "not much impartial scientific method is to be discerned in our administrative practices." Beyond this, because administration seems to be a "foreign science," largely European, "it employs only foreign tongues" and its principles seem "alien" to the American mind.[32]

Wilson is clear why a science of administration must be developed. To begin with, "[t]here is scarcely a single duty of government which was once simple which is not now complex." Moreover, whereas in authoritarian regimes "government once might follow the whims of a court," the rise of democracy requires it to "follow the views of a nation." This, in turn, means that governments are "steadily widening to new conceptions of state duty; so that, at the same time that the functions of government are every day becoming more complex and difficult, they are also vastly multiplying in number." Since "every day" there are "new things the state ought to do, the next thing is to see clearly how it ought to do them." Given this expansion of governmental tasks, as well as the need for expertise and knowledge in executing them, the goal of a "science of administration" should be "to straighten the paths of government, to make its business less unbusiness-like, to strengthen and purify its organization, and to crown its duties with dutifulness."[33]

Wilson is under no illusion that administrative reform will come easily. He points to the enormous difficulties posed by "popular sovereignty" to any such efforts. In a monarchy, one has only to convince the king to achieve reforms, while in a democracy "to make any advance at all we must instruct and persuade a multitudinous monarch called public opinion." This popular sovereign "will have a score of differing opinions"; its members "can agree on nothing simple" and this necessitates "compromise, by a compounding of differences, by a trimming of plans and a suppression of too straightforward principles." A related difficulty is that the people "have no single ear which one can approach" but rather "several thousand persons" who are "selfish, ignorant, timid, stubborn, or foolish" with "no definite locality." If this were not enough, "the sovereign also is under the influence of favorites"—favorites produced by prejudices that are not susceptible to reason.[34]

Unlike Mill, Wilson sees a need to gain popular support for reforms, something he regards as no small task. But this desire to garner public support, despite the enormous difficulties involved, illustrates the contours of a basic tension in Progressive thought that emerges full blown over the first half of the twentieth century. On the one hand, a distinguishing characteristic of Progressivism, at least in the political arena, is its commitment to direct popular control and participation in political processes through such devices as referendum, recall, and initiative. On the other hand, many theoretically oriented Progressives share Wilson's rather low estimate of the character of the general population; these figures think the broader social and economic goals of Progressivism could only be obtained through elite leadership, not unlike that envisioned by Mill.[35] Wilson identifies some of the conditions and circumstances from which this tension arises. He considers tradition to be an obstacle impeding acceptance of new reform principles and, more important, reflecting the "unphilosophical" character of the "bulk of mankind."[36]

This unphilosophical bent—more pronounced, he opines, in the United States than in most other countries—threatens any wide embrace of needed administrative reform. It also leads to a more general and critical concern. That concern stems from Wilson's conviction that "better officials" are needed to man the "apparatus of government." To secure such officials, Wilson argues, "[i]t will be necessary to organize democracy by sending up to the competitive examinations for the civil service men definitely prepared for standing liberal tests as to technical knowledge."[37]

Civil servants should be "prepared by a special schooling and drilled, after appointment, into a perfected organization, with appropriate hierarchy and characteristic discipline." Wilson realizes that many "thoughtful individuals" might regard such a "corps of civil servants" to be "an offensive official class—a distinct, semi-corporate body with sympathies divorced from those of a progressive, free-spirited people." Any such "class," he understands, "would be altogether hateful and harmful in the United States." Yet, Wilson maintains, any such apprehension would be out of place. Why so? The answer comes down to Wilson's firm belief in the separation of politics and administration. "Administrative questions are not," he insists, "political questions." He quotes an "eminent German" authority, Bluntchli, to the effect that "policy does nothing without the aid of administration," to which he adds, "but administration is therefore not politics." Exhibiting the same mind-set on this issue as Mill, he writes, "[T]his discrimination between administration and politics is now, happily, too obvious to need further discussion."[38]

We note the clear opposition between Wilson's model and that of the Framers. Vincent Ostrom notes that Wilson's lodestar, Bagehot, saw the American Constitution as the result of a misunderstanding of the British constitution, with its unitary structure placing sovereignty in the prime minister and cabinet. The American "composite" system produced different "ultimate powers" on different issues, leading to needless confusion.[39] Wilson, too, saw in America's overlapping structures and realms of responsibility needless confusion and the opportunity for corruption. He did not see in the constitutional system an intentional separation of powers, checks and balances to maintain that separation within the federal government, and an intentional reliance on more local associations as a means by which the people might conduct their own business as an aspect of self-government. Wilson's concern was to simplify, rationalize, and centralize the apparatus of state power so as to make it more efficient in putting a single, national general will into action. Not only his vision of public administration but also his vision of what it means to be a self-governing people was fundamentally opposed to that of the Framers and that of the American people up until that time.

Thus, to those who might look upon his well-trained "corps of civil servants" with some trepidation, Wilson responded with a vision eliding the central problem of his system's incompatibility with the polycentric nature of American culture and the American federal system.[40] As Wilson put it, "[T]hat such a body will be anything un-American clears away the moment it is asked, What is to constitute good behavior?" For him, this "question obviously carries its own answer on its face," namely, "hearty allegiance to the policy of the government they will serve." The "bureaucracy can exist only where" the distinction between politics and administration is observed, "where service to the state is removed from the common political life of the people." "Policy," he insists, "will have no taint of officialdom about it" since "the whole service of the state is removed from the common political life of the people." At the same time, as we might expect, and in a telling contrast to Mill, Wilson insists "that administration in the United States must be at all points sensitive to public opinion" through representatives "whose responsibility to public opinion will be direct and inevitable."[41] In this formulation there is no intimation that Wilson shared Mill's views on the incapacity of the legislature to legislate, that is, to draft a coherent program to handle the wants or concerns of the people.

Wilson, again unlike Mill, seems unconcerned about the legislature intruding on the legitimate domain of the bureaucracy. Rather, he worries about the people of the United States who, unlike other peoples, are accustomed to "'having their own way.'" The major problem in this respect is making "public opinion efficient without suffering it to be meddlesome." This means it should avoid the direct "oversight of daily details and in the choice of daily means of government," which would amount to a "clumsy nuisance, a rustic handling delicate machinery." But "public criticism is altogether safe and beneficent," even "indispensable," when "superintending the greater forces of formative policy alike in politics and administration." And one of the objectives of "administrative study" would be to set the boundaries of constructive public interference and criticism.[42]

Wilson also is concerned about accountability or, as he puts it, the "placing of responsibility." He is clear that the bureaucracy ultimately is accountable to the people, but he points out that the capacity to exercise this authority wisely and constructively is a function of the distribution of power. One task, then, for the development of a science of administration would be to "discover the simplest arrangement by which responsibility can be unmistakably fixed upon individuals." To do so would immeasurably help the public perform its oversight function: "Public attention must be easily directed, in each of good or bad administration, to just the man deserving of praise or blame."[43]

Wilson is aware that the distribution of functions and power must accord with the Constitution, but, in this vein, he charges those developing an administrative science to discover what kinds of constitutional structures and processes will simplify the task of fixing responsibility. He is "convinced" that "Montesquieu did not . . . say the last word on this head."[44] This comment anticipates the position of later Progressives that our constitutional system, with its separation of powers, is structurally and procedurally incapable of operating in accordance with sound principles of administration.[45]

In arguing for a science of administration, Wilson emphasizes the universality of its principles and application: "So far as administrative functions are concerned," he writes, "all governments have a strong structural likeness; more than that, if they are to be uniformly useful and efficient, they *must* have a strong structural likeness." This is true of "Monarchies and democracies" since they "have in reality much the same business to look to." Nor, he continues, should we "be frightened" to look "into foreign systems of administration for instruction and suggestion" since "for all governments alike the legitimate ends of administration are the same." To answer those who believe foreign examples would lead to "transplant[ing] foreign systems into this country" or be "incompatible with our principles," he answers that this is not at all likely and, in any event, the principles derived from such comparative studies would have to be "filter[ed] through our constitutions." The "prejudices against looking anywhere in the world but at home" must be overcome: "[N]owhere else in the whole field of politics, it would seem, can we make use of the historical, comparative method more safely than in this province of administration."[46]

Central to Wilson's conviction that we can "with safety and profit" study foreign governments is his distinction between politics and administration. "If I see a murderous fellow sharpening a knife cleverly," he notes, "I can borrow his way of sharpening the knife without borrowing his probable intention to commit murder with it." By the same token, Wilson continues, "if I see a monarchist dyed in the wool managing a public bureau well, I can learn his business methods without changing one of my republican spots." "We can," he concludes, "scrutinize the anatomy of foreign governments without fear of getting any of their diseases into our veins."[47] Whether Wilson was correct in his view that a monarchical public administration is best for all societies, or whether the habits of such an administration better lend themselves to an authoritarian than a self-governing political system, is a question we take up in Chapter 6.

Goodnow: Politics and Administration

Frank Goodnow, one of the more prominent Progressive students of public administration, wrote some thirteen years after the appearance of Wilson's essay, developing certain of Wilson's more important ideas and concepts. The central purpose of Goodnow's work *Politics and Administration* was to establish the central role of political parties as instrumentalities through which the "will of the State" could find expression. But in so doing he provides a conceptual framework that deals with ideas and concerns expressed by Wilson. Goodnow accepts Wilson's belief that a science of administration is possible. He also perceives a basic "similarity" in the "real political institutions of different peoples" that can be attributed "to the fact that . . . man is man everywhere and at all times, and that all political organizations of men must therefore have ultimately the same ends, and must adopt in a general way the same methods for their satisfaction." He thus seems to accept Wilson's methodology for the discovery of the principles of scientific administration.[48]

Goodnow also accepts, with minor modifications, the politics/adminis-tration dichotomy advanced by both Wilson and Mill. "Political functions," he writes, "group themselves naturally under two heads," that is, "opera-tions necessary to the expression of its will" and "operations necessary to the execution of that will." Likewise, as with both Mill and Wilson, he is adamant that there are limits to the proper role of the state's political arm within the administrative realm. Political control, he insists, "should not be permitted to extend beyond the limits necessary in order that the legitimate purpose of its existence be fulfilled." Like Mill, he notes the "tendency" of legislative bodies to intrude on the "execution of the state will in such a way as to influence improperly the expression of the state will." "The evils arising from the partial and interested administration of the law," he continues, "are so great that the most progressive political communities have felt obliged to take" measures to secure "the indepen-dence of certain of the authorities intrusted with the administration of the law."[49]

Establishing the proper boundaries between politics and administra-tion is no easy task, according to Goodnow. While there is a difference between "expressing" and "executing" "the will of the state," "the organs of government to which the discharge of these functions is intrusted cannot be clearly defined." For example, in his view the legislature is not the only organ that legitimately can express "the will of the state." The courts in passing on the constitutionality of legislation do so as well. Moreover, Goodnow does not believe it possible "to assign each of the functions [i.e., policy formation and execution] to a separate authority, not merely because the exercise of governmental power cannot be clearly appor-tioned, but also because, as political systems develop, these two primary functions of government tend to be differentiated into minor and sec-ondary functions."[50]

Goodnow is concerned particularly to determine the grounds for polit-ical bodies to legitimately exercise control over those entrusted with the execution of policy. Like Mill and Wilson, he is clear that the executive function "must be subjected to the control of politics" or, more precisely, "to the control of the body intrusted ultimately with the expression of the state will."[51] Like Mill and Wilson, he sees the need to limit or curtail this control.

As a general rule, Goodnow would exclude from political control "that part of the administration not distinctly of an executive character" save "to insure administrative integrity."[52] His exclusions would include the judiciary and "quasi-judiciary" for a number of reasons, including prevention of corruption.[53] Also removed would be "governmental authorities intrusted with the discharge of the administrative function," who also should have permanent tenure, "because the excellence of their work is often conditioned by the fact that they are expert, and expertness comes largely from long practice." As well, their missions are nonpolitical, characterized by "the exercise of foresight and discretion, the pursuit of truth, the gathering of information, the maintenance of a strictly impartial attitude toward the individual with whom they have dealings, and the provision of the most efficient possible administrative organization." These individuals are not unlike those who comprise Mill's bureaucracy, though Goodnow does not entrust to them any legislative prerogatives. Finally, also excluded from political control would be the "vast class of clerical and ministerial officers who simply carry out orders of superiors."[54]

Who, then, should be subject to control by the political agencies? Stated negatively, such control "should not be permitted to extend beyond the limits necessary" for "securing the execution of the state will."[55] Stated positively, control can be exercised legitimately over those engaged in executive as opposed to administrative functions. Executive authorities, whose major objective is implementation or realization of the state will, necessarily are involved in politics and must have a far wider discretion than those engaged in purely administrative functions.

On Goodnow's showing, then, the distinction between administration and politics is not as clear cut as for Mill and Wilson.[56] Because executive authorities often must fill in necessary details for the full articulation of the state will, they possess "considerable ordinance or legislative power." "These details," Goodnow insists, "must conform with the general principles laid down by the organ whose main duty is that of expression," in democratic regimes, normally the legislature.[57]

Goodnow seeks coordination and "harmony between the functions of politics and administration," conditions he regards as essential to successful governmental operations.[58] What this comes down to, in light of the responsibilities of the executive authority, is a means whereby the political agency can exercise effective control over the executive function. While this poses no problems, for example, in the English system where the majority party in Parliament appoints the principal executive officers, it does in the United States, with its constitutional separation of powers.

To this point, Goodnow writes, "It has been impossible for the necessary control of politics over administration to develop within the formal governmental system on account of the independent position assigned by the constitutional law to the executive and administrative officers." This is a recurrent theme in Goodnow's work and leads straightaway to his discussion and treatment of political parties. Parties in the United States have taken on the necessary "burden of coordinating the functions of expressing and executing the will of the state in the American governmental system."[59]

Particularly at the state and local level, according to Goodnow, political parties have not performed their function very well, largely because they have not paid due heed to the distinction between politics and administration. Parties look upon "ministerial appointive officers" in the same light as "discretionary elected officers" in order "to keep up the party organization and to maintain its strength." The resulting "spoils system" has "seriously impaired administrative efficiency" and fostered the growth of "political party machines," "making the party an end rather than a means."[60]

Goodnow sees improvement coming, albeit slowly at the state level, through reforms that centralize accountability in keeping with the politics/administration separation. The American people, he contends, "have already" perceived "the need for change" and with this the necessity "to centralize the administration in the nation, the state, and the city." In this respect, he observes, the national government enjoys an inherent advantage over municipal and state governments because from the beginning the constitutional order contained "the germs of administrative centralization." By the middle of the nineteenth century, he writes, the "conception of the centralized character of the national administration" emerged with the president possessing "large if not complete powers of appointment, removal, direction and supervision."[61]

Throughout his advocacy of administrative reform, Goodnow has nothing but praise for administrative centralization so long as the administrative apparatus does not fall into "the hands of irresponsible party leaders." Centralization, accompanied by an understanding of the distinction between politics and administration, he maintains, not only produces greater administrative efficiency; it allows as well for more effective control

over those with executive or discretionary authority.[62] In this, he is as one
with both Mill and Wilson.

Herbert Croly and the Progressive Vision

Herbert Croly was perhaps the leading Progressive thinker of the early
twentieth century. His major work, *The Promise of American Life*, which
appeared in 1909, has had a lasting impact on American politics.[63] We will
review the impact of this work on the scope of governmental functions and
activities after surveying his views on matters surrounding democratic control of the bureaucracy. This survey, for reasons that will be evident, also
must include his less comprehensive work, *Progressive Democracy*, published in 1914.[64]

While *Promise* does not offer a comprehensive treatment of the issues
raised by Goodnow, Mill, or Wilson, it is not devoid of observations relevant thereto. Croly devotes an entire chapter to various aspects of state
institutional reform, which he believes must be "radical," involving "a different relation between the executive and legislative branches and a wholly
different conception of the function of a state legislative body." Such is not
the case with the "Federal Constitution," which "is very much less in need
of amendment than are those of the several states." He deems it "on the
whole" to be "an admirable system of law and an efficient organ of government" that "at present" requires only authority to control corporations in
order to implement "an efficient national industrial policy."[65]

Croly finds governance in most states deplorable. State governments,
he charges, are both "corrupt and inefficient" mainly due to the fact that
"they have been organized for the benefit of corrupt and inefficient men."
It would be difficult to overstate the contempt in which he holds state legislatures. They have, he contends, "betrayed the interests of their constituents, and have been systematically passing laws for the benefit of corrupt
and special interests."[66]

Croly elaborates upon state evils and deficiencies at some length to
arrive at one of his central points, namely, that these conditions can be
attributed "chiefly to the lack of a centralized responsible organization."
He then proceeds to outline the measures and changes he regards as necessary to provide for responsibility, accountability, and centralization within

the context of popular government. There are, he postulates, but "two ways" a "concentration of responsibility" can be achieved: "either by subordinating the legislature to the executive or the executive to the legislature."[67]

Traditionally, Croly acknowledges, American practice has been to subordinate the executive to the legislature. But, he warns, "[W]hatever the theoretical advantages of legislative omnipotence," such as that found in the English parliamentary system, "it would constitute in this country a dangerous and dubious method of concentrating local governmental responsibility and power." Concentrating power and responsibility in the legislature might be beneficial if the legislators were of high quality, but Croly sees little hope of this: "American political practice has and always will tend to give mediocrity to the American popular representation." Indeed, he goes on to maintain that the shortcomings of the legislators—"at best . . . committee-men . . . at worst mercenaries . . . paid to betray their original employers"—has lent both "strength" and "propriety" to "the contemporary movement" for "the initiative and the referendum."[68]

Clearly, Croly is moving away from the legislature as the primary institution for articulating Goodnow's "will of the state." So much is confirmed when he introduces the notion of a "legislative council." On broad issues of policy—for example, whether gambling should be allowed or whether liquor sales should be curtailed—"an American electorate is or should be entirely competent to decide." But the people "cannot be expected to decide with any certainty of judgment about amendments or details, which involve for their intelligent consideration technical and special knowledge." Nor can such tasks be entrusted to the "existing legislatures," whose "members are experts in nothing but petty local politics" and "wholly incapable . . . of passing intelligently on matters either of technical or financial detail." Thus, according to Croly, American government requires a legislative council, "an experienced body of legal, administrative, and financial experts, comparatively limited in numbers, and selected in a manner to make them solicitous of the interests of the whole state." The functions of this council bear some resemblance to those of Mill's Council of Legislation. "The work of such a council," according to Croly, "would not be in any real sense legislative." Rather, "it would be tantamount to a scientific organization of the legislative committees, which at the present time exercise an efficient control over the so-called legislative output."[69]

Croly envisions the council not only as mediator between law-enacting people and a law-administering governor, but also as a check on the governor, who, in turn, would check the council. A main function of the council would be to act as a "technical advisory commission," preparing legislation for popular enactment or rejection. And, in keeping with Croly's goal of providing "an efficient concentration of governmental responsibility," the council would give priority to bills introduced by the governor. The council, for its part, could amend or even reject the governor's proposals, but if the governor persists, "the question at issue would be submitted to popular vote."[70]

Croly defends executive dominance on the grounds that the governor, "elected by the whole constituency," is far more "representative of public opinion than are the delegates of petty districts." This dominance would be enhanced by Croly's insistence on ensuring concentration of power and responsibility in the executive branch. Here he introduces the idea of an "executive council," "similar to the President's cabinet." This council would consist of chief administrative officers—"Controller, Attorney General, Secretary of State, Commissioner of Public Works, and the like"—all appointed by the governor to ensure that its members agree with him on "all essential matters of public policy." If and when such agreement no longer obtained, the governor could use his unilateral power of removal and appoint a successor. Beneath the members of the executive council, who clearly are political, Croly sees the need for a more or less permanent bureaucracy consisting of "experts," individuals who are "absolutely the masters of the technical business of the offices and of the abilities and services of their subordinates."[71] On this score, his thoughts parallel those of Mill, Wilson, and Goodnow.

Croly's executive would be "an enemy of the machine," a "real 'Boss'" who "would destroy the sham 'Bosses.'" With a strong governor "there could be no trafficking in offices, in public contracts, or in legislation." There would no longer be a need for the "professional politician," and those who "wished to serve the state unofficially would have to do so from disinterested motives."[72]

At least equally important, the centralization of power, Croly insists, would enhance responsible, efficient, and popular government. In this respect, Croly is fully aware of limitations on the executive's power. Even an empowered governor might not win battles with the legislative council;

he might even be removed from office through popular vote. Yet, with public opinion on his side, Croly is convinced that the chief executive would be an enormous force in advancing Progressive principles and goals.

Croly's recommendations for reform in *Progressive Democracy* differ in some respects from those he advocates in *Promise*. Moreover, his focus shifts to, for example, the compatibility of Progressive democracy with the existing party system. Nevertheless, belying somewhat his comment in *Promise* that all is reasonably well at the national level, he strongly states his commitment to the centrality of the national as well as state executive.

The executive's "primary business," in Croly's system, "is that of organizing a temporary majority of the electorate, and of carrying its will into legal effect." The primary responsibility of the executive, accordingly, would be that of "a law giver," with a secondary responsibility for "administrative efficiency." Also important in this regard is his discussion of "the proper function of administrative agencies in the realization of a progressive democratic policy," which anticipates in many respects developments during the New Deal.[73]

At the outset of his discussion delineating proper administrative functions, Croly remarks that delegation "of any considerable responsibility and power to administrative officials has been repugnant to the American political tradition both in its legalistic and democratic aspects." Nonetheless, "[l]egislatures have been compelled to delegate to administrative officials functions which two decades ago would have been considered essentially legislative" and even the courts have broadened "the scope of the valid exercise of administrative discretion." Croly has no difficulty accounting for this change: it is due to "the large volume of progressive legislation," implementation of which is "left increasingly in the hands of administrative commissions." He amplifies upon this later in his analysis: the success of highly complex and experimental social legislation that seeks to modify "social behavior" depends "more and more" on both "the good faith and competence of its administration."[74]

In noting this departure from our tradition, Croly is not unmindful that these broad delegations might undermine Progressive democracy—that they might lead, as they have in certain European countries, to arbitrary government or the growth of an "enlightened class" above the law. But he dismisses any such worries by recurring to the democratic character of American political culture. "Administrative action cannot very well become an agency of oppression in the United States" because administrators' authority flows from "the consent of public opinion." Administrators in a democracy, on this view, will find themselves in an entirely different "political and social" environment "from that of a continental bureaucrat."[75]

For Croly, however, America's environment need not constrict the latitude of discretion accorded to the bureaucracy. He anticipates that some parts of Progressive social programs will be "embodied in law," whereas "other aspects of it will still remain in a much more experimental condition," still the subject of "active political controversy." This, he maintains, points to a great need for "political continuity and stability" that can only be provided by "a permanent body of experts in social administration." Such an agency, he believes, "would give continuity" to policies, allowing "profitable lessons to be drawn from" their more experimental aspects.[76] The success of such laws, he concludes, rests upon "the ability and the disinterestedness with which" they are "administered." This means, in turn, that the administrators must be accorded "large discretionary powers" becoming, in effect, "official custodians of a certain part of the accepted social program[s]."[77]

Because bureaucrats will know best whether social programs are serving their intended purpose, Croly envisions them as having the executive's ear in recommending needed modifications in the law. Their recommendations would be looked upon as the professional judgment of a "conscientious," "independent authority" that the legislature would be bound to respect.[78]

As Croly proceeds in outlining the bureaucracy's functions, its discretion appears to broaden. First, he would accord considerable discretion to a "commission," not unlike Mill's Council of Legislation, charged with achieving general goals or conditions upon which the people have agreed. For instance, if the people have agreed on the goal of protecting factory workers' health and safety, a commission would draw up a set of regulations to achieve that goal. This it would do after "a comprehensive investigation of the conditions upon which the health and safety of the industrial employees depend." In this process, as Croly describes it, "industrial commissioners" would ideally consult extensively with "manufacturers and their employees . . . to frame a reasonable and effective group of regulations." Croly fully recognizes the unusual character of such a commission. In giving "specific expression to the general policy of the state," it can be regarded as a "fourth department of government" because "it does not fit into the traditional classifications of governmental powers." Being "in part executive, in part legislative . . . in part judicial, and . . . sharply distinguished from administration in its conventional sense," it can be regarded as "simply a convenient means of consolidating the divided activities of the government for certain practical social purposes." This he regards as a "permissible and useful" partial consolidation of powers. Croly argues here that the powers invested in the commissions are in less "danger of usurpation as would result from the grant of legislative power to the executive, or executive powers to a legislature." Moreover, their effectiveness relies on the support of "public opinion" and this, in turn, rests upon their ability to effectively implement "positive popular social program[s]."[79]

Further insight into Croly's understanding of the function or discretion of such commissions is to be found in his contention that administrative courts, independent of the regular courts, should handle disputes that arise in the process of administering programs. He argues here that commissions are not bound by rules. He takes up the objection that while the commissions are to advance "social justice," their justice is "justice without law—a justice which lacks the relative certainty and impartiality which can be obtained only from judgment according to accepted rules." Croly denies this, pointing out that decisions of a commission can serve as precedent for future decisions in like matters, so that rules can develop over time. But he does insist that a commission must have flexibility in adjusting the rules to different conditions and circumstances. Administrative courts are, in his judgment, better suited to understand the purposes of the commissions, namely, "to discover and define better methods of social behavior and to secure cooperation in the use of such methods by individuals and classes."[80]

In addition to administrative courts, according to Croly, a "general staff" is needed "for a modern progressive democratic state." Such a staff would acquire knowledge, would plan "as far ahead as conditions permit," and "must have a hand in creating the social experience which it is recording." While Croly does not go so far as to suggest that this general staff actually should initiate policy or articulate what Goodnow calls the will of the state, he does realize that responsible critics might say that, given its wide-ranging responsibilities, it should be subject to some form of popular control. As we might expect, Croly calls for administrative independence. "The administrator," he writes, has no control over controverted policies, except insofar as he can exert personal influence on elected officials or public opinion." To this, he adds, "[H]is authority, in so far as it exists, is essentially scientific." He does hold, however, that "an administration" should be "representative without being elective," a state of affairs he believes could come about through the proper "method of recruitment" aimed at shaping "its behavior, its sympathies, and its ideals."[81] Above all, Croly wants bureaucrats deeply committed to the goals of the programs they administer.

The Progressive Program

The foregoing survey shows agreement among Willson, Goodnow, and Croly on certain central propositions widely accepted today concerning the role of the bureaucracy in a republican form of government. We see agreement that experts not only should administer but also present detailed plans for the execution of policies to achieve ends directly or indirectly sanctioned by the people. We also see agreement that there is a point, somewhere beneath the very top levels in the bureaucracy, beyond which political influences ought not to hold sway. All agree that experts ought to enjoy tenure; their positions should not depend upon party affiliation. The Jacksonian motto "to the victors belong the spoils" is thoroughly repudiated by all in one fashion or another. In addition, with some differences, all thinkers discussed here subscribe to the politics/administration dichotomy; indeed, it is this distinction that opens the door wide to the experts. All also are strong advocates of centralization that, in the American context, comes down to executive control over the major departments of administration. The chief reasons for this are responsibility and accountability. That is, there is a need to have a ready target in case the bureaucracy fails to perform properly its duties. Finally, in one way or another all seek popular sanctions for activation of the bureaucracy; they seek popular support, expressed through the legislature or by the people themselves, for policies pursued or programs undertaken by the administrative arm of the state.[82]

In many ways Croly's *Promise of American Life* and its central message provide a convenient point of departure for understanding developments in the Progressive program. Croly argues for reforms going beyond those of most of his fellow Progressives. But those changes are in keeping with the overall reformist trend. In them we can see the intellectual roots of subsequent changes in the Framers' constitutional morality.

Clearly, realization of Croly's "promise" requires a more expansive and positive government, both state and national, than that contemplated by the Framers' Constitution. National authority had to be expanded so that the goals associated with Croly's promise could be uniformly and efficiently achieved. As he points out, to attain the degree of "comfort, prosperity, and opportunity for self-improvement" held out to us "by our patriotic prophecies" is well beyond the "competence" of "voluntary associations," no matter how "resourceful or disinterested" they may be. Likewise, their attainment could only be partial or at best uneven if left to the states. Consequently, realization of the national promise can only be achieved "by means of official national action." This is why Croly's program is so widely considered a precursor of Franklin Roosevelt's New Deal; it would expand the range of national authority in order to enact economic and social policies not unlike those advanced during the New Deal era. In some senses—for example, in calling for a "higher level of associated life" or in seeking subordination of self-acquisitiveness to the "dominant and constructive national purpose"[83]—Croly sets goals beyond those of the New Deal. Clearly, then, his understanding of the role of the bureaucracy forms a backdrop against which to appreciate developments during the succeeding era of reform.

Progressives generally seek to link the activity of government, and hence the bureaucracy, to the popular will. Thus, to take the most obvious example, Goodnow speaks of the will of the state that is normally articulated by the elected representatives. This will comes down to the deliberate sense of the people or, short of this, the deliberative will of a majority. The bureaucracy, for its part, simply executes what the legislature determines to be the will of the majority. Croly, on the other hand, would elicit from the people what amounts to a will of the state through a process that would determine their general sentiments, leaving to the bureaucracy the task of transforming their expression of will into a coherent and detailed legislative package.

In either case, Progressives seem to assume that most individuals would embrace proposals advanced in the name of the people and the common good even if they adversely affect their own interests. Progressives do not seem to anticipate the difficulties confronting a bureaucracy implementing the will of the state in the face of affected groups unwilling to cooperate. To be sure, Croly provides that affected groups should be consulted in working out policy details. But he does not deal with the critical question of which inputs are legitimate, which might be self-serving, and which might actually undermine the very purpose of the policy.

Another feature of Progressive thought, perhaps most prominent in Croly's work, relates to the role of administrative experts. It might appear that a major tenet of Progressivism, that of advancing direct popular control, precludes entrusting experts with authority to initiate policy. Croly, however, comes close to suggesting that these experts might, in effect, be able to advance policy initiatives given the deference policy makers might (or should?) accord them.

Moreover, Croly pictures the experts as public spirited, genuinely supportive of the policies they implement in the name of the people, and thoroughly capable of discerning social complexities that would bear upon policy implementation. Given these and like attributes, one is left to wonder why these experts should not be able to initiate policies by submitting well-designed programs to the legislature for its approval. Put another way, Progressive thought places a great emphasis on the beneficial role of experts, as well as their devotion, judgment, and professionalism, all of which stand in contrast to legislative bodies whose procedures and personnel fall far short of ideal. One senses that the Progressives are tempted, but reluctant, to embrace Mill's placement of experts at the very center of lawmaking processes. Yet their treatment would lead a reasonable person to ask, why not?

The Bureaucracy and the Public Interest

The relevance of these observations can be seen in Pendleton Herring's work *Public Administration and the Public Interest*, written in the early years of the New Deal. Herring clearly sees that there has been a transformation in the scope and purposes of the national government along lines very similar to those urged by Croly: "The government has assumed a general and positive responsibility for the management of industrial and social relations. The 'general welfare' is no longer regarded as a by-product inevitably ensuing from the profitable operations of the competitive system."

The general welfare now requires the regulation of interest groups "in such wise as to produce a balanced and harmonious whole" or a "dynamic synthesis." In this process, Herring emphasizes, the bureaucracy must play a central role. Indeed, "government today is largely a matter of expert administration," if for no other reason than that Congress increasingly has ceded wide discretionary powers to the bureaucracy. More specifically, the bureaucracy is charged with implementing laws in the "'public interest, convenience or necessity,'" even empowering "boards and quasi-judicial commission to determine the public interest."[84]

As to what should constitute the "linkage" between popular will and the bureaucracy, Herring categorically rejects the earlier Progressive answer and its reliance on "direct democracy." "Our experience with the direct primary, the initiative, the referendum and recall, and the long ballot," he avers, "have demonstrated that the mass public cannot be treated as though it possessed a unified and responsible will." Against Goodnow, Herring also maintains that political parties are incapable of reflecting the popular will by way of giving directions to the bureaucracy. In his view, not only does "the citizen put little faith in the ballot as a means of influencing the vast operations of government," but "the political party has proved inadequate" in "formulating a program and standing responsible for its consummation." Nor can Congress, "torn by blocs and dominated by organized groups," serve this function: "there is need for promoting a purpose of the state over and above the purposes of the medley of interests that compose it."[85]

Because, in the last analysis, Herring looks upon "the 'voice of the people'" as "a pleasant fancy and not a present fact," he insists that "if democracy is to succeed as a form of government," the initiative "for positive political action must be deliberately imposed at some strategic point." He puts this thought somewhat differently when he writes that in order to prevent "the domination of organized minorities," a democratic state must have some means whereby "the public interest can be formulated and presented to the voters." By way of pulling various strands of his analysis together, he holds that democratic government is possible so long as its institutions are "fitted to the limited capacity of the citizen to participate in political decisions."[86] This means, of course, that the initiative for political action to advance the public interest must belong to a political institution, presumably one accountable to the people.

Herring perceives potentially insurmountable difficulties to achieving this state of affairs in the United States. "We are left," he writes, "with a governmental apparatus of eighteenth century design whose obsolescence becomes the more striking in the light of present-day demands." While he has kind words for the British parliamentary system and expresses a sympathetic understanding for the position of those calling for constitutional reforms, he feels obliged to "seek a solution in terms of" existing institutions. That solution, not unexpectedly, is to be found in "Presidential control and leadership"; "the President has time and again been better able to uphold the public interest than a Congress controlled by blocs and organized minorities." It is, he believes, the responsibility of the "executive branch" to provide "the people generally with an interpretation of the public interest that they can accept or reject through the established channels of representative government." In advancing this position, he recognizes that as the power of the president is increased so, too, is "the importance of the bureaucracy."[87]

At this point the question arises whether, under the arrangement Herring envisions, the role of the bureaucracy would conform with democratic principles. Might it become an independent source for "positive political action"? What would be the nature of its input into the formulation or execution of public policy?

As Herring would have it, ideally the bureaucracy should work out the details of legislation with representatives from the affected interests. Not only are administrators better able to withstand the special pleading of these interests than are congressmen, but their "special knowledge" would enable them "to understand the merits of the proposed legislation in terms of what is possible of enforcement and of accomplishment." According to Herring, the bureaucrats, in consulting with affected interests, should not seek compromise or cater to their demands. While "the bureaucracy must be responsive to groups," it also must "be responsible to those political leaders who are designated to speak for the people." To this he adds, "[I]t must seek to act always in the public interest." In fact, a major purpose of his book is "to explore the implications" of his call for responsiveness to interests and, at the same time, an overriding concern for administrators to advance the public interest.[88]

Even where "certain guiding criteria" for decision making are "supplied by statutes," Herring comments, "a margin of discretion remains inherent in the administrative process," a discretion that must be exercised in accordance with the public interest. While difficulties (such as discerning the nature of the public interest itself in a given situation) inhere in the processes he recommends, he sees significant benefits resulting. Among them would be an agreement among involved interests that would "forestall opposition later in Congress" and produce sound legislation because the most competent individuals would work out its details and "technical provisions."[89]

Herring recognizes that his project would require greater coordination between the executive and legislative departments. He acknowledges that this would involve the cultivation of a "responsible bureaucracy" that would in its expertise and professionalism resemble that found in England. And he is highly critical of Congress, particularly its committee system, which "has nothing to offer in our search for integration and responsibility in political affairs."[90]

Whence, then, the necessary coordination? Here Herring looks to the "greater demands" that increasingly are placed upon the bureaucracy, often without any guidance provided by statutes "that set clear limits to [its] activities." "With this greater degree of discretion," he observes, "a very much broader field of jurisdiction" has been accorded the bureaucracy without any institution that might coordinate its activities. As a result, "it is more difficult for" an official in one field "to measure his activities against" those in "related fields." Worse still, "there is no place where a broad comparative view is taken of the various administrative activities of the federal government," a very serious shortcoming that prevents assessment of the "relative importance" of programs and policies. To alleviate this lack of coordination, Herring recommends an "administrative council" that would operate along the lines of a "general staff." While he provides only a sketchy outline of this council's composition and organization, he is clear about its primary function: "to discover how the laws passed by Congress could be most effectively and harmoniously executed."[91]

It is apparent that Herring's reforms could not be fitted into the politics/administration dichotomy. As we have seen, from policy formulation through policy implementation, Herring's bureaucracy would exercise a discretion that most would regard as political. It would, for instance, bear primary responsibility for working out policy with the involved interests, and in the process of implementing policy it necessarily would have to exercise discretion in formulating rules consonant with the public interest.

There can be no question that Herring's experts would have considerable influence over their elected overseers, if only in pointing to problems requiring attention. This breakdown of the politics/administration concept is far from unique to Herring. His understanding that in practice administration and politics cannot be entirely separated—an understanding that seems implicit in Croly's reforms—was advanced during the early stages of the New Deal and, as we have noted, has come to be accepted wisdom in modern times.

Implications for Constitutional Morality

The Progressive reform program calls for a constitutional morality substantially different from that attached to the Framers' Constitution. It would, in essence, blur the separation of powers, creating a fourth branch of government in which the powers of the other three would be mixed. It also would substantially increase the powers the president would be called upon to exercise. It clearly calls for virtues, particularly on the part of bureaucrats. But those virtues are of a different sort, or attach to different parties in different ways, from those of the Framers' constitutional morality. For example, the people's representatives would be called on to exercise much less in the way of judgment in lawmaking, ceding this judgment to the commissions and other institutions of the executive branch. Further, the president would be called on to act in a more active, expansionist fashion.

Restraint would no longer be a central virtue for those in any of the Framers' three branches. Judges actively would oversee all aspects of government. Presidents actively would promote national policies of their choosing. And even members of Congress actively would engage in their new role as overseers of the bureaucracy in defense of their constituents' rights and interests. As for the bureaucrats, while called on to act with restraint in the realm of policy making, they also would be called on to act as policy makers as well as administrators, arbitrators as well as executors of the laws—in effect as a nexus of three forms of action the Framers sought to keep separate in order to prevent arbitrary government. Most important, political officers under this new, Progressive constitutional morality would not be called upon to defend their turf. Instead, the government would be one of "shared powers." All would be active—in different ways but on the same turf. Bargaining and cooperation on the basis of varying "deals," rather than restraint and wariness, would be the chief virtues underlying a system no longer centered on formal structures and procedures, but on the formation and implementation of programmatic policies and political reforms.

This new constitutional morality requires analysis and appraisal. First, however, we turn to Progressive arguments and later actions regarding the Framers' Constitution. Our purpose: to show the manner in which the new constitutional morality was developed and how it has affected the structure of the Constitution, the practice of governance, and the rule of law.

5

Progressive Reformers
and the Framers' Constitution

THE CENTRAL DIFFICULTY facing Progressive reformers during the early twentieth century was that of reconciling an expansive bureaucracy exercising broad discretionary powers with democratic governance. Believing that administrators should have wide latitude to make public policy effective and efficient, Progressives nonetheless were convinced that these administrators should receive their marching orders, in some sense, from "the people." But who spoke for the people?

The natural representative of the popular will in a republic is, of course, the legislature. And Wilson and Goodnow, at least, argued at times that legislative action could be taken to reflect the popular will. Croly and Herring, on the other hand, had significant doubts in this regard. They saw legislatures as subservient to special interests, riven by political divisions, and characterized by rank incompetence, making them unreliable conduits for the popular will. In addition, concern for responsibility to the public, shared by all Progressives, moved Croly and Herring to look to the single, united executive as best able to speak for the people.[1]

This favoritism toward presidential governance was problematic, of course, because the Framers' Constitution was built upon not just the separation of powers but also the primacy of the legislature as lawmaker. Today, however, in both theory and practice, the president's claim to embody the popular will is widely accepted and taken to be more legitimate than that of Congress.[2] The presidency-centered view received early reinforcement, beginning with Theodore Roosevelt's vision of expansive executive authority and Woodrow Wilson's *Constitutional Government*, which in holding the president to be the only authentic voice of the people broke with his own earlier work.[3] It was institutionalized to a significant degree in the New Deal and continues to shape reform ideology and governmental practice to this day.

In this chapter we first turn our attention to the key elements of the constitutional transformation set forth by Wilson, Progressivism's most influential advocate. We next discuss, in summary form, the actual changes wrought in governmental practice during the first half of the twentieth century, changes producing what is properly termed a presidential or administrative republic. From here we proceed to an examination of later reformers justifying these transformations, and demanding more. For many decades now, critics of the Framers' Constitution have advocated reforms along lines marked out by Wilson, a large number of them requiring structural and procedural change through constitutional amendment. These reforms seem aimed at completing and securing Wilson's vision and the institutional changes begun in earnest under the New Deal.

The New Deal did not suddenly produce a new republic. Rather, its programs were part of a longer, still-ongoing transformation of constitutional morality and with it the government in action, or what might be termed our operational constitution. With this understanding, we turn to reformers' critiques of the separation of powers and the motives of the Framers in ensuring that adequate provision for it was made in the Constitution. This examination provides a backdrop for comprehending the causes for the triumph of Wilson's vision and the effects of that vision on constitutional practice and the rule of law.

Woodrow Wilson and the Constitutional Transformation

In many ways, Wilson may be regarded as the father of the modern Constitution. Two of his major works dealing with the Constitution, *Congressional Government* (1885) and *Constitutional Government in the United States* (1908), are most interesting. The first, *Congressional Government*, presents a picture of our constitutional system that in a number of important particulars corresponds with that of the Framers, most notably in affirming that Congress is, and was intended to be, the predominant branch. His later work, *Constitutional Government,* represents an abrupt about-face, setting forth the major themes that have served to alter the character of our constitutional morality and operational constitution without altering the written Constitution's formal structure. Put another way, Wilson's change of heart is reflected in his charge that the branches of government—their respective powers and duties, as well as their representative character—should be looked upon in a new and markedly different light than that of the founding generation. Wilson's arguments influenced formation of a still-developing, new constitutional morality, changing the manner in which the Constitution is, or is not, followed and upheld.

In *Congressional Government,* Wilson contends that Congress has overstepped its legitimate boundaries, the very condition the Framers sought to prevent since they regarded it as a prelude to tyranny. But Wilson's take on this development, while highly critical, is far from alarmist. "The Constitution in operation," he cautions, "is manifestly a very different thing from the Constitution of the books." The "unquestionable" reality is that in practice "the predominant and controlling force, the centre and source of all motive and of all regulative power, is Congress. All the niceties of constitutional restriction and even many broad principles of constitutional limitation have been overridden." This congressional dominance "gives a very rude negative to some theories of balance and some schemes for distributed powers, but . . . sits well with convenience, and does violence to none of" the underlying constitutional "principles of self-government."[4]

Wilson stresses that there are no really effective checks on federal congressional power. He maintains that from the time of the nation's founding there has been "a steady and unmistakable growth of nationality of sentiment," and that the Civil War had "finally and decisively disarranged the balance between state and national powers." In sum, the Union victory in the Civil War marked "the triumph of the principle of national sovereignty." "For all practical purposes," he writes, "the national government is supreme over the state governments, and Congress predominant of its so-called coordinate branches."[5]

Wilson is prescient in seeing even greater centralization of power at the national level: "[T]here is a distinct movement in favor of national control of all questions of policy which manifestly demand uniformity of treatment and administration such as cannot be realized by the separate, unconcerted action of the States." He sees as well that the national government, in this case Congress, will expand its powers either by "constitutional amendment, or by still further flights of construction." Nor, he observes, can the judiciary—that institution best equipped to preserve the residual power of the states—effectively curb Congress since "the national courts [even the Supreme Court] are for the most part in the power of Congress." Before the courts will ever interpose, he holds, "Congress must wantonly go very far outside the plain and unquestionable meaning of the Constitution," clearly contravening both "right and precedent."[6]

Likewise, Wilson believes that Congress has little to fear from the presidency. As an admirer of the early presidents, he is convinced that the caliber of those holding the office underwent a decline with the emergence of nominations by party conventions. Rather than strength of character, power brokers at these conventions sought political deals and presidential candidates with short and uncontroversial, hence undistinguished, public records. The basic underlying reason, however, for the decline of the presidency was not the decline in the "prestige of the office," but its waning power and the increasingly "predominant" role of Congress. The incursion of Congress on executive powers, Wilson takes pains to point out, is both subtle and somewhat indirect. For instance, he views Congress as increasingly entering "into the details of administration" to such a degree that "it has virtually taken into its own hand all the substantial powers of government." What is more, in this process Congress "does not domineer the President himself, but it makes the Secretaries its humble servants."[7]

Although Wilson believes Congress has "always" harbored the desire to expand its authority, he does not regard its ascension to be the result of any "scheme of conscious usurpation." Rather, over time "it found means and opportunity" to expand its powers "so naturally and so silently that it has almost always seemed of normal extent" and very seldom "much beyond its acknowledged constitutional sphere."[8] Or, as he puts this more generally, "our Constitution, like every other constitution which puts the authority to make laws and the duty of controlling the public expenditure into the hands of a popular assembly, practically sets that assembly to rule the affairs of the nation as supreme overlord."[9]

Wilson is not overly concerned with Congress's dominance; he seems to accept the proposition that representative assemblies are the institutions that most accurately reflect the will of the people. At the same time, however, because he does not regard Congress as an "effective representative body," he dwells upon what he regards as its major shortcomings, that is, those that detract from its effectiveness. On this score, while he is disturbed by Congress's lack of transparency, deliberation, and accountability, his major concerns seem to be twofold. First is the lack of coherency in the legislative "debates" and in the legislative output. In his words, "no two measures consciously join in purpose or agree in character, and so debate must wander as widely as the subjects of debate." In this vein, he continues, "there is no one policy to be attacked or defended, but only a score or two of separate bills."[10]

Somewhat related is Wilson's second concern, the almost total separation of the legislative and executive branches. This separation in his view prevents Congress from fulfilling the duties and functions it has assumed. On this point, Wilson notes a number of shortcomings. Congress, for instance, finds itself incapable of "superintending all matters of government," very much unlike the British parliamentary system. "It is," he contends, "the proper duty of a representative body to look into every affair of government and to talk much [about] what it sees." He insists that an effective Congress should "have and use every means of acquainting itself with the acts and the disposition of the administrative agents of government" so that the "country" may "learn how it is being served." "The only really self-governing people," he writes, "is that people which discusses and interrogates its administration." He is one with John Stuart Mill in asserting that this "informative function," resulting from investigation and oversight of the administration, "should be preferred even to its legislative function." As "the sphere and influence of national administration and national legislation" widen, he warns of the imperative need of Congress to "be equipped with something besides abundant powers of legislation" in order to ensure uniform administration of its policies in a manner "diligently obedient to the more permanent judgments of public opinion."[11]

Wilson is aware that constitutional change would be necessary to overcome the difficulties he cites. He believes the Framers' desire for a Congress that would not be "subservient" understandably led them to provide for its "absolute separation" from the executive branch.[12] He pleads with the American people to overcome their blind veneration of the Framers and their handiwork so that they may make those changes necessary to render "self-government among us a straightforward thing of simple method, single, unstinted power, and clear responsibility."[13] Oddly, though, he makes no specific recommendation. We say "oddly" because he makes essentially the same points, along with a specific recommendation, in an article he wrote in 1879, while still an undergraduate.[14] In this article he seeks to bridge the gap between Congress and the executive by proposing that the president select his cabinet secretaries from among congressional or even state party leaders.

Without overtly rejecting the Constitution itself, Wilson in *Congressional Government* moves away from the constitutional morality undergirding that Constitution. He seeks to make the Constitution operate so as to undermine the separation of powers in favor of a system supporting Progressive notions of democratic accountability. He would call for greater changes later in his career.

While in subsequent writings Wilson offered up other piecemeal "reforms" designed to produce greater coordination between the executive and legislative branches, we see a paradigmatic shift in his thinking with the publication of *Constitutional Government*. Strong hints of this shift can be seen in the short preface to *Congressional Government's* fifteenth printing in 1900, wherein he writes in the final paragraph that "[i]t may be . . . the new leadership of the Executive, inasmuch as it is likely to last, will have a very far-reaching effect upon our whole method of government." This "new leadership," he adds, "may also give the heads of the executive departments a new influence upon the action of Congress," thereby providing "an integration which will substitute statesmanship for government by mass meeting." He concludes by observing that this new presidential leadership "may put this whole volume hopelessly out of date."[15] And, in fact, it is in this light that *Constitutional Government* can best be viewed; it marks a radical transformation of Wilson's thought. In this work, he abandons his mission of reforming Congress to provide for an effective representative system and dwells on the potentialities of a presidentially centered constitutional order that can, he believes, overcome virtually all the difficulties enumerated in *Congressional Government*.

Wilson concludes that an active, responsible, and effective government— one capable of achieving the goals associated with the Progressive movement of the early twentieth century—could only be achieved under the forms of the Constitution through presidential leadership. In so doing,

Wilson is aware that he is proposing what amounts to an overhaul of the Constitution. In his new constitutional order the executive branch, not the Congress as the Framers had intended, would predominate.

Two major extraconstitutional developments serve to facilitate and, in a sense, justify the "reform" Wilson seeks in *Constitutional Government.* The first of these, thanks largely to the efforts of Jefferson and Madison, was the emergence of organized political parties that could potentially serve as a bridge between branches, thereby overcoming whatever barriers the formal constitutional separation of departments might present to concerted action.[16] Andrew Jackson can be credited with the second development of presidential leadership—a development that probably could not have come about without the first. Simply put, Jackson's route to the presidency in 1828 through nomination and election by the people allowed him to claim that he was just as representative of the American people as Congress.

In *Constitutional Government,* Wilson acknowledges that the Founders scarcely envisioned a president assuming a dominant role in the process of government. But Wilson believes that these extraconstitutional developments have enabled modern presidents to assume such a role without the need for any basic constitutional changes. To this effect, he observes, the president "has become the leader of his party and the guide of the nation in political purpose, and therefore in legal action. The constitutional structure of the government has hampered and limited his action in these significant roles, but it has not prevented it." This understanding, as well as the history of the office, leads Wilson to conclude that the presidency is largely what its occupant at any given time "has the sagacity and force to make it."[17]

In contrast to his earlier position acknowledging congressional supremacy, Wilson now sets forth a conception of the separation of powers in which the president is the centerpiece, "the unifying force in our complex system, the leader both of his party and of the nation." He points to the inherent advantages that a president, as a unifier and leader, enjoys over Congress. Because the president alone represents "no constituency, but of the whole people," he is the "only national voice in affairs." Aside from the fact that only the president, and not Congress, can speak for the people as a whole, Wilson insists that other factors and forces point to his dominance: the country's "instinct is for unified action, and it craves a single leader" so that once he has gained "the admiration and confidence of the country . . . no other single force can withstand him, no combination of forces will easily overpower him." Or, again, "if he rightly interpret the national thought and boldly insist upon it, he is irresistible."[18]

And what would be the role of the people in such a national government? Presume for a moment that the American system was organized to achieve the conditions sought by the Progressives. Under an ideal arrangement there would be disciplined parties, with the majority party headed by the president, capable of enacting its programs with the necessary input from administrative experts. Despite Wilson's gestures toward popular rule, there is room to wonder about the level of democratic accountability such an arrangement would evince, and through what mechanism. There is, of course, the question of how the parties would go about formulating their programs and whether they could do so without bending to special interests or allowing expert opinion to trump politics. But, in the last analysis, competition between the parties for majority support through the electoral process would be the means by which policies would obtain the democratic or popular seal of approval. The election, to put this in other terms, would provide the marching orders for the bureaucracy under the watchful eye of the president.

Would such a system produce democratic accountability? One should consider, to begin with, the hierarchical structure of the parties though which policy alternatives are formulated. More telling, it is highly questionable whether popular support for any given program or policy can be derived from popular elections, that is, whether such elections can legitimately be viewed as giving the executive and bureaucracy their marching orders.[19] A mandate or approval for any given part of the party's program, it would seem, is simply assumed; it cannot be empirically or logically shown to be the case on the basis of election results, which reflect broader concerns of character, personality, responsibility for overall economic conditions, war, and various other factors. In any event, reforms designed to overcome the separation of powers, while retaining the veneer of democratic accountability, allow not only for a wide degree of discretion on the political side (and this quite aside from any popular support), but also allow considerable latitude for the experts to flesh out the means of policy implementation.

Rejection of the cultural unwritten constitution entails rejection of its focus on self-government among that variety of overlapping associations characterizing American life, increasingly as one looks back before the expansion of federal power. As noted by analysts from Tocqueville in the nineteenth century to Ostrom in the twentieth, this culture was associated by nature with administrative decentralization. Thus, centralization of authority entailed centralization of administration and replacement of local associations with the machinery of monarchical administration.

We see, then, in Progressive thought adherence to a view of politics, of constitutional order, and of the role of the people in making law, distinctly at odds with that of the Constitution's framers. Along with this contrasting political vision comes a contrasting constitutional morality. The Framers and their successors were devoted to the structure of the Constitution, to its formal requirements, and to the limited roles it assigned each branch of government. The goal was maintenance of ordered, limited government and the rule of law. The Progressives put forward a quite different conception of the proper nature and goals of government, one rejecting formalism and restraint, instead emphasizing the need for efficiency in pursuit of a substantive common good.

The New Deal: Normative Antecedents and Institutional Outcomes

Decades ago, Fred Greenstein argued that the Franklin Roosevelt administration fundamentally altered the nature of American government, in large part through the "metamorphosis" of the presidency. This metamorphosis had four key components: the president began establishing a policy agenda, actively seeking congressional support and using his veto power to further that agenda; he began exercising unilateral powers, particularly through executive orders, to make policy; he built an administrative apparatus within his own executive office to formulate policy and pursue his legislative agenda; and he took on the role of national symbol, projecting reassurance and other qualities identified with "great" presidents of the early republic, thus personalizing the presidency.[20]

Clearly there were antecedents to the New Deal in the establishment of a "strong" presidency. David Nichols argues that the New Deal was not, in fact, transformative, because the presidency is accorded a breadth and depth of power by the Framers' Constitution that is overlooked in most of the literature. He asserts, "The increased activity of the President can be attributed to broad changes in the character of government and society and not to a change in the balance of power between the President and the other branches." On Nichols's view, "the constitutional office of the presidency" has not, in fact, undergone significant change; the change has come about primarily in the manner and especially the extent to which the president exercises powers he already had.[21] The thrust of Nichols's argument is that the powers of the modern presidency exist in the text of the Framers' Constitution, there to be utilized more or less aggressively and developed through more or less elaborate forms of statutory and informal institutionalization.

In one sense this is a radical claim, rejecting as it largely does the vast literature on the creation of the administrative state, and the state-building of the first and second Roosevelts in particular, as having altered the nature of the American regime.[22] In a more important sense, however, Nichols's claim accords with contemporary notions of constitutions as possessing an intrinsic elasticity beyond that envisioned by the Framers. But such elasticity was not in the Framers' text—though it was, as it must be, intrinsic to the Progressive constitutional morality.

In addition, it is important to note the antiformalist tendency of democratic peoples (and Americans in particular) and the institutional ramifications of this hostility. As Tocqueville noted, *"Men living in democratic ages do not readily comprehend the utility of forms: they feel an instinctive contempt for them . . . Forms excite their contempt and often their hatred; as they commonly aspire to none but easy and present gratifications, they rush onwards to the object of their desires, and the slightest delay exasperates them. This same temper, carried with them into political life, renders them hostile to forms, which perpetually retard or arrest them in some of their projects."*[23]

Forms irritate democratic men because they stand in the way of their goals, of their desires of the moment, and, more systemically, of progress. By the late nineteenth century, irritability in the face of formal obstacles to their immediate wills had been transformed among many Americans into an ideology of practicality. In the philosophical sphere it was called pragmatism; in politics it went by the name of Progressivism. Long before the New Deal, Wilson had set in motion policies and supported a public ideology committed to breaking down the forms of American politics, and of American constitutionalism in particular.

While not perhaps a revolution, the New Deal marked a high point in the long-term Progressive move away from the constitutional morality of the Framers' Constitution. The Framers' constitutional morality clearly had begun undergoing fundamental changes by the time of FDR, and it was further changed by him. Moreover, institutional innovations clearly played a role in expansion of the presidential office. To take one example, the Bureau of the Budget was formally established in 1921. It added significantly to the president's power to take control of the legislative agenda. The bureau began with limited powers and the aim of imposing economy on an unruly, free spending congress. But it developed as part of a program, realized over ensuing decades, to build a more activist federal government requiring greater presidential guidance, and it aided presidential dominance of the legislative agenda.[24]

As important, the Great Depression produced economic suffering on a scale that, when combined with previous normative and institutional changes, fomented a general demand that the federal government "do something." It did not merely encourage FDR to use aggressively powers he clearly had. It helped create a further shift in the constitutional morality of the people itself. Urged along by material distress, the people came to demand of their representatives a different code of conduct from that previously seen as fit. In previous crises, systematic (let alone ongoing) federal action had been all but unthinkable.[25] Now, however, voters and, increasingly, their representatives came to accept the idea that the federal government would provide substantive goods rather than focus on maintaining the rule of law and balance among mediating groups to which the people might look for material assistance. Thus, the shift in constitutional morality already experienced by elite thinkers became electorally important, bringing changes in the operations of American government inconsistent with the Framers' Constitution.

Over the course of the early twentieth century, few would deny that there was significant movement toward a president-centered system. Important in this regard was Theodore Roosevelt's stewardship theory of presidential authority. According to this theory, the president was the "steward of the people," and as such had a duty "to do anything that the needs of the nation demanded unless such action was forbidden by the Constitution or the laws."[26] During the first Roosevelt's presidency (1901–1909), such thinking spawned much strong rhetoric. Some of this rhetoric had substantive implications. Such was the case with Roosevelt's threat to order, unilaterally, that U.S. armed forces take over coal mines shut down in the midst of a labor dispute—a threat from which Roosevelt stepped back only on the condition management and labor submit to federally appointed mediators, not then provided for in any legislation.[27] Administratively, Roosevelt successfully pushed for expansion of the discretionary power of the Interstate Commerce Commission and formation of the Bureau of Corporations, along with legislation establishing food inspections and expanding civil service reforms to "professionalize" administration.[28]

Wilson's direct contribution to Progressivism's institutionalization was ambiguous. His primary, but not his only, state-building enterprises came about in the heat of World War I. Before the war, Wilson established a variety of commissions and other independent agencies (e.g., the Federal Trade Commission to regulate corporate mergers and securities trading and the Federal Reserve Board to regulate banking). He also promoted a wide-ranging Selective Service Act, combined with various forms of morals legislation institutionalizing federal police powers. In addition, he secured legislation establishing the Council of National Defense, the first federal agency established to coordinate war production; the Lever Act, granting him power to regulate food and fuel businesses; and the Overman Act, which delegated to the president the power "to make such redistribution of functions among executive agencies as he may deem necessary" for the duration of the war and the following six months. The Espionage Act spawned thousands of prosecutions for sedition. Finally and more generally, the sheer size and expense of government grew to levels never before seen, and ensured that "never again would federal revenue be less than five times the pre-war average."[29]

There were, of course, other crucial developments during this era. Perhaps most important, the character of the Senate was altered fundamentally through the Seventeenth Amendment, which provided for direct election of senators. By changing senators' constituencies—by making them answerable directly to the masses rather than to the legislatures of their states—this amendment changed the relevant constitutional morality of that body. It undermined the set of counteracting structural ambitions called for in *Federalist* 51, weakening the reliance of senators on state-level support and encouraging them to support expansion of federal policies at the expense of state prerogatives.[30] Other electoral reforms, including institutionalization of the referendum and recall, encouraged the idea that government should be directly responsive to the substantive desires of popular majorities.[31]

As important as these developments were long-term changes in Supreme Court doctrine. Of special note were the court's determination to protect "freedom of contract" and other "fundamental rights" under the due process clause of the Fourteenth Amendment, and its use of this doctrine to strike down state legislation regarding various forms of economic activity.[32] Also important was the court's increasing acceptance of expanded federal power to regulate commerce. Where before Congress's power in this area had been limited to regulating goods actually in interstate commerce, the court came to see the reach of this power extending to the manufacture of goods that later might enter the stream of commerce.[33]

Substantive due process and extension of the commerce power both helped produce changes in the structure of government. They encouraged changes in the constitutional morality of the American people by allowing greater federal action (commerce power) and, in effect, forbidding or at least trumping attempted reforms at the state level (substantive due process). Thus, they focused the people's attention on the federal government as the necessary locus of power to affect public policy. Decisions rendered under these doctrines also altered the operational constitution—the actual habits of governance—by making the federal courts intermediaries between state governments and individuals claiming particular rights. This was in marked contrast to the courts' previous position as intermediaries between the federal government and the people, taken principally as corporate wholes in their states and communities.[34] And these decisions evinced and furthered a change in judges' constitutional morality in that they entailed courts reaching beyond the text and history of the Framers' Constitution to a variety of philosophical and economic theories and issues not traditionally held to be within the definition of judgment according to judicial duty.[35]

These changes added up to a significant reformation of governmental conduct in the United States. At the same time, however, the formal structure of the Framers' Constitution remained largely intact and received general support among political actors within all three of those branches. In particular, much of Wilson's wartime expansion of presidential power and the nascent administrative state, reliant as it was on presidential war powers, did not last. It would take the "moral equivalent of war" during the Great Depression to advance the Progressive program and institutionalize it for the long haul.

Prepared by previous administrations and by a change in the constitutional morality of countless political actors, the ground was fertile for FDR's New Deal. There was, of course, a flurry of legislation during FDR's first one hundred days in office—a flurry that in itself showed a change in the demands of the people and the determination of political actors to act with dispatch rather than restraint.[36] That this was, in fact, a shift in constitutional morality is shown perhaps most clearly by the frequent reliance of FDR and his supporters on analogies to war. The administration called for powers that previously had been granted presidents (e.g., Wilson) during wartime in order to combat a crisis it likened to foreign invasion.[37]

The legislative result: the Federal Emergency Relief Administration, the Civil Works Administration, the Public Works Administration, and the Civilian Conservation Corps all were established to provide emergency relief, as was the Emergency Banking Act. The Federal Deposit Insurance Corporation, the Tennessee Valley Authority, and the Agricultural Adjustment Act all aimed at more systemic institutionalization of administrative agencies. Succeeding initiatives, including the Securities Exchange Commission, the National Labor Relations Act, the Works Progress Administration, and the Rural Electrification Administration, also were intended to institutionalize administrative agencies responsible for regulating wages, hours, prices, production levels, and working conditions in the name of national public health, safety, and welfare. Perhaps most significantly, the Social Security Act set up a two-tier state/federal system of unemployment and old-age payments institutionalizing dependence on the federal government (directly or indirectly) for a minimum level of financial well-being.[38]

FDR was far from universally successful in his attempts to institutionalize administrative regulation of economic and social welfare activities. Moreover, he was not able to gain full control over the bureaucracy he created. His recommended executive branch reforms were resisted, forcing him to scale back his attempts at administrative control under a new executive office of the president formed through a combination of legislation and unilateral executive action.[39] But succeeding presidents would continue to institutionalize federal economic and social welfare responsibilities and regulation, perhaps most significantly through the Administrative

Procedure Act,[40] which essentially laid out a form of "law" governing the conduct of administrative rule making.[41]

At the end of the day, the New Deal succeeded in changing the character of the American constitutional morality and its form of governance. Where before the Constitution, the constitutional morality, and the actual form of governance had at least generally conformed to the model of a mediating constitution, now the call clearly was made for a government that would command a "new deal" for the people in the form of federally mandated changes in social and economic as well as political structures. This was at least the stated intention of FDR himself. In answering the charge that he was establishing government regimentation of the American people, FDR responded that "the federal government was liberating individuals from plutocratic regimentation. Vast inequalities of wealth had produced 'a kind of private government, a power unto itself—a regimentation of other people's money and other people's lives.' "[42] Various permanent programs from Social Security to unemployment insurance to electrification and price supports now would provide substantive goods to the people, "freeing" them from various conditions and private actors by shaping their economic lives through bureaucratic rules and administration.

Thus the change in constitutional morality was significant. The masses now demanded, and political actors thought it their duty to provide, substantive goods through the federal government. These "goods" would include a more equal division of power within society, as commanded from the political center. Moreover, the means chosen to produce those goods, including oversight of industry so as to protect health and safety, was not to be the legislature, but rather the executive branch, overseen by a powerful president.

Still, as Theodore J. Lowi has pointed out, in the liberal mind there is no stopping point for governmental regulation or the formulation of public goods the government may provide.[43] This being the case, the New Deal was not the end of the Progressive push for administrative and, eventually, constitutional reform. Indeed, the call for Progressive reform was still just beginning.

Wilson's Legacy beyond the New Deal

The central feature of the Framers' Constitution—the separation of powers—had made activist government difficult both during and prior to the New Deal. This structure was, after all, central to what was by design and intent a mediating rather than a commanding constitution. It is not surprising, then, that the separation of powers continues to be perceived as an impediment to good government. The basic problem has been put in the following terms: there are "three centers" of power, "the presidency, Senate, and House of Representatives . . . elected at different times and responsible to different constituencies. And each center is structured to prevent any 'faction'—such as political party—from establishing control over the machinery as a whole."[44] From the Progressive perspective, the separation of powers, among its other shortcomings, is the source of "grid-lock" or "deadlock."[45] According to Progressives, this separation renders legislation in the public interest extremely difficult.

The New Deal was in itself a victory over the separation of powers— but only a partial victory. It was a special case, in which a powerful or "great" president facing a national crisis managed to push through an ambitious legislative program. Circumstances, powerful rhetoric, and political maneuvering were combined to overcome an already weakened constitutional morality embodied in checks and balances and so found a substantial though incomplete administrative state. But not even FDR, on the Progressive view, was able to overcome deadlock fully and provide all that the people needed from their federal government.[46]

From the Progressive perspective, then, the New Deal left the nation with a new problem. While the operational constitution had been altered significantly, the written constitution had not; and the constitutional morality, while weakened, had yet to be extinguished or replaced. Not surprisingly, then, post–New Deal reformers have sought to further erode separation of powers from a perspective openly hostile toward the Framers' constitutional morality, especially as embodied in checks and balances.

Virtually all contemporary schools of administrative thought, and most certainly the Progressive, see the separation of powers as contravening the most important tenets of sound administration and democratic accountability. At least since the New Deal's abortive "third phase,"[47] reforms have been set forth attempting to overcome these shortcomings. Some relate to only certain elements of the present system. More comprehensive reforms, which certainly would bring about the changes necessary from the Progressive perspective, center on disciplined political parties, with the president as party chief, to overcome constitutional separation. The comprehensive reforms are patterned after the British system, with its disciplined parties and concentration of powers in the hands of a prime minister and his or her cabinet; this hardly is surprising, given the praise bestowed on it by Progressives for its providing accountable and efficient government.

Yet, as we have seen, Progressive reform proposals emphasize the virtues of unity in the executive and the drawbacks associated with the composition and operations of the legislature. Over time, Progressives came to demand a president-centered government reliant on only very general and sporadic popular oversight. Over time, they have tended to get what they demanded.

Even a cursory examination of reforms of our constitutional system advanced in recent decades is sufficient to show that they, like Wilson's, do not keep house with the Framers' separation of powers. So much is evident from the character of those reforms set forth by prominent political scientists and others with considerable practical experience in government.[48] We note in particular reforms proposed during the 1980s—an era of limited success for reformers, after Johnson's Great Society and before the systemic health-care and other reforms of the Obama administration, and during the presidency of Ronald Reagan, a man of rather limited popularity among Progressive reformers.

First, most of these proposed reforms are designed to move the present system more into line with the British parliamentary system for reasons that Wilson set forth, namely, that the system of separated powers designed by the Framers makes it difficult, if not impossible, to fix responsibility. To this point, C. Douglas Dillon writes of "the inability to place responsibility on any one person or group." The president is elected every four years on a program for which he feels he has a mandate. But the Congress, no matter which party is in control, "practically never implements these policies." "The result," Dillon observes, is that "the President blames Congress, the Congress blames the President, and the public remains confused and disgusted with government in Washington."[49]

The statement of the bipartisan Committee on the Constitutional System (1983) offers a slightly different twist to the absence of responsibility, one that also echoes Wilson's concerns over coherency in its legislative product: "Even when policies are produced, after arduous delays, they are often a contradictory hodge-podge that no one supports as a whole. Neither the President nor any legislator wants" an astronomical budget deficit, "but none of them feels responsible for legislating such a result; and none of them can be held accountable for it. The President blames the Congress; members of Congress blame the President," with the result that "people lose confidence in government itself."[50]

Further, again echoing Wilson, critics of the existing system have viewed it as ineffective in handling the problems facing the nation. To recur again to the collective judgment of the Committee on the Constitutional System, "the checks and balances inspired by the experience of the eighteenth century have led repeatedly, in the twentieth century, to governmental stalemate and deadlock, to indecision and inaction in the face of urgent problems." And the committee agrees with Wilson as to the reasons for this system of checks and balances, to wit, it "was deliberately designed in the aftermath of the revolt against George III to protect the young republic against a new despotism."[51] The committee, as we might imagine, is far from alone in this assessment. Lloyd N. Cutler, for instance, recognizing that separation of powers might have been appropriate given the world of the Framers, finds it inadequate to handle the "problems that all contemporary governments must resolve" in the "interdependent world society we have become."[52]

Bruce Ackerman continues the call for president-centered reform. He has blamed the inability of American administrations to implement Progressive policies in a definitive fashion on the splintered nature of the American regime. "New ideas" or political coalitions must persevere through several election cycles before they come to dominate both houses of the legislature and the executive branch, and even then may face a hostile judiciary. Deadlock, Ackerman avers, is the inevitable result of a system that fails to put public opinion into effect in an immediate fashion.[53]

Ackerman merely repeats criticisms from decades earlier. Virtually all reformers see the need to avoid divided government if possible—that is, the president of one party serving while one or both chambers of Congress is controlled by the other. Thus, various schemes are set forth, even amending the Constitution to provide for the election of the president and all members of Congress, senators and representatives, on the same day. A suggested statutory reform would provide that "presidential elections be conducted two-to-four weeks before congressional elections," with the hope that "this would tend to reduce divided government" since the voters would know which party would be occupying the White House.[54]

Thus, more recent and contemporary Progressives continue to advocate reforms that effectively would alter the basic structure of the Framers' Constitution without evincing any seeming awareness of why the Framers provided for this structure. As our analysis of the deliberations in the Philadelphia Convention has shown, for instance, the Framers' aversion to an executive with the powers of King George III—widely cited by reformers as a reason for the predominance of the legislature—reveals very little about their intentions regarding the separation of powers.[55]

More generally, reformers—including Wilson but also figures from throughout the twentieth century and up until today—in their concern to point up the deficiencies of the present system have ignored or, more often, misconstrued the question of what values the Framers sought to realize or perpetuate through the separation of powers. In so doing they have mischaracterized the nature and virtues of the constitutional morality associated with the Framers' Constitution. As a consequence, they have not confronted systematically the question of how these values might be lost or diminished in a president-centered system.

The Separation of Powers and Democracy

A central school of thought among reformers, beginning with James Allen Smith in the early twentieth century, emphasizes criticism of the Constitution for being undemocratic. Such thinkers attribute the Constitution's emphasis on the separation of powers to this antidemocratic program. We again note the near unanimity among reformers that the existing system produces "deadlock" or "gridlock." Daniel L. Robinson, the editor of *Reforming American Government,* comments on this trend, noting at the outset of a section entitled "Breaking Deadlock" that "the tendency of the American political system to fall into deadlock when confronted by difficult and controversial issues" is one of the recurrent themes stressed by reformers.[56]

To be sure, some critics of the present system, perhaps even Wilson, hold that in simpler times with a far less extensive republic these constitutional checks and balances did not serve as a serious impediment to effective action. But others see the Framers' attachment to the separation of powers as an effort to thwart popular government or, more exactly, majority rule. Indeed, underlying Progressive thought from its inception has been the conviction that the Constitution was designed to thwart majorities.[57] If anything, it would appear that critics of the system increasingly have emphasized its departure from "democracy" due largely to the separation of powers.[58]

Robert Dahl's widely heralded *Preface to Democratic Theory,* first published in 1956, is testimony that many students critical of the Constitution see the Framers' motive behind the separation of powers to be a perceived need to protect certain minorities.[59] In his work, Dahl critically analyzes in considerable detail the concepts and principles of the "Madisonian theory of democracy," which Dahl abstracts almost entirely from key essays of *The Federalist.* What is more, Dahl assumes, as he unfolds his analysis, that this Madisonian theory provides the theoretical underpinning of the processes and structure of the Constitution.

Dahl grants that Madison's theory embodied "'the republican principle'" of "majority rule," containing as it did "the idea that all the adult citizens of a republic must be assigned equal rights, including the right to determine the general direction of government policy." "On the other hand," reflecting the Progressive view of the founding, Dahl contends that "Madison wished to erect a political system that would guarantee the liberties of certain whose advantages of status, power, and wealth would, he thought, probably not be tolerated indefinitely by a constitutionally untrammeled majority." "Hence," Dahl concludes, Madison believed that "majorities had to be constitutionally inhibited."[60] As such, he views "Madisonianism" as a "compromise between two conflicting goals"—majority rule and protection of select, privileged minorities—that cannot be theoretically reconciled. At the same time, Dahl perceives "Madisonian ideology" providing "a convenient rationalization for every minority that, out of fear of possible deprivations of some majority, has demanded a political system providing it with an opportunity to veto such policies."[61] Again, we come back to the notion that the system is wired to produce gridlock; that such was an inevitable outgrowth of the Founders' efforts.

James McGregor Burns, in his *Deadlock of Democracy,* written a few years after Dahl's *Preface,* poses in stark terms a key question arising from Dahl's analysis: namely, on Madison's own showing, was not the separation of power superfluous?[62] In somewhat abbreviated form, the background for Burns's concern is as follows: in *Federalist* 10, Madison/Publius argues that the election of "fit characters," along with the multiplicity and diversity of interests in the proposed extensive republic, would be sufficient to prevent factious majorities—that is, majorities bent on oppressing minorities or acting contrary to the "permanent and aggregate interests of the community"—from getting their way. As Madison put it at the very end of this essay, "[I]n the extent and proper structure of the union, therefore, we behold a republican remedy for the diseases [majority factions] most incident to republican government."[63]

In recapitulating this basic argument in *Federalist* 51, Madison/Publius maintains that in the extended republic envisioned in the proposed Constitution, "the society . . . will be broken into so many parts, interests, and classes of citizens, that the rights of individuals, or of the minority, will be in little danger from the interested combinations of the majority."[64] In other words, as Madison would have it, a problem inherent in popular government, the majority oppression of minorities, is "solved" by conditions and means having nothing to do with the separation of powers.

In light of this, Burns asks a logical question: "[I]f, as Madison said, the first great protection against naked majority rule was the broader diversity of interests in the larger republic and hence the greater difficulty of concerting their 'plans of oppression,' why was not this enough in itself?"[65] Why, since the problem posed by factions was "solved," did Madison also want a separation of powers? Clearly, as this question suggests, and as Burns subsequently makes abundantly clear, he holds that Madison, contrary to what he writes as Publius in *Federalist* 10 and 51, really did not believe that the election of "fit" representatives coupled with a multiplicity and diversity of interests was sufficient to prevent majority oppression. In fact, as Burns would have it, Madison believed that a separation of powers also was needed for this purpose, but "not . . . a flimsy separation of powers that lunging politicians could smash through." Rather, demonstrating his "genius as a political scientist," "he was calling for barricade after barricade against the thrust of a popular majority—and the ultimate and impassable barricade was a system of checks and balances that would use man's essential human nature—his interests, his passions, his ambitions—to control itself." Madison's solution, in Burns's eyes, is the "archpin of the whole constitutional framework" and, at the same time, the source of deadlock.[66] The reform of political parties, along with firm presidential leadership, is Burns's formula for overcoming the obstacles to democratic rule implanted by Madison. His ultimate goal is largely indistinguishable from that advanced by Wilson.[67]

Reformers on the Framers' Concerns

Over the course of the last century a consensus has emerged that the American people would benefit from a president-centered national government. Justifications for this view generally center on greater accountability and responsibility, while stress also is placed upon the increasing complexity of affairs, both national and international, that point to the imperative need for centralized leadership. Connected in one way or another to all these justifications, but also advanced as an end in its own right, is the greater degree of democracy that presumably would result from party reform and presidential leadership. Finally, the greatest impediment to the realization of this system is felt almost universally to be the separation of powers broadly conceived to embrace bicameralism and checks and balances.

Pursuit of a president-centered system in recent years has been facilitated by constitutional scholars who have constructed novel paradigms that justify expansive executive powers. Indeed, there can be no question that the constitutional system has been transformed over the course of the last century along the lines that Wilson and others desired. This transformation has not, obviously, been as thorough as most reformers would like because even one chamber of Congress still can reject executive proposals. Nevertheless, it has resulted in a constitutional order fundamentally different from that which existed at the time of its ratification. And this change has come about largely through informal and extraconstitutional developments that Wilson identifies, not by formal amendments to the Constitution.[68]

From the reformers' point of view, the separation of powers seems to have no redeeming virtues; it can be discarded without adverse consequences. But if this is not the case, if the Framers looked upon the separation of powers as playing an integral role in our constitutional system, then one is obliged to take this into account. Would the effective elimination of separated powers involve the sacrifice and endangerment of other ideals or goals that normally are associated with constitutionalism, properly understood? Likewise, could reforms in the name of democracy, such as those we have canvassed, actually result in the diminution of democracy or lead to conditions that would undermine both constitutional and popular government?

As we explained in some detail in Chapter 3, the Framers' concern in seeking to secure the separation of powers within the Constitution was not antidemocratic, but instead was pro-ordered liberty. That is, the Framers sought not to put into action whatever a majority of the moment happened to desire nor to thwart the will of majorities in any systematic fashion. Rather, they sought a government that would provide the tranquility of mind necessary for the people, as groups and as individual persons, to go about their lives unmolested, to seek their individual and common goods, and to plan their futures for themselves and their communities. Following Montesquieu, the Framers were convinced that such a state required stable, predictable laws and a governmental structure that would ensure that the governors would be subject to their own rules, thus encouraging them to enact only mild, rational laws. And, for Montesquieu and the Framers, such a structure must be characterized by the separation of legislative, executive, and judicial powers so that each might guard the people and the law from incursions by the others.

A New Political Universe

Our analysis to this point shows a wide gap between the prevailing understanding of our system and that which the Framers seemed to possess. The significance of this gap, as we also have endeavored to show, is enormous because it indicates that we live under a virtually new constitutional order that, in effect, overrides the safeguards the Framers provided in order to secure the rule of law. To put this another way, as the deliberations of the Constitutional Convention and *The Federalist* unmistakably show, a belief prevailed at the founding that a separation of powers would provide for the rule of law, which itself was regarded as essential for both political liberty and the stability of the political order. These conditions, in turn, were regarded as prerequisites for an enduring constitutional republic. As we have noted, Article XXX of the Declaration of Rights in the Massachusetts

Constitution of 1780 is only one of many public declarations made in the founding era to the effect that the separation of powers is necessary to republican constitutions "to the end it may be a government of laws and not of men."[69] Today, this view is treated as antiquated.

Departures from the original understanding are clear, numerous, and definitive of a new dispensation. For example, whereas the Framers regarded the legislature as the predominant branch, as well as the one most representative of the people, this, beyond any question, is no longer the case. We can readily imagine a situation that illustrates just how far Congress has descended relative to the executive and judicial branches. Recall that in *Federalist* 49 Publius contends that, were disputes between the branches submitted to the people for resolution, Congress likely would prevail. To support his position he cites a variety of factors and concludes that the legislature would have stronger and deeper bonds with the people than either the executive or judicial branches. But today, it seems safe to say, students of the system would in all probability reach the opposite conclusion; that is, in any popular showdown the president and even the Supreme Court would win out over Congress. We do know that for the better part of the twentieth century popular allegiance has shifted to the president to such a degree that he would be a prohibitive favorite in any such hypothetical showdown.[70]

It seems evident as well that Wilson's vision regarding presidential leadership largely has been realized; that is, the president has assumed the role of a unifying force in our national politics. By the middle of the twentieth century, particularly after FDR and World War II, few doubted that the presidency had become the dominant institution in the American system. The historian Clinton Rossiter, writing during the Eisenhower administration, reflected this consensus in setting forth the president's constitutional "functions": "Chief of State, Chief Executive, Commander in Chief, Chief Diplomat, [and] Chief Legislator." To these roles he added "five additional functions:" "Chief of Party," "Voice of the People," "World Leader," "Protector of the Peace," and "Manager of Prosperity."[71] This is not to say that there have not been ups and downs in the growth of presidential power, but as Edward Corwin notes in his monumental work, *The President: Office and Powers, 1787–1957*, "the history of the presidency is," by and large, "a history of aggrandizement."[72]

Parties and Motivations

Beyond question, political parties, and their development over the decades of the early republic, were a decisive force in elevating the presidency to what would become its current, predominant position. For Andrew Jackson, party nomination and popular election were sufficient to link the president to the people and thereby legitimate the claim that he was on equal footing with Congress as a spokesman for the popular will. Wilson, of course, went beyond this to assert that the president was the only authentic voice of the people; he also perceived that party allegiance could be a bridge to overcome the barriers posed by the formal constitutional separation of powers. Reforms to the nominating system instituted after the 1968 presidential election thoroughly democratized the presidential nomination process, eliminating any possibility of nominations brokered by local bosses, favorite sons, and the like. Central party structures and even party discipline in the legislatures have suffered.[73] But, significantly, there is no question that presidents are the leaders of their party, a position that assumes enormous significance when the president's party controls both chambers of Congress. Finally, and quite apart from their status within their party, modern presidents, largely because they speak with a single voice, are far more effective than Congress in utilizing the mass media to advantage. This new avenue provides presidents, probably to a degree that Wilson could not envisage, the means to give "direction to opinion" and to make known their views on "the real sentiment and purpose of the country."[74]

The cohesion required within the political parties for success in their quest for the presidency has served to undo the Framers' design. To see why this is so, we can return fruitfully to Publius's solution for maintaining the separation of powers. As we have seen, he perceived that there would be a union between the "interest" of the officeholder and the "constitutional rights" of the office. This union, he believed, would be sufficient, when combined with the limited and partial virtue called forth by attachment to the constitution as law and political system, to preserve separation. Exercising this virtue, officeholders of one branch naturally would repel efforts by officers of another branch to aggrandize their powers and functions. Once set in motion, the separation would perpetuate itself, each branch possessing the wherewithal and constitutional virtue to resist the encroachment of the others. With the emergence of president-oriented political parties, however, even in Congress—the centerpiece of the Framers' Constitution—party considerations trump institutional interest. This is to say, over the years, particularly when one party has simultaneously controlled all the branches, majorities in Congress have put institutional interest to the side to support the president, their party leader. The incentives to do this are great, among them being the commitment to programmatic government instantiated by the new, still-forming constitutional morality, and the display of party unity important for continued electoral success.[75] We should also note in this respect that even when presidents are rebuffed, usually because their party does not control both chambers of Congress, partisan considerations remain dominant.

Thus, party unity serves to trump institutional interest among members of Congress. Members refuse to defend their turf as an institution so that they may better defend their turf as members of programmatic parties. On the other hand, by all accounts institutional interest does play a significant role impelling the president to expand the powers of the office. A number of factors account for this. Presidents are singular individuals, obviously high powered and ambitious, who cannot help but focus on leaving a legacy that will be looked upon favorably by future generations. In this regard, we can be reasonably certain that presidents are going to compare themselves with other occupants of the office, knowing that the "strong" presidents—Jefferson, Jackson, Lincoln, Wilson, the Roosevelts I and II—are not only those who asserted and expanded presidential prerogatives and powers, but who also are generally considered to be among the greatest.

No president, we may safely assume, wants to leave the office weaker than when he or she entered. In sum, the interests of the individual and of the office naturally are joined in the presidency. Indeed, they are joined so well as to weaken severely any self-restraint rooted in constitutional morality. But, as we might expect, this is not the case with Congress. Its members are numerous so that cohesion on institutional as opposed to partisan interest is understandably much weaker, more diffused, and more likely to dissolve in the face of other, more immediate, individual interests.

In addition, the president now is called upon to fulfill an expanded role as representative of the will of the people. This, of course, stands in sharp contrast to the Framers' view that in republican governments legislatures are the institutions through which the people make known their will.[76] Robert Nisbet has explored the theoretical foundations underlying this highly significant reversal. He notes that an important element of French revolutionary thought was transforming "the ideal of oneness," which has roots in Western rationalistic theories, "into new techniques of centralization." "If the interests of a political population could safely be entrusted to five hundred men," he argues, "why not to one hundred, to fifty, to ten men." This line of reasoning, Nisbet points out, leads straightaway to the proposition that "the interests of a political population" can be vested in *"one* man who, by his virtue and devotion to the whole of the people, could be depended on to interpret and give actuality to the will of the people in a way that no cumbersome parliamentary system could."[77]

That this mode of thinking provides the foundation for Wilson's views, as well as for those who advocate reforms that would expand or consolidate presidential leadership, seems clear. But, to be exact, reformers do not dwell on the "virtue and devotion" of presidents, although they are convinced, consistent with Enlightenment thought, that the president sees the national interest and common good more clearly than does Congress. Moreover, they seem to share a conception of the political community upon which this centralization of power finds ultimate justification: it is a community wherein, to use Nisbet's formulation, "the people" are viewed "as simply a numerical aggregate of individuals regarded for political and administrative purposes as discrete and socially separated." This conception of community seems to have eclipsed the older one shared by the Framers, in which the people are regarded "as indistinguishable from a culture, its members inseparable from the families, unions, churches, professions, and tradition that actually compose a culture."[78]

These conflicting views of society are relevant because the character of republican government largely depends upon which prevails. The second, that which views individual persons in a cultural context as members of a myriad of associations, would allow for a mediating constitution and a federal government of narrower scope. It also would point to the need for a representative institution, such as Congress, that would reflect the diversity and complexity of the society. The first, which conceives of society as "an aggregate of individuals," opens the way for centralization, a commanding constitution, and the modern presidency. Legislatures are the legacy of the second conception so that, as we shall see, critical questions emerge as to what their role ought to be, particularly in our system, where the first and newer conception apparently has come to prevail.[79]

New Concerns

That we now live in a system in which the executive authority predominates is generally conceded. What this means, however, is that we have eliminated or scrapped vital elements of the structure and procedural provisions of the original Constitution—that which we associate with the separation of powers—intended to prevent arbitrary and capricious rule. This state of affairs prompts two observations. First, if the Framers were correct in their belief that the people should be ever wary of the legislative branch given its nature and powers under the Framers' Constitution, then, by the same token, today we have every reason to redirect our attention to the executive branch. Put otherwise, Madison's injunction to keep "watch" on "the source of danger" tells us now it is best we keep our eyes focused on the executive.

Our second observation must be this: those seeking reform of our constitutional system, as our survey indicates, seem to be concerned with changes that will make it more responsive to the will of the people. They find the dispersion of power within the system leading to deadlock or distortions of the popular will. What is missing in their quest for a more perfect democracy, however, is a replacement, institutional and/or procedural, that might perform the functions for which the separation of powers was designed. Missing as well is apprehension about a president-centered system. To put this matter in its starkest terms, we cannot help but go back to what Publius contends in *Federalist* 9, to wit, that without the separation of powers, the core of the new and improved principles of political science, republican regimes have a distinct tendency to vibrate between the extremes of anarchy and tyranny. But, to once again emphasize our basic concern here, it is not at all apparent that the reformers share these concerns, or, perhaps, their evidently keen desire for a more democratic order has diverted their attention.

More generally speaking, and leaving to one side their views on executive power, those who would reform our system primarily to attain a greater degree of "democracy" pay scant attention to what is necessary for the rule of law. The Framers' concerns in this regard simply seem to be cast aside. This can be concretely illustrated by revisiting Robert Dahl's *Preface to Democratic Theory,* in which he both analyzes "Madisonian democracy" and develops his "Polyarchy,"

As we have noted, Dahl finds Madisonian democracy wanting; it institutionalizes political inequality presumably to advantage certain privileged minorities. In Dahl's more detailed analysis, as we have remarked, he sets out to show that Madison's definition of tyranny is, in the end, meaningless, which allows him to proceed—even in the face of the deliberations at Philadelphia—as if the Founders' concerns about oppressive government were baseless. Indeed, his preferred governmental system of "polyarchy" can be regarded as specifying the conditions for a model democracy by maximizing the principle of political equality upon which the populist, majority-rule conception of democracy rests. In his polyarchy, for instance, citizens express their preferences—or "scheduled alternatives" at the stage of voting—with that alternative favored by the greater number being "declared the winning choice." And, at the "prevoting" stage an individual "who perceives a set of alternatives, at least one of which he regards as preferable to any of the alternatives presently scheduled, can insert his preferred alternative(s) among those scheduled for voting."[80] While there are other conditions associated with polyarchy, they all are means fashioned to ensure that the preferences of the greater number should prevail.

To be clear, our concern here is not with the coherence or practicality of this model. Our concern with polyarchy, and to only a slightly lesser degree with principles underlying the bulk of reformers' constitutional reform proposals, centers on the fact that no provision is made to guard against arbitrary or capricious rule. For instance, polyarchy has no hooks to grapple with the "effects of mutable policy," which, as Publius would have it, "poison . . . the blessings of liberty itself."[81]

Publius's overriding fear is that the "laws" might become "so voluminous that they cannot be read, or so incoherent that they cannot be understood." This concern is heightened if, he continues, "they be repealed or revised before they are promulgated, or undergo such incessant changes, that no man who knows what the law is to-day, can guess what it will be tomorrow."[82] He concludes with a rhetorical question: "Law is defined to be a rule of action; but how can that be a rule, which is little known and less fixed[?]"[83] In fact, there can be little doubt that this mutability contributed to the vibrations between anarchy and tyranny of the "petty republics" to which Publius refers. What seems clear is that if the fear of mutable policy is well grounded, a democratic system that places a premium on liberty would be well advised to take preventative measures to guard against it. This, in turn, might well require some brake on the popular passions along with the provision of institutions and procedures that assure deliberation—safeguards against mutability that might well require some modification of or deviation from the conditions of a "model" democracy such as those embodied in polyarchy.[84] Without such safeguards, to put this another way, the entire superstructure of democracy might well collapse.

Many of the constitutional changes called for by reformers have not been and almost certainly will not be adopted. Nevertheless, we must note once again that through more or less informal developments, the system has in practice moved in the direction that these reformers have advocated so that major components of Wilson's vision now are an operational reality. These developments present us with a new political landscape in which new questions and concerns arise concerning popular control, account-ability, and, inter alia, the rule of law. In the following chapter, we will examine this matter in detail. For now it is sufficient to remark that we must explore these questions and concerns in a context markedly different from that envisioned by the Framers: the president, not Congress, now poses the greatest threat to those values we cherish. Our attention now must focus on executive power and the degree to which it now encroaches upon the legislature's legitimate domain and what effects this has upon the rule of law, accountability, and popular control. In this endeavor, of course, we cannot overlook the reality of a highly complex society and the need for the expertise of a bureaucracy to identify and fashion solutions to problems that arise within it.

Finally, we should make clear that we are not among those who would urge that we simply return to the Framers' understanding of the Constitution. The Framers' constitutional morality, while not dead (for example, voters at times explain their split-ticket voting as intended to "maintain checks and balances"), no longer serves as a reliable guide to action, especially among political elites. Moreover, the people continue to demand ever more substantive goods from their government and, increasingly, accept its commanding role in society. Such tectonic shifts in political culture—the unwritten constitution—are not liable to easy or technical political reform within the confines of ordered liberty and the rule of law. Our point, to repeat, is that as the Progressive reforms have taken hold little regard has been shown for the potential dangers of mutable policy and arbitrary and capricious laws; those dangers were uppermost in the minds of our forebears because they undermine ordered liberty and, ultimately, republican government. We are convinced that any efforts to rectify this situation must necessarily be undertaken in the new constitutional context that Wilson envisioned if they are to have any chance of success.

6

The New Dispensation
and the Rise of Quasi-Law

OUR VIEW that the administrative state was institutionalized as part and consequence of a change in constitutional morality and in opposition to the Framers' design is, no doubt, quite clear. Our purpose in this chapter is to examine what impact formation of that state, given the particular manner and shape of its formation, has had on the rule of law. The administrative state may be inevitable, but this does not mean that we must accept as good every consequence of the particular form it has taken, or that we should suspend judgment regarding all of its effects, including those on the manner in which we are governed. In particular, we are concerned with the internal morality of our juridical order. That is, we are concerned with the extent to which rules handed down by our governing authorities now fail to abide by procedures and/or fail to include crucial elements necessary to conform to the rule of law and so are incapable of providing that rule's ordering benefits to our society.

At its root, the problem is constitutional. To the extent our laws are no longer formulated and promulgated according to the processes laid down in the actual text and corresponding morality of our Constitution, the Constitution is no longer operative and our governors are no longer bound by the rule of law. Some recent academics have sought to dismiss such criticism of the new dispensation by pointing to political checks on power that may still exist in our society.[1] But political checks are not law. They

183

neither rely upon nor encourage a habit of obedience to formal, constitutional structures and procedures. And the loss of such habits constitutes a significant loss to social order, the possibility of liberty, and resistance to the political pursuit of evil.

The loss of constitutional structure and formalities not only has led to lawmaking that fails to abide by law in the higher, constitutional sense; it also has produced laws that increasingly fail to conform to basic standards of internal morality. And to the extent our laws no longer have the fundamental characteristics of law—are no longer predictable, known, consistent, and in accord with the other standards recognized as essential by Lon Fuller, among others—it is safe and necessary to say we no longer live under the rule of law. The American government increasingly fails to maintain the most fundamental elements necessary for what is called a law to in fact be a law—that is, a rule capable of being followed by those required to follow it. The worse a regime is at achieving minimal consistency, clarity, and predictability in its rules, the closer it is to falling into simple lawlessness, in which abiding by the law becomes pointless and impracticable.[2] We do not claim that we have reached such a point in the United States, but do argue that the American government has moved perilously far in that direction. We have moved distressingly far toward a regime of nonlaw, endangering peace of mind, liberty, and even the most basic social good of the ability to plan.

We are aware that the current model of governance has created winners as well as losers. Some may find our concerns overwrought given the continuing vitality of the technology industry in particular. This is not a book of political economy, nor is our central concern that of making arguments for the best way to maintain America's edge in a global marketplace. The pragmatic concern to value constitutional structures according to their seeming economic by-products is a significant part of the problem we seek to address in this book. That said, it is not unimportant that the prime examples generally given of economic success in recent decades are (high-tech) companies that rely on extensive governmental largesse, including subsidies and massive waivers from immigration and other laws, and that employ a miniscule number of regular Americans.[3] Moreover, Progressives in particular should be alarmed that "some 94 percent of the income gains during President Obama's first term have gone to barely one percent of the population while incomes have declined for the lower 93 percent."[4]

Wealth will continue to be created even in the absence of the rule of law. Ironically, the pursuit of a more equal distribution of that wealth often results in formation of oligarchies consisting of those who know best how to manipulate rules, regulations, and especially discretion-wielding officials to serve their own ends. None of our current troubles provides any reason to embrace such discretion. Nevertheless, our focus remains where we are convinced it belongs, on the increasing prevalence of arbitrary power in our once-limited constitutional system.

In this chapter we lay out the results and implications of the new dispensation of law freed from constitutional constraints. Several decades ago, Theodore J. Lowi pointed out that in the liberal state, which is dedicated to and justified by the popular will, all things are good to do. There is no end to the wants of the people or to the dangers against which they might be protected. Thus, Lowi argued, there is no end to the objects appropriate for regulation.[5] The formalities of our Constitution were established to see to it that only those measures commanding support from a majority of governmental actors (particularly in the legislature) that is so substantial and varied as to approach consensus, would become law. These formalities having collapsed under the weight of repeated demands for swift, broad action, restraints on governmental conduct have been reduced to a more basic level. Public opinion, elite pressure, and the practical constraints of time, interest, and expertise on the part of lawmakers now are the chief factors constraining the making of government policies.

The demand for "action" being constant while the means (principally time, skill, and interest) to make law remain highly limited, the result has been a regime that rules by something akin to but less than law. We have chosen to refer to the chief instrumentality for governance under the new dispensation as *quasi-law*. By *quasi-law* we mean rules that have the impact of law—they alter the rights of people in our society—yet lack essential elements of law.

We did not coin the term *quasi-law*. It has been used for some time to denote "constructive" or fictional laws—directives that are not law but are treated as such for practical reasons and purposes.[6] Quasi-law also has been defined as almost or near law, lacking certain essential aspects such as general enforceability; in this sense the term applies to forms of traditional, indigenous laws in many countries because they do not apply to everyone in all circumstances.[7] In addition, the term may be used in reference to an officer assuming the function of "quasi-law maker."[8] All these definitions of quasi-law are applicable and important, constituting, when taken together, a regime that neither conforms to nor rules according to law in a reasonably full sense.

Some commentators have argued against the search for essential aspects of law, opining that all laws are imperfect, hence not fully "law" in any ideal sense. Thus, the term *quasi-law* could be applied more or less to all law and so is not a useful term.[9] We have argued that such a continuum of law exists, but assert the importance of the fact that our laws have moved noticeably far down the spectrum toward unlawlike directives. Moreover, Americans, including the judges and lawyers whose duty it is to uphold the law, no longer recognize the necessity of law's internal morality. In terms of the eight canons constituting law's internal morality elucidated by Fuller,[10] quasi-laws often violate several at a time and produce a system in which none of the canons are applied with consistency. And the prevalence of these severely flawed laws constitutes a veritable system of quasi-law, undermining public order and the possibility of liberty.

In summary form: our quasi-laws often are not general, instead being written for the benefit of some individual or interest group.[11] Quasi-laws may be promulgated by such a wide variety of offices and bodies and in such a way that promulgation fails to meet its intended purpose of providing proper notice of their requirements. Quasi-laws in our administrative state frequently lack clarity, leaving broad discretion to powerful government officials to act as they will. While particular quasi-laws generally do not require contradictory actions, the overall requirements of our administrative state often point in contradictory, confusing, and delegitimizing directions—as when some laws subsidize tobacco farming and others authorize spending to discourage smoking. Our quasi-laws fail to remain relatively constant over time. Finally, our quasi-laws, complete with waivers and other provisions involving vast amounts of discretion, often are administered in a manner that differs wildly from that in which they are declared. Emanating from areas throughout our political structure, granting rights and imposing duties, these quasi-laws bind us but do not provide us with the certainty necessary for a free society.

The growth of quasi-law may be directly tied to the rise of our administrative state, with its independent agencies formulating rules with the power of law. But it is important to note that the construction of the "fourth branch" of government, whether or not inevitable, is only one element in the regime of quasi-law. It would be wrong to simply point to the federal bureaucracy as the source of the breakdown in the rule of law in the United States.[12] Each branch of the government—the original three as well as the newer fourth—not only shares responsibility for these new developments, but itself issues quasi-laws. Indeed, one of the factors constituting our regime of quasi-law is the inability of citizens to know from what direction a new "law" may arise, as rules affecting their rights may come from almost any powerful source. Here we look to the various manners in which quasi-laws are produced under the new dispensation, along with the impact of quasi-law and its formation on the rule of law.

Congress: The Great Enabler

It is a sign of the demise of our traditional constitutional morality that Congress—the subject of the Constitution's first article and the predominant force under the original dispensation—today comes, at best, a distant second to the president in terms of legislative power. Congress's dramatic loss of power under the new dispensation can be ascribed to the central role its own members have played in undermining constitutional morality and the consequent aggrandizement of presidential power. Congress, intended by the Framers to be the locus of federal lawmaking power, has enabled the other branches to seize that power both through acquiescence in their actions (not, for example, moving to impeach and remove presidents who ignore laws they have signed) and, even more, by passing statutes that fail to embody the essential characteristics of law.

One central cause of Congress's loss of power has been its refusal to do the hard work of negotiating and drafting statutes that comport reasonably well with the requirements of the rule of law. We note, for example, the role of "omnibus" legislation in empowering and even, in political terms, demanding that presidents use tools such as waivers, budgetary and interpretive gamesmanship, and signing statements to in effect veto portions of bills taking up hundreds and even thousands of pages of text, covering a wide variety of issues and policy areas. While presidents should, of course, veto such legislation as a matter of constitutional morality, it is to say the least not surprising in an era beyond constitutional good and evil that they instead choose political expediency.

Omnibus legislation generally is passed in areas crucial for the continuation of necessary programs such as national defense. Because the omnibus legislation includes very important provisions, members of Congress are empowered to attach scores of additional provisions of only marginal relevance to the bill's stated purpose, often inserted to gain a few votes for passage or score political points. The result is legislation that lacks clarity of purpose and may even contradict statutory or constitutional principles. In this context, presidential use of various tools that make it possible to refuse to enforce laws as enacted is just another development in a quasi-legislative process.[13]

More telling and fundamental has been "enabling" legislation establishing administrative agencies of various sorts and otherwise delegating power to executive branch officers. For reasons of political self-interest well elucidated, for example, by Morris P. Fiorina,[14] members of Congress pass vague statutes directing executive agencies to "solve" various problems such as workplace safety, pollution, and drug use. In one sense such statutes constitute claims of increased power, ignoring the federal structure of the Framers' Constitution and the limits of its enumerated powers.[15] But, in practice, these claims to new power actually have disempowered Congress. Why? Because, rather than do the hard work and risk the political fallout of crafting specific rules aimed at promoting specific goods or ameliorating specific evils, members of Congress prefer to take credit for enacting broad, well-meaning legislation, and then overseeing, investigating, and blaming agency personnel for the problems and failures that inevitably follow. The result is a frighteningly high rate of reelection for particular members, along with a downgrading of the institution's role from that of principal lawmaker to chief ombudsman. This practice and its political implications are, of course, entirely in keeping with Progressive theory and goals.

The Supreme Court has accepted the notion that power may be delegated by Congress to executive agencies. While its decision in *Schechter Poultry,* holding that Congress may not delegate its lawmaking powers to the executive branch,[16] has not formally been overturned, the court has ignored it, allowing it to become a dead letter. Again, one need take no position as to the substance or the goals of legislation (e.g., regulation of railroads, as was done with the seminal executive agency in this area, the

Interstate Commerce Commission [ICC])[17] in order to take issue with the manner in which Congress increasingly has chosen to regulate: through quasi-laws granting broad discretionary power.

Defenders of the new dispensation have argued that the wide discretion left to administrators in enabling legislation is necessary to maintain our administrative state.[18] Yet, as Lowi has pointed out, such claims rest on the mistaken view that complexity itself renders clear legal standards impossible. In fact, the problem in regard to discretion relates not to complexity but to abstraction.[19] Lowi does not argue that all laws must state explicitly every single rule and how it is to be applied—that would exclude the common law itself. Rather, what is required is a set of standards, along with prestatutory development and statutory language sufficiently "freighted with meaning" to provide objective rules and procedures.[20] For illustration Lowi looks to the original language of the Interstate Commerce Act, which applied to a specific industry (railroads, defined in section 1) and forbade specific practices (rebates, short charges, and the like, defined and enumerated in section 2). Lowi terms the ICC legislation "good law" "because standards concerned with goals, clientele, and methods of implementation were clear."[21]

To see the (early) descent of law into quasi-law one need only compare the original ICC standards with those encompassed in the 1914 legislation for the Federal Trade Commission (FTC). This legislation forbade "unfair methods of competition . . . and unfair or deceptive acts or practices."[22] The original ICC legislation provided for enforcement of specific rules against specific persons. The FTC legislation gave power to administrators to determine what practices were unfair, meaning that those regulated (defined as those operating in interstate commerce, thus capturing many citizens unawares) would not know what standard would be applied to them until informed of their violation of the "rule." To its credit, in the early days of delegation, the Supreme Court repeatedly struck down as overly vague regulations based on this quasi-law.[23]

Already by the early twentieth century, Congress was neglecting its duty to provide standards in enabling legislation. As to the ICC itself, the 1920 amendment gave the commission the right to raise minimum rates on the basis of its determination of what was "just and reasonable."[24] Lowi traces development in regulatory law from the concrete, specific, rule-bound, and proscriptive legislation establishing the ICC to enabling legislation establishing agencies like the Occupational Safety and Health Administration (OSHA) with the purpose of assuring "so far as is possible every working man and woman in the nation safe and healthful working conditions and to preserve human resources."[25]

Noble goals, to be sure, but how to accomplish them? By establishing standards deemed by the agency (or secretary of labor) appropriate to provide such safe and healthful working conditions.[26] And whence would such standards come? By what statutorily defined methods would administrators formulate the rules by which people would live? By an in-house advisory committee or, more often, through adoption of a "national consensus standard," that is, any standard already adopted by a "nationally recognized standards-producing organization under procedures where it can be determined by the Secretary that persons interested and affected by the scope or provisions of the standard have reached substantial agreement on its adoption."[27] So long as those deemed interested were given the opportunity to participate in the formulation of the standard, the standard would be deemed appropriate.

One might see the OSHA rulemaking formula as a demand for lawlike rules for developing regulations. But this delegation of power constitutes lawmaking by interest group. It includes little genuine representation of the interests of the general public (including the general working public), who have neither the time nor the wherewithal to help set "consensus standards" because they do not control powerful organizations. The results often have been highly favorable to the regulated industries.[28]

Congress's broad delegation of lawmaking power to OSHA is scarcely unique. The Consumer Product Safety Act of 1972 provides an equally broad mandate for the Consumer Product Safety Commission: "to protect the public against unreasonable risks of injury associated with consumer products."[29] The responsibility of the Environmental Protection Agency set forth in the Clean Air Act (1970) is "to protect and enhance the quality of the Nation's air resources so as to promote the public health and welfare and the productive capacity of its population."[30] Examples of similar congressional delegations of broad authority to commissions, agencies, and departments could be multiplied many times over; one indication of the extent of such rulemaking is *The Federal Register;* this compilation of the rules issued by these authorities ran to seventy-five volumes and over seventy-nine thousand pages in 2014.[31]

What we have in our administrative agencies, be they executive or "independent" of direct presidential oversight, is not lawmaking, but rather the making of quasi-law—of vague and mutable standards that may, or may not, be enforced. Congress has abdicated its constitutional role as law-maker, opting instead, with court encouragement, to pass enabling quasi-laws containing some "intelligible principle" to guide agencies in drafting regulations that then are given the force of law.[32] Only the goal of the leg-islation and its "principle" receive full congressional consideration. The rulemaking itself is ruled by a procedural statute—the Administrative Procedure Act—or by procedures set out in specific legislation. These procedures dictate a form of investigation, consultation, and reasoning generally incorporated in "notice and comment rulemaking." Under this procedure, agencies formally propose new rules, or indicate areas under consideration for regulation, take and evaluate public comments, and then issue such new rules as they think fit, along with a "concise statement" that in reality is a rather lengthy explanation of the rationale for the new rule.[33]

Administrative law scholars may debate the proper nature and limits of judicial review of this process, which by its nature is highly deferential.[34] Moreover, Philip Hamburger recently has shown that adjudication—actual treatment of persons and entities operating under these regulations—lacks the essentials of due process.[35] Our point is that the rulemaking process itself is quasi-legislative. That is, a nonlegislative body is, in direct violation of the Constitution's explicit granting of that power to Congress, legislating. This criticism may be dismissed as formalistic, as concerns with constitu-tional form generally are dismissed, and it may be seen as impractical. But the concern that Congress pass legislation constituting rather than directing the formulation of laws is hardly meaningless. Not only does delegation violate constitutional morality, but it also has set in motion a lawmaking process that is partial, highly discretionary, and lacking in appropriate gen-eral publication.

Moreover, we would argue that the descent into administrative discre-tion is inevitable. This is true because of the fundamental, structural flaw intrinsic to our current administrative state: its assignment of legislative and—more often glossed over—judicial duties to agencies fundamentally executive in their character and motivations. Even the original ICC legisla-tion concerned the quasi-judicial enforcement of rules by a "commission" that was executive in character.[36]

Administrative personnel in the late nineteenth century began being given the power not only to flesh out (and later draft) regulations but also to interpret and enforce them, including by potentially massive fines that in turn could trigger criminal prosecution for noncompliance. As Montesquieu noted, such a combination of powers is by nature arbitrary. Defenders of this system may point to the use of administrative law judges as "solving" the problem of arbitrariness. But these judges, themselves executive in character, preside over adjudications lacking the essential elements of due process we expect in dealing with genuine laws, from formal indictment on independent evidence in front of a grand jury to rights against self-incrimination; their involvement does nothing to cure the arbitrary nature of rule by bureau or the tendency of such power to expand beyond any natural bounds.

Agencies can provide neither the full procedure nor the clarity of enforcement appropriate for law in the full sense. Indeed, they increasingly are moving away from these procedures in the name of necessity, bringing back the absolute, that is, nonlegal, powers of prerogative courts. Administrative tribunals exercise powers we would not tolerate, and that the Constitution specifically forbids, in regular courts, complete with the ability to force the accused parties to testify against themselves in an inquisitorial proceeding.[37]

We hasten to add that the means for establishing a truly lawlike procedure capable of producing law in the full sense are not beyond reach. Agencies developing particular rules to put into effect the stated goals of Congress might do so under congressional control, being reconstituted as congressional committee staff, answerable directly to the legislature, and presenting their findings to that legislature for its use in drafting laws as it deems appropriate. Such safeguards would require realignment of agencies from executive to congressional management, leaving the president to preside over a robust enforcement apparatus exercising only the limited discretion appropriate to that appropriately executive function and pursuing prosecutions through appropriate, Article III courts.

We do not expect enactment of reforms along these lines. They would require significant effort and impose substantial responsibilities on members of Congress—responsibilities those members have spent decades constructing institutions and practices to avoid. We merely point out the practicality of such measures, along with their consistency with that portion of the Framers' constitutional morality concerned with maintenance of the separation of powers. The adherence of such a system to a constitutional morality of federalism and enumerated powers would, of course, be much more problematic, as would its ability to adjudicate disputes in accord with due process rights. But these problems merely bring to light the choices the people should openly have been asked to make in weighing their attachment to traditional liberties and/or the promises of a full-blown federal administrative state.

Congress's Stepchildren: Executive (and "Independent") Agencies

Created through the delegation of broad lawmaking authority from the appropriate—legislative—branch to the executive branch, executive agencies and their "independent" counterparts (which enjoy additional protections regarding employment tenure) are overseen by methods of questionable constitutional status. For example, a significant means of congressional oversight remains the legislative veto. This mechanism has in the past allowed Congress to pass legislation ceding some power to an executive agency while reserving to itself the right to overrule that agency's decisions through a resolution of one or both houses. It was declared unconstitutional because in effect it allowed Congress to pass legislation (reversing or amending the agency action) without going through the proper constitutional procedure of securing passage in identical form by both houses, and then presenting the legislation to the president for signing (or veto).[38]

Despite the Supreme Court's clear disapproval, however, legislative vetoes make their way into myriad pieces of legislation and, while not enforced by courts, are respected (out of necessity) by agencies in their dealings with congressional committees. Over two thousand "legislative veto" provisions have been enacted since the practice was ruled unconstitutional in 1983, though their enforcement has been relegated to policy manuals and committee and subcommittee practice.[39] Such a pragmatic arrangement certainly appears convenient. But it does not give potential objects of regulatory compromises the means by which to predict the rules under which they must act at any given time. Moreover, while such forms of quasi-legislative oversight may maintain some semblance of congressional control over the agencies, they do little to establish congressional responsibility for the laws they (quasi-) draft.

Their lack of responsibility allows members of Congress to hand over to executive agencies the power (and motivation) to develop quasi-laws that are loose, vague, overly discretionary, and, exacerbating all of these, simply too voluminous and complex for citizens to understand or even, at times, know of. Many argue, of course, that complex postindustrial societies require a complex legal structure if they are to be governed with fairness and efficiency. And this may be true—up to a point. But, we submit, our legal structure long ago exceeded the point of complexity at which the rule of law begins to dissipate.

It is well to remember here the view of the drafters of our original Constitution. For example, in *Federalist* 62, Publius observes that the laws may "be so voluminous that they cannot be read, or so incoherent that they cannot be understood." And they may "undergo such incessant changes, that no man who knows what the law is today, can guess what it will be tomorrow."[40] Such fears, pointing to a loss of the rule of law, hardly seem overwrought when, for example, our tax code has been amended more than three thousand times in the last decade.[41]

Publius notes the injustice of this kind of statutory volume and mutability. "Every new regulation concerning commerce or revenue" or "affecting the value of property," he maintains, "presents a harvest to those who watch the change, and can trace its consequences; a harvest, reared not by themselves, but by the toils and cares of the great body of their fellow citizens." Publius contends that this state of affairs lends weight to the contention "that laws are made for the *few,* not for the *many.*" He also points to the "unreasonable advantage" this gives "the sagacious, the enterprising, and the monied few, over the industrious and uninformed mass of the people." At least as important, however, would be the effects this loss of predictability would have on commerce, for who would move forward with any long-term project knowing he might fall "victim to an inconstant government?"[42] No one, we would venture, but those powerful enough to take part in the bargaining over what that inconstant government would decide next and, as important, have the wherewithal to bargain over potential prosecutions under the resulting quasi-laws.

Publius's concerns remain highly relevant because the federal government has assumed vast responsibilities in fields such as education, health, civil rights, and the environment—areas where Congress has set down broad goals, leaving the promulgation of regulations that have the force and effect of law to the bureaucracy. The history of OSHA well illustrates the difficulties that have arisen with the emergence of the modern administrative state. Already by 1994 OSHA had issued over four thousand regulations in an effort to fulfill its mission.[43] OSHA regulations range over a wide variety of concerns and conditions—e.g., where to store rags, the composition and structure of ladders, what substances are toxic (there are over sixty thousand listed, including sand),[44] and the height of railings[45]—and they are so numerous it is unlikely that even OSHA inspectors (much less managers in the workplaces) know them all. Thus, those who must take responsibility for "regulatory compliance" may regard each OSHA inspection as "a kind of negative lottery: 'Every inspector knows different rules,' and will always find a violation," even when the company inspected has sought to maintain compliance for decades with the same agency's rules.[46] Clearly, the number of regulations and their inevitably arbitrary application, coupled with the fact that they have the force and effect of law—their violation carrying with them enforceable penalties—constitute a breach of the rule of law, that is, the uniform, equal, and predictable application of set, known rules.[47] Moreover, it seems equally clear, this state of affairs is precisely what Publius inveighed against.

Waivers

Congress has not sought to address the problem of mutability through a return to law. Instead, the congressional response to increasing complexity and discretion in rulemaking and enforcement has been to increase executive discretion yet further. In particular, Congress has increased the power of the executive to "waive" statutory provisions and requirements in an attempt to show flexibility in the demands it makes on states, localities, and nongovernmental parties. A waiver is a "statutory provision exempting certain persons, projects, or categories of activities from some or all of the requirements" of some statute.[48] But the waiver is rarely specific. Rather, it sets forth criteria the agency may use in guiding its discretion as it determines who is to be released from their statutory responsibilities—and who is not to be so released.

For examples we look to two relatively recent statutes. The first is President Obama's Patient Protection and Affordable Care Act (ACA). The

ACA provides temporary waivers to a large number of unions, employers, and insurers, allowing them to retain annual caps on health insurance coverage. The waivers were intended to prevent these entities from dropping health insurance for part-time and low-wage workers prior to 2014, when the administration originally said they would be able to purchase subsidized insurance through mandated "exchanges." In January of 2012 the Department of Health and Human Services (HHS) reported that it had awarded more than twelve hundred waivers under the ACA.[49]

These exchanges themselves are subject to waiver. Section 1332 of the ACA, entitled "Waiver for State Innovation," offers a provision that allows each state to apply to the HHS secretary for a waiver from the statute's provisions regarding required health coverage, costs, and mandates on employers. The secretary may grant such waivers if he or she determines that the state's alternative plan "will provide coverage that is at least as comprehensive," is "at least as affordable," and "will provide coverage to at least a comparable number of" state residents as the legislation itself.[50]

The George W. Bush administration's No Child Left Behind Act (NCLB) likewise includes waiver provisions.[51] These provisions have been emphasized by the Obama administration in an attempt to answer complaints from states that the law is misguided and impossible to implement. Ten years after the act's passage, a *Washington Post* article reported, "Most states are concerned about the law's sharply escalating demands, culminating in the goal that 100 percent of students must be proficient in reading and math by 2014 or their schools will face serious sanctions, including the loss of federal aid." These fears have been cited in reports of "rigged" test scores and other abuses by state and local education entities.[52] In response, the Obama administration has made aggressive use of NCLB waiver language. The relevant provision provides that the Secretary of Education "may" waive any statutory or regulatory requirement if the Secretary determines, in his or her discretion, that the alternative plan will produce the outcomes demanded by the statute, here increasing the quality of instruction for and academic achievement of students. Forty-five states, the District of Columbia, Puerto Rico, and the Bureau of Indian Education had submitted requests for flexibility by May, 2014; forty-three states, the District of Columbia, and Puerto Rico had received waivers.[53]

Thus, under the guise of "encouraging innovation," the Obama administration is using broad discretion provided by legislation to in effect negate central provisions of that legislation. This practice has been defended and even championed as the next stage in the fight against gridlock. Indeed, some scholars, such as David Barron and Todd Rakoff, have seen waivers as presenting a new paradigm shift toward a lawmaking process (dubbed "big waiver") by which yet more "flexibility" (discretion) may be granted to executive agencies in translating congressional statements of policy preference into (quasi-) law. Barron and Rakoff state,

> By allowing Congress to take ownership of a detailed statutory regime—even one it knows may be waived—big waiver allows Congress to codify policy preferences it might otherwise be unwilling to enact. Furthermore, by enabling Congress to stipulate a baseline against which agencies' subsequent actions are measured, big waiver offers a sorely needed means by which Congress and the executive branch may overcome gridlock. And finally, in a world laden with federal statutes, big waiver provides Congress a valuable tool for freeing the exercise of new delegations of authority from prior constraints and updating legislative frameworks that have grown stale. We welcome this new phase of the administrative process.[54]

This "new phase of the administrative process" frees Congress from having to codify actual rules for people and other governmental entities to follow. It allows Congress to submit grand statements of preferences ("let there be better education" or "let there be affordable health care") and demand that others achieve these goals, without providing clear, consistent, or even abiding rules by which they are to achieve them. Such commands are approved as granting "flexibility" to agencies and those they regulate to achieve the (putatively good and achievable) goals as they see fit. The next frontier in this elimination of settled rules is bureaucratic inertia, which provides its own form of latent predictability. Rather than let rules "ossify," now agencies are to keep busy changing up rules to meet new circumstances, new policy preferences, and new personalities.

The gridlock of democracy is ended by ending the process of lawmaking. Members of Congress agree to decree that good things happen, then leave it to the agencies to make it so. Gridlock—otherwise known as the legislative process, by which debate, compromise, and bargaining produce something approaching consensual support for any successful legislative proposal—remains the enemy, as it was for the Progressives. But now "progress" demands that the quasi-law adopted include provisions for its own negation. This safety valve, by which ill-considered provisions may be negated through administrative discretion, allows Congress to pass laws declaring goals it does not know how to achieve, confident that such "details" will be worked out later. Indeed, in the case of NCLB, waivers appear to have "saved" legislation fast on its way to repeal or irrelevancy by empowering the executive branch to eliminate mandated reforms in favor of its own waiver criteria—in effect its own law.[55] As for the ACA, Richard Epstein has explained the process of quasi-lawmaking by waiver as follows: "As a matter of grand legislative policy, ObamaCare decreed that firms would be required to knock out wasteful administrative costs by attaining favorable 'medical loss ratios,' which in turn require them to slash their administrative expenses for individual and group health care plans . . . The numbers are often little more than half of the current expense ratios for various kinds of plans."

In demanding such cuts, the ACA simply assumes that existing administrative costs are waste, allowed for by faulty markets. Yet the legislation does not identify the sources of such waste, or even what might constitute an administrative cost.[56] The result has been massive flight from healthcare provision, with employers, unions, and insurers eliminating health benefits of any kind for millions of workers. Perhaps most dramatic, McDonald's announced that it would cut off limited health benefits from thirty thousand of its low-paid workers because high employee turnover rates made administrative costs too high for them to meet the statutory requirements.[57]

Obama has used waivers to try to rescue the program from its own flawed assumptions. Not surprisingly, however, the waivers themselves, by the very fact that they lack express standards and rules, end up increasing administrative costs as they undermine the rule of law. Waivers provide extremely valuable competitive advantages for those who secure them, fostering fierce conflict among those required to provide insurance to get their own—and prevent their competitors from receiving waivers in turn. Under such circumstances, "administrative expertise quickly takes a back seat to old-fashioned political muscle and intrigue."[58] And this waiver process is unceasing. Waivers typically only last for short periods and often are "given on condition that the firm take steps to bring itself into compliance during waiver period." Thus, the agency repeatedly decides whether another short-term compromise is called for or whether to withdraw the dispensation it had granted from enforcement and potential punishment.[59]

As Epstein sums up his critique, "[W]hat matters systematically is not the outcome of any particular case but rather the long-term toll that extensive rulemaking exacts from the administrative process. The safeguards of the rule of law are always undermined by fierce short-term pressures on administrative agencies." The guidance and predictability provided by the rule of law are sacrificed on the altar of "results." And regulated people and entities become more or less influential supplicants before the agencies, seeking special favors in the discretion of persons, not of laws.[60]

Consent Decrees

Consent decrees are another means by which executive agencies may "waive" statutory/regulatory requirements. Here the agency, or a related section of the Department of Justice, utilizes its prosecutorial discretion to let regulated entities off the hook for putative regulatory violations—for a price. With a consent decree the regulated company avoids prosecution under terms bargained out with the agency.[61] Through them Congress, in effect, enables agencies to make deals with the regulated industries, requiring them to uphold policies the agency favors (whether or not embodied in legislation)[62] on a case-by-case basis. Such case-by-case, ad hoc power is intrinsically unlaw-ike.[63] And this rejection of law in application has spread through our legal culture even into the realm of criminal law, where plea bargaining has become standard operating practice. The proportion of guilty pleas rose from under 65 percent in 1908 to over 95 percent in 2002.[64] Between 1980 and 2002, the federal criminal trial rate dropped from 23 percent to less than 5 percent.[65]

Whether termed a consent decree or plea bargain, the central concept is, of course, bargaining—and it is not a term of law. Rather, bargaining is a process whereby parties assess the strength of one another's positions. The clarity of the evidence and severity of the accusation are relevant, but so are the reputation of the lawyers and the amount of influence the regulated entity and/or defendant has with higher-ups in government. Influence and personality become key factors determining the outcome, as befits a process of bargaining rather than law; a process that relies on who one is, and who one knows, rather than what one has done; a process that constitutes the rule of men, not of laws.

Courts and the Perversion of Common Law

Executive agencies are able to coerce individuals and groups into consent decrees precisely because they promise to keep them out of court, saving them from crippling or fatal legal costs. This is an especially effective threat when the court actually is an administrative tribunal providing only the limited procedural rights appropriate to a prerogative, executive court. But regular Article III judicial courts themselves are not free from the difficulties we have noted. And we would not want to be seen as charging them solely with excessive activism. In part the courts are responsible for our current predicament on account of their failure to act—in particular their failure to enforce the nondelegation doctrine. Nonetheless, the principal reason for the lack of judicial conformance with the rule of law stems, as we have remarked above, from the abandonment of judicial duty, the morality that prevailed at the time of founding. As Hamburger notes, this morality was "so clearly evident" during the founding era that "it could be left implicit"; that is, it needed no formal constitutional grounding. Unfortunately, the dictates of judicial duty—along with its prescriptions regarding the functions of the courts and the strict limitations on their power to invalidate legislation—"have almost been lost to view."[66]

Over a number of decades, modern historians and legal academics have misconstrued exercises of judicial duty in the early American states as mere precursors to "judicial review." From here they have developed an extremely malleable understanding of judicial power, one far more malleable than that embodied in judicial duty. Moreover, as we might expect, this "judicial review" is taken to be largely an American "invention" and, therefore, like many other developments of the founding period, a matter of abiding uncertainty as to its origins, scope, and intended uses.[67]

With the emergence of judicial review, a question involving the basic underlying principles of the rule of law emerges, namely, what is the extent of judicial power? To put this another way, as Hamburger notes, at various time in the English experience there were those who urged the abandonment of the restrictions imposed by judicial duty. Some sought to turn the intrinsically limited practice of equitable interpretation into a power to fully control legislation.[68] That is, they sought to abandon their duty to look to the intent of the legislature, only filling in interstices where the language is unclear and incomplete, and only endeavoring to fulfill the legislature's perceived intent in accordance with the law of the land and the customary assumptions regarding what is fair and reasonable embodied therein. Instead, they sought to subordinate the law of the land to their own "rational" conception of the dictates of justice they ascribed to an abstract reading of natural law (or, today, the demands of "justice" defined in terms of civic republican virtue) and individual conscience.[69]

Hamburger emphasizes the basic disagreement that perennially has surrounded the source and content of any higher source for judging human law.[70] Common law judges came to recognize that, if an abstract understanding of natural law were used as a measure for the legitimacy of the law of the land, there would be no uniformity in adjudication of the laws. Thus, the growth of precedent and known principles of adjudication at the very heart of the rule of law would be undermined. Indeed, once free of the limitations of judicial duty, judicial power is theoretically limitless.

The problem of judicial power has become very real and acute in the United States as judicial review has been interpreted to embrace the notion that the Constitution embodies rights whose realization and enforcement fall to the courts. Perhaps the decision in *Missouri v. Jenkins* best illustrates the extent to which the courts go to secure these rights; specifically, they may compel local governments to tax at a rate in excess of state statutory limits in order to force compliance with judicially determined constitutional obligations.[71]

The Supreme Court's decision in *Roe v. Wade*, however and whatever one's views on the underlying policy issue,[72] best illustrates the range of difficulties with this conception of judicial authority. In *Roe*, to begin with, we find a pattern of circular reasoning common to virtually all decisions, going back to the infamous proslavery decision in *Dred Scott v. Sandford*,[73] which embrace "substantive due process." There is no articulation of a theoretical foundation or framework for determining why the right to an abortion is "fundamental" or why, it would seem to follow, other recognized rights may be less than fundamental. In other words, we are left to speculate how we are to determine the relative status of rights that comprise generally understood limitations on the scope of governmental authority.[74]

The decision in *Roe* closely resembles the infamous decision in *Lochner v. New York*, in which "liberty of contract" was read arbitrarily into the Due

Process Clause of the Fourteenth Amendment as a right beyond the legitimate control of the legislature.[75] Certainly, the *Roe* decision partakes of this same arbitrary character by relying on the "right of privacy"—a right of its own invention, not specifically enumerated in the Constitution—to find abortion a "fundamental" right protected by the Due Process Clause of the Fourteenth Amendment.[76] The lack of any grounding in the text of the Constitution on which to base a right that is claimed to be fundamental clearly indicates that subjective values determined the outcome in *Roe*. If a court may root around in the text of various constitutional amendments to find a set of rights with some tangential relationship, abstract them into a general "penumbral" right like "privacy," then respecify that right down to a concrete particular like abortion (after having first traded "marital privacy" for a purely individual right) the field is wide open; courts may find whatever rights they like within a "Constitution" the meaning of which they have assumed the power not merely to interpret but to determine. Such conduct suggests that future courts would be free to look beyond the Constitution's express provisions to "discover" new rights that should be shielded from legislative control.

The court's arbitrariness, both real and potential, undermines and weakens the basic framework necessary for the rule of law. If the law as enacted by the legislature is not the law as applied by the courts, the citizenry will not be able to predict what the law will be as applied to them; their success or failure in arguing that they have not violated the law will depend, not on their ability and willingness to abide by the law, but rather on their ability to appeal to the moral and political convictions of the judges. Some may find naïve Blackstone's admonition that judgments are the sentence of the law, merely pronounced by the court.[77] But that formulation marks the distinction between the rule of law and the rule of those entrusted to apply the law.

Another related and equally serious problem concerns whether in this and like cases involving rights the court has not usurped a legislative function. Certainly the *Roe* court took a bold step in invalidating legislation, particularly on the grounds that it did. Beyond this, the court set down rules regarding what legislatures may or may not do during the "trimesters" of pregnancy, and certain of these rules have some attributes of law. For instance, the stipulation that in the first trimester "the abortion decision and its effectuation must be left to the medical judgment of the pregnant woman's attending physician,"[78] although it takes the form of a judicial command, is legislative; it is a generally applicable rule of action, albeit only quasi-legal in nature, given its nonlegislative source and arbitrary rationale. What is more, the trimester rules and related regulations over the decades themselves are, much like Congress's delegations, susceptible to varied interpretations. Subsequent to its decision, for example, the court has had to resolve key issues such as what constitutes the "health of the mother," which it acknowledged as legitimate grounds for state regulation in the third trimester.[79] Many of the court's decisions following upon *Roe* also take the form of laws in marking out whether a state "interest" is sufficiently "compelling" to justify regulation of abortion.[80] And significant uncertainty still exists at the state level over what constitutes legitimate regulation in the court's eyes.[81]

Much of the controversy surrounding *Roe* and subsequent decisions stems from the American constitutional understanding that legislatures would be better forums than the courts to accommodate and balance the claims and interests of contending parties. This would suggest that prudential considerations should come into play in determining which branch is best capable of handling contentious issues. While concern with observing the rule of law does not necessarily exclude such considerations, it does point to the need for establishing criteria to determine when the judiciary legitimately can remove an issue from the political arena. What kinds of issues should be handled in this manner, and why? Are all "rights claims" to be handled exclusively by the judiciary? Is it possible to formulate relatively precise rules or standards for determining the legitimacy of rights claims? These questions arise once judicial duty is abandoned and replaced with a broad and amorphous conception of "judicial review." Yet these issues remain unresolved. So long as this is the case, the capacity of our institutions to act in accordance with the rule of law remains severely compromised.

It is unnecessary to rehearse here the entire, well-known panoply of judicially active decisions and their impact on public policy. Sometimes for good ends, sometimes for bad, depending on one's social and political convictions, courts have become instigators of public policy and authors of quasi-laws intended to shape and reshape American politics and culture. In so doing, they have rejected the Framers' constitutional morality and undermined both it and the rule of law.

Rule by Decree? Presidential Quasi-Law

Whatever the pretensions of some federal judges, and whatever may remain of the pretensions of members of Congress, the focus of attention and the locus of power under the new dispensation is the president, not merely as putative head of executive agencies, but as a quasi-lawmaker in his or her own (quasi-) right. In a nation committed to swift action aimed at solving all significant problems, the most effective means by which to end the "deadlock of democracy" is to concentrate power in as few hands as possible, particularly when crises occur. Indeed, the Framers recognized the link between concentration and efficiency in opting for a unitary executive. As Publius notes, putting the executive power in one set of hands would ensure that it could be used with energy. And energy, Publius writes in *Federalist* 10, "is essential to the protection of the community against foreign attacks; it is not less essential to the steady administration of the laws; to the protection of property against those irregular and high-handed combinations which sometimes interrupt the ordinary course of justice; to the security of liberty against the enterprises and assaults of ambition, of faction, and of anarchy."[82]

Publius focuses on the need for energy in times of war and emergency. Yet the president has numerous roles to play and, with them, opportunities to take the lead in political affairs—including as commander in chief, head of state, chief law enforcement officer, and head of the executive branch.[83] All these roles are directly attributable to the Constitution. Yet there is another role that has been ascribed to the president for some decades: that of "chief legislator."[84] Oddly, however, while such ascriptions mention the president's role within the formal legislative process, in which his constitutional power is officially limited to potential exercise of the veto, mention is not often made of the president's increasing ability to essentially make law by decree through various presidential directives.

Presidential directives may be called executive orders, proclamations, memoranda, or even signing statements. The terms all refer to more or less formal, written commands from the president, all with the same force and authority, none defined within the Constitution itself.[85] These directives increasingly have assumed the force of law, creating and imposing specific, legally enforceable burdens on citizens.[86]

One crucial element missing from presidential "legislation" is Congress. Presidential directives are just that, directives. Through them the president rules, where he so desires and is not blocked by other political actors, by his own decrees. As President Clinton's advisor Paul Begala noted, "[S]troke of the pen . . . law of the land. Kind of cool."[87] The Supreme Court quite properly has struck down attempts by Congress to check presidential action through the so-called "legislative veto." The court has not been so vigilant, however, in checking the president's exponentially growing power to issue decrees with the force of law.

As with most alterations undermining American constitutional morality, that regarding presidential directives was set in quick motion during the Progressive era. It was during this period that President Theodore Roosevelt expounded his stewardship theory, according to which the president is empowered to take any action he deems necessary for the public good not specifically prohibited by statute or the Constitution.[88] Of course, such a view exactly reverses the structure of government established by the Framers' Constitution, which grants the federal government only limited, enumerated powers. Consistent with this older view, Theodore Roosevelt's successor, William Howard Taft, warned against giving the president an "undefined residuum of power." Taft saw such powers transforming the president into a kind of "Universal Providence" empowered to and responsible for setting "all things right."[89]

Like most forms of power, the president's ability to issue directives has been used in good causes and bad, wisely, foolishly, and at times disastrously in both political and moral terms. Racial integration in the military, the Teapot Dome scandal arising from the transfer of property to an official of President Harding's cabinet,[90] and the internment of Japanese Americans during World War II all were products of presidential directives. Our concern, then, is not to evaluate the moral quality of particular presidential directives in either intent or effect taken as political acts. It is, rather, to show the manner in which expansion of their use has given to our government a quasi-law character. We will examine this growth and its implications for the rule of law in the development of presidential executive orders and signing statements. We will, however, frequently refer to each of these acts as simply "presidential directives" to highlight the overall impact of rule by unilateral presidential action.

Executive Orders

The term *executive order* has come to be applied to the most formal and clearly powerful type of presidential directive. Stemming from the "executive power" vested in the president by Article II, Section 1 of the Constitution, the executive order is a necessary tool for carrying out the duty, set out in Article II, Section 3, to "take care that the laws be faithfully executed." Generally used by the president to manage operations within executive departments, executive orders today may be used "to create and impose legal burdens on private citizens."[91] Yet their beginnings were relatively humble.

President George Washington issued directives on a number of occasions. These early orders accorded with a restrictive understanding of the president's need to direct the actions of subordinates in carrying out specific presidential duties.[92] Thus, for example, Washington directed officers having served under the Articles of Confederation to provide reports to him sufficient to take account of their status and activities.[93] More controversially, Washington issued a declaration of neutrality regarding the position of the United States in the conflict between Great Britain and revolutionary France. This last directive was criticized, despite being in the area of foreign affairs and despite Washington's contention that it only stated the nation's preexisting policy at the time, because it was seen as seeking to influence congressional conduct.[94]

Even in the area of national defense and war, it was left to later generations for presidents to expand the power of presidential directives. Where Washington had acted against the Whiskey Rebellion only after receiving congressional direction, President Lincoln first responded to the secession of the southern states from the union with a series of far-reaching unilateral decrees. These orders called forth the militia, established a blockade of southern ports, ordered construction of warships, provided war funding, and suspended the writ of habeas corpus, thereby subjecting citizens to imprisonment without formal charges.[95]

The last of these orders, suspending the writ of habeas corpus, was brought into question by the courts, especially in *ex parte Merryman*. In that case Chief Justice Taney expressed surprise at the necessity of pointing out that the Constitution specifically and exclusively grants to Congress the power to suspend the writ, and then ordered it issued (which in effect would have freed the person in question).[96] Within the same constitutional realm, and within a few years, in *ex parte Milligan* the Supreme Court denied President Lincoln's assumed right to subject civilians to military law where the courts were open and functioning.[97] But, in part out of concern that unity be shown in time of crisis and in part because many of Lincoln's congressional opponents had left that body when their states had seceded, no specific congressional action was taken to overturn these orders, and the courts did not formally strike down any of them. The orders went far toward establishing the massive power of presidents in time of war.

In the domestic sphere, it was many decades before the legality of an executive order was brought into serious question, and then the focus was not so much on the order as on the legislation giving rise thereto. In addition to the direct authority of the Constitution, most clearly and expansively seen in the realm of foreign affairs and national security, the power to issue presidential directives may be based in statute.[98] The Supreme Court has been loathe to hold that presidential directives have no basis in one or the other of these—having done so less than a handful of times. But the directives generally have some basis in statutory or constitutional language.

One potentially important exception involved Franklin Delano Roosevelt's use of executive orders to implement the National Industrial Recovery Act. The legislation empowered the president to give "codes of fair competition" the force of law. These codes established enforceable standards regarding wages, length of employee work weeks, minimum numbers of employees, licensing, and other key elements of trade and business. In giving the president the power to establish such rules in his discretion, that act, according to the court, violated the Constitution by delegating its essential legislative function to the executive branch.[99] This decision, potentially limiting presidential power, has been allowed to atrophy as the administrative state has grown in size and complexity.

Another Supreme Court decision specifically invalidating an executive order has had a longer lifespan, though arguably no greater impact on presidential conduct. In refusing to countenance President Truman's executive order seizing control of American steel mills during the Korean War, the court in *Youngstown Sheet & Tube Co. v. Sawyer* held that the action, which was not authorized by any statute, also was not authorized directly by any constitutional power of the president in the area of national defense.[100] In a concurring opinion, Justice Jackson set forth a doctrine regarding presidential power that has served ever since as the basis for court review, such as it is, of presidential directives. That opinion constructed an amorphous three-part categorization of presidential power. Such power was at its height, according to Jackson, where the president acted with the express or implied authorization of Congress. It was less expansive where Congress had not made its desires known; here there might be a "twilight zone" of concurrent presidential and congressional power, the outlines of which would be determined by the court's reading of the facts of particular cases. Finally, presidential power was at its lowest in any realm in which the president acted in opposition to Congress's express or implied will.[101]

It has been in the second, "concurrent" realm that presidential power has grown most. The court over several decades developed a doctrine of congressional "acquiescence" according to which that body's failure to reject presidential actions has been taken as approval of any relevant presidential directive.[102] In effect, this doctrine puts the onus on Congress to pass a law undoing a mere presidential decree. The result is legislatively torturous. If faced with a presidential decree establishing a new law, even one its members had no inkling was in the offing, and which they find utterly abhorrent, Congress must put together the majority needed to pass legislation—and possibly the two-thirds supermajority to override a veto—in the face of presidential prestige and a political fait accompli.[103] Moreover, in at least one area, that of the presidential power to keep documents secret, the language of any restriction must be explicit and specific, lest it be brushed aside in accordance with assumptions of presidential power.[104]

This is not to say that executive orders are never struck down. In addition to those mentioned already, President Clinton's executive order forbidding employers from hiring permanent replacements for striking workers was rejected by the Supreme Court because it directly violated an existing statute.[105] But an executive order has been directly vacated only three times by the court, indicating that an extensive realm of lawmaking power has been ceded to the president. Today, an aggressive president may seize control of the policy initiative by simply issuing executive orders, secure in the knowledge that they, and even entire federal agencies they establish and wars to which they commit the nation, almost certainly will stand.[106] Such orders have been used to wage wars, to change policies, and to establish new agencies of government. A president may achieve all this without his or her policies, language, or implementation being subjected to the full consideration and development of broad support required by legislative lawmaking.

Not only does the law instituted by these decrees lack the procedural origins called for by the higher, constitutional law, but it also often lacks proper publication. Executive orders do not appear in the *United States Code;* they instead are included in the more obscure, voluminous, and difficult-to-navigate *Federal Register* and *Code of Federal Regulations.*[107] Only directives of "general applicability and legal effect" need appear even in the *Federal Register*—and only if the president does not determine, for national security or other reasons, that they should not be published.[108]

Executive orders that are not "secret" also may be considered too minor for publication. And this leaves even greater room for presidents to make law without congressional input or full discussion among various constituencies. Thus, for example, President Clinton used memoranda to heads of departments (officially less important than executive orders because limited to setting internal policy) to effect such significant policy changes as requiring performance of abortions on military bases overseas.[109] In the same way Clinton directed the Environmental Protection Agency (EPA) to develop new rules and regulations in accord with the president's own (that is, not statutorily codified) policy preferences.[110]

Implications for the rule of law are far reaching. Take, for example, President Obama's Executive Order 13535 in regard to abortion funding under the structures established by the ACA.[111] The executive order was the result of bargaining between the president and Congressman Bart Stupak, who had expressed fear that the legislation would allow federal funding for most abortions, a policy with which he said he disagreed. Rather than convincing Congress to amend the bill, however, the president promised that after signing it he would issue (as he did issue) an executive order barring the use of federal funds for most abortions.[112] Whatever one's opinion regarding the substance of the law in question, it seems clear that such a course of action violates and undermines the rule of law.

The deal was needed because Congress has understood, ever since *Roe v. Wade* declared a right to abortion, that federal health-care funds are assumed to be available for abortions unless specifically prohibited by Congress.[113] This is why Congress consistently included in relevant legislation a Hyde Amendment specifically forbidding the expenditure of Medicare funds for abortions.[114] The 2010 health-care bill did not include that ban, so the proper reading of the statute is that it leaves public money available for abortions.

Again, the issue here is not the wisdom or virtue of the underlying policy but the deviance of the lawmaking methodology from that required by the rule of law. Customary interpretation of statutory law dictates that the health-care legislation be read as allowing federal funding for abortions, until and unless a more general statutory policy or more specific statutory amendment is enacted. But the president signed this legislation and then simply and clearly contradicted it through an executive order—a decree issuing from his office, under his authority alone. And the president could undo this act by simply replacing this executive order with another one authorizing public funding of abortions. The president signed one law, issued a quasi-law contradicting a portion of that law, and potentially could use another quasi-law to undo his contradiction—all on his own.

Certainly such a deal was convenient in securing enactment of legislation on which supporters lacked a common understanding as to its applicability. But the impact of such deals on the rule of law is devastating. A law passed according to the rules of the game[115] has been contradicted specifically by a presidential decree. The result can be looked at in either of two ways: the law passed by Congress is in mere contradiction with the law decreed by the president, meaning that we have inconsistent laws, or we have a clear inconsistency between the law as passed and the law as it will be applied. In either case the government has failed to make law; it has declared rules inconsistent with one another and/or a rule that is in practice different from the rule as published.[116] It has rendered the law difficult to find, understand, and follow, undermining the ability of those to whom it is applied to recognize it as law, let alone follow it. The only other possibility: today presidential decrees trump legislation, rendering statutes mere advice to the new legislator in chief. To say that such a situation gives people a set rule to follow—that is, the declaration of the president—is to say that arbitrary power may be exercised in consistent fashion. The power remains arbitrary and the consistency a matter of potentially changing personalities, policies, and moods.

Signing Statements

Another common and seemingly different form of presidential directive is the signing statement. The origins and logic of signing statements are simple: presidents since the early republic have issued public statements when signing bills into law. The vast majority of these statements are purely ceremonial, emphasizing the importance of the legislation, thanking particular constituencies, and expressing other sentiments in connection with the signing.[117] Even today, signing statements constitute something more than ceremonial rhetoric only when they also contain presidential directives relevant to the legislation signed.[118] But these directive signing statements, in which the president instructs executive branch personnel as to how (and whether) to implement provisions of the new statute, have become increasingly common and powerful in recent decades.

Directive signing statements exist, by nature, in a realm of conflict and potential uncertainty. The president is charged by the Constitution to "take Care that the Laws be faithfully executed." But there often is room, and even necessity, for discretion in such execution. Signing statements provide a means by which the president may signal the manner in which he will (or will not) execute the law he is signing. It is this parenthetical issue—when will the president *not* execute the law he has signed, or at least not as the plain meaning of the words would dictate?—that shows the danger of directive signing statements to the rule of law.

After a fashion, directive signing statements may be seen as serving the rule of law because they announce circumstances under which presidents will only selectively implement statutes. Such actions clearly are preferable to those by which the president secretly acts in violation of clear statutory language and then claims, when his actions come to light, that he was constitutionally required or empowered to violate the statute. This latter was the conduct engaged in by President George W. Bush in regard to his domestic surveillance program. Relevant legislation had required those conducting such surveillance to gain particularized preapproval from a specified judicial body.[119] Bush signed the legislation without objecting to this mechanism, yet ordered that surveillance be undertaken without approval from the statutory court. When forced to justify his surveillance actions after they were discovered, the head of the National Security Agency argued that he was faced with the choice of either obeying the statute or obeying a contrary presidential directive. He chose to obey the presidential decree, a choice he, and the Bush administration more generally, justified on the grounds that the legislation improperly infringed upon the president's "inherent" power to protect the nation's security.[120]

Such secretive annulment and replacement of duly enacted legislation clearly violates and undermines the rule of law. Even were one to agree with Bush II claims to "unitary executive power," particularly in areas related to national security, respect for law and the Constitution would require vetoing rather than surreptitiously undermining contrary legislation. But we submit that announcing the intention of ignoring or misinterpreting a statute one is signing is at best a marginal improvement over secretly doing so. Such statements are, even if published in some form, not promulgated as law or published in the *United States Code.* They are not dispositive in court. They too often are simply assertions by the president of his intent to violate the law just promulgated.

In certain areas, particularly those concerning appropriations of federal funds, there is a natural realm of debate and conflict encapsulated within signing statements. But directive signing statements, as they have developed over the last several decades, have worsened rather than ameliorated the problem of laws being enforced and implemented in a manner and extent contrary to those dictated by their announced meaning. Indeed, the spectacle of a president announcing, as he signs a bill into law, that portions of that law are unconstitutional and hence will not be implemented constitutes a blow to constitutional morality, sending the signal to all involved that duly enacted laws remain mere suggestions to be followed, or not, as dictated by political opinion and/or expediency.

In the area of appropriations, signing statements have been used at least since the time of President Andrew Jackson to announce the president's intent to go against the letter of the law—the claim being that such contrary action is necessary in order to follow the perceived dictates of constitutional or divergent statutory principles. In signing a bill authorizing funds to build a road from Detroit to Chicago, for example, Jackson's signing statement declared that he would interpret the bill to provide for funding only within Michigan. Jackson considered internal improvements to be a matter for the states and, while Michigan remained a territory, Illinois was at this time a state, making it an inappropriate place, in Jackson's view, for federal monies to be spent on roads.[121] In recess at the time, Congress later, while acceding to the action, deemed the signing statement's interpretation and impact to constitute a "line item" veto. That is, the president had used his statement to in effect veto a portion of the bill— something disallowed under the Constitution, which requires the president to either sign or veto bills in their entirety.[122]

Appropriations bills are most open to selective presidential enforcement because the statutes often allow for presidential discretion in spending up to a given amount on roads, grants for a given program, and the like. However, where Congress clearly rules out such discretion the spending becomes a mere "ministerial" act the president, in theory, cannot avoid. Thus, for example, Richard Nixon was ordered by the courts to spend funds he had impounded in contradiction to clear statutory language.[123]

The contemporary, expansive use of directive signing statements arguably has its roots in memos written by future Supreme Court Justice Samuel Alito, then working in the Reagan administration's office of legal counsel. Alito aimed to counter the problem of courts placing improper emphasis on (often intentionally misleading) legislative history, which consists of committee reports, legislative debates and other materials purporting to establish a particular meaning or intent for a statute. On Alito's view, signing statements could be used to announce a more appropriate (and friendly to the president) reading of a particular statute.[124] In point of fact, courts rarely rely on signing statements in construing statutory language, in part because the statements generally are too vague and have not gone through the constitutional requirements of bicameralism and presentment.[125] But these statements do publicly signal that the president is implementing the law in a manner he himself deems consistent with his own conception of his authority.

Out of concern over statutory construction, and from a desire to centralize executive branch decision making in the Oval Office, the Reagan administration developed a policy of using signing statements to announce particular constructions of statutory language and to direct agency heads to enforce laws in accordance with constitutional interpretations included in those statements.[126] The result was a substantial increase in the number and importance of directive signing statements. More important, Reagan's signing statements frequently questioned the constitutional validity of particular provisions of bills the president was signing into law. And such questioning has skyrocketed since. As one study showed, "the average annual number of legislative provisions that signing statements challenged prior to 1981 was 0.5; in contrast, under Ronald Reagan, George H. W. Bush, William Clinton, and George W. Bush, the average numbers have been, respectively: 8.9, 58.0, 17.5, and 146.0."[127]

It is important to note that during the Clinton administration, when the numbers of legislative provisions challenged by signing statements dropped, there nonetheless was significant doctrinal development increasing their power. Clinton actually used a signing statement to create, on his own, a new federal agency—the National Nuclear Security Administration.[128] More often, however, Clinton signing statements announced the president's refusal to enforce provisions he claimed were likely to be declared unconstitutional by the courts.[129]

The quasi-legislative logic of Clinton's directive signing statements, spelled out in a series of memoranda authored by then Assistant Attorney General Walter Dellinger, established a pattern in use ever since: directive signing statements inform subordinates how they are to interpret and/or implement the statute, assert the president's view (where applicable) that portions of the statute present constitutional questions and/or conflicts, and announce that the president will enforce such provisions only when and to the extent he or she believes doing so would not cause a constitutional violation.[130] Central to such a strategy is the view that the president has no duty to veto bills he believes include unconstitutional provisions, but rather may decide unilaterally what parts of legislation to enforce.[131] That is, the president may, at his discretion, choose to violate the Constitution by promulgating and enforcing an unconstitutional law.

In a follow-up memorandum, Dellinger argued that the president should only make such constitutional assertions and "corrections" after flagging constitutional issues early in the legislative process. In such cases a directive signing statement might be seen as creating a justiciable issue for Supreme Court consideration and clarification.[132] Such refined parameters for the quasi-legislative use of signing statements have, to say the least, not been uniformly respected.

Signing statements came to wide and alarmed attention among academics, politicians, and the public during the presidency of George W. Bush. Bush II went far beyond his predecessors in the use of directive signing statements. He not only used them much more often to question the validity of far more statutory provisions, but he also used them in a more aggressive fashion to further his vision of presidential power.

An example showing the extent to which Bush II signing statements contradicted the laws they accompanied is provided by the McCain amendment, or the Detainee Treatment Act of 2005.[133] The McCain amendment explicitly directed that detainees not be subjected to cruel, inhuman, or degrading treatment.[134] On signing the relevant legislation into law, Bush issued a directive signing statement declaring that the executive branch would construe the statute "in a manner consistent with the constitutional authority of the President to supervise the unitary executive branch and as Commander in Chief and consistent with the constitutional limitations on the judicial power."[135]

Here, Bush II indicated his intention to see that the McCain amendment was applied only when and to the extent it was in accord with his own views regarding the "unitary executive" and the lack of room for judicial review thereof. Not only would the law not be enforced as written, but there would be no published law informing people of the rules to be applied, and indeed no set law of any kind in this area; actions taken regarding detainees would comport with whatever the executive branch deemed fitting in accordance with its own reading of its own powers. There would be no law, only actions dictated by presidential will—the very definition of arbitrary power.[136]

The signing statement for the McCain amendment was no aberration. According to the Congressional Research Service, "the large bulk" of Bush II signing statements "do not apply particularized constitutional rationales to specific scenarios, nor do they contain explicit, measurable refusals to enforce a law. Instead, the statements make broad and largely hortatory assertions of executive authority that make it effectively impossible to ascertain what factors, if any, might lead to substantive constitutional or interpretive conflict in the implementation of an act."[137]

Directive signing statements generally lacked specific statutory construction and argumentation before Bush II as well.[138] But the clear quasi-legislative program of the Bush II administration, in which fewer than a dozen bills were vetoed while more than 150 signing statements called into question well over one thousand provisions in the statutes being promulgated, marks it as unique up to its time in its drive for executive discretion beyond law.[139] Bush II intentionally avoided confrontation within the legislative process in favor of declarations that he would act as he saw fit outside it. Moreover, it seems clear that in the case of Bush II the lack of specific statutory discussion in these statements was intended to support a particular doctrine—that of a "unitary executive" exercising "inherent powers" in important areas, especially regarding national security and foreign relations.[140] The Congressional Research Service noted in the Bush II signing statements a pattern intended "to object systematically to any perceived congressional encroachment, however slight, with the aim of inuring the other branches of government and the public to the validity of such objections and the attendant conception of presidential authority that will presumably follow from sustained exposure and acquiescence to such claims of power."[141]

In our terms, the Bush II signing statements were intended to eliminate any vestigial remnant of constitutional morality hostile toward unchecked presidential power. But it would be wrong to ascribe this intent solely to the Bush II signing statements. Some attempts to put the inherent powers doctrine into action were not embodied in anything so formal as a signing statement; this was the case with the controversial "torture memos" of John Yoo advising the executive branch to ignore congressional limitations on interrogation techniques if they encroached on the commander-in-chief powers of the president.[142]

In addition, Bush II has not been the only president to issue directive signing statements claiming wide presidential power. One more recent example: President Obama's signing statement regarding legislation directing the secretary of the treasury to adopt specific positions in dealing with the International Monetary Fund. Obama's signing statement declared, "I will not treat these provisions as limiting my ability to engage in foreign diplomacy or negotiations."[143] That is, Obama declared his intention to treat provisions specifically directing him to take certain positions in negotiations as not limiting his ability to take whatever positions he thought proper in those negotiations. He was stating his intention to disregard specific statutory provisions on account of their encroaching on his "inherent" powers. He was placing himself above a statute he had signed into law.[144]

Another example: in signing the National Defense Authorization Act for Fiscal Year 2013, Obama said he intended to "avoid constitutional conflict" in interpreting a section limiting the military's authority to transfer third-party nationals detained in Parwan, Afghanistan. The constitutional principle was the president's power as commander in chief. In addition, Obama questioned provisions limiting his ability to try detainees in federal court; close the military base in Guantanamo Bay, Cuba; and transfer detainees to foreign countries. Obama's response, while not atypical, is telling in its refusal to provide specific criteria or guidelines: "My Administration will interpret these provisions as consistent with existing and future determinations by the agencies of the Executive responsible for detainee transfers. And, in the event that these statutory restrictions operate in a manner that violates constitutional separation of powers principles, my Administration will implement then in a manner that avoids the constitutional conflict."[145]

In this one directive signing statement, Obama questioned the validity of twenty-one specific provisions in the legislation. And his list of objections was not drawn as exclusive. In each case, Obama promised to interpret the provisions as he saw appropriate given his own reading of his own presidential power.[146]

Over several administrations a practice has developed by which presidents sign into law bills they believe are unconstitutional—itself a violation of any coherent constitutional morality. Presidents then question the laws they are promulgating, reserving to themselves a power to suspend or dispense from laws as they see fit. The president rejects his essential legislative role and means (the veto power) in favor of assertions of discretionary authority and power. Citizens (and others) are left with only their political judgment as a tool for predicting governmental action over time—the very calculus the rule of law by nature is intended to replace with set, predictable procedures.

Rule of Law or Rule by President?

As with presidential waivers and executive orders, signing statements have a technical origin in statutory language. But in all these cases that origin is paradoxical; these unilateral actions aim to supplement, and more often subvert and/or counteract, the legislation in question. Hamburger has pointed out that the Obama administration's use of waivers is reminiscent of medieval and early modern uses of the dispensing power. Monarchs at one time were able to except certain persons from the effects of generally applicable laws. It was well understood in these cases that the ruler was acting above or "notwithstanding" the law. That is, the ruler was using his or her putatively unlimited sovereign power to dispense with the law in cases where he or she judged it unfair or inconvenient. Of course, the British ended such uses of the dispensing power with the Revolution of 1688. In the United States, constitutions uniformly rejected any such power to dispense with laws. Presidents might pardon particular persons, or refrain from prosecution (potentially at great political cost). But there was no pretense that the law did not apply to everyone it said it did—until recently.[147]

Today, the president may dispense with laws for certain persons by directing agencies in their exercise of the waiver power. The president also may change the law through directive signing statements ordering administrative underlings to ignore parts of the law or interpret it in a manner clearly at odds with that envisioned by the legislature. And the president may make quasi-law unilaterally through executive order.

When combined with Bush II's assertions of a "unitary executive" power to supervise his subordinates, these powers to change or create quasi-law through decree create a kind of prerogative in presidents under the new dispensation. That is, presidents increasingly are claiming for themselves, and being accorded, the old, royal power to act outside the law so long as it is in some sense "in the public interest." Small wonder, then, that we are seeing greater emphasis on political and moral as opposed to formal, constitutional, and legal limitations on the powers of the office.

Customary restraints were crucial to the British monarchical tradition. But ours is not the British monarchical tradition. Indeed, the British system itself dispensed with the royal prerogative centuries ago because of its tendency to make the executive arbitrary. By statute and developing tradition, the British reshaped their (unwritten) constitution into one of formal parliamentary supremacy. Americans, on the other hand, made a conscious choice in framing their written Constitution to bind, limit, and check power through formal procedures and a formal structure of separated powers.

The Framers' Constitution succeeded for many years in maintaining the rule of law and the possibility of ordered liberty. It did so through its formal structures and procedures, which required deliberation and development of supermajority support for most significant changes in policy. These formal structures worked well for many decades. But they could not have done so without a supporting constitutional morality emphasizing restraint and acceptance of formal limitations on power. Checks and balances themselves limited arbitrary power only to the extent they were applied moderately and in support of a mediating constitution.

A mediating constitution, supported by a morality of restraint is, of course, difficult at times to accept in an unjust, tragic world. It requires accepting that many bad things and even evil institutions cannot be eliminated immediately, or even soon, through political force. But such a constitution provides the procedures and mechanisms by which people, as individual persons and in their more local, natural associations, can govern themselves, pursue decent lives, and come to recognize and address injustices in a way that may preserve peace, order, and the possibility of virtue for generations to come.

The question we face now is how to maintain or reestablish the rule of law at a time when our written Constitution is ignored in favor of an operational constitution impatient, at best, with formal structures, clear rules, and categorical limitations on the rulers' powers to "do good." The moribund state of our constitutional morality points to changes in the character of the people (our political culture or "unwritten constitution") not amenable to simple, programmatic reform. It would be pleasant to believe that a simple statement of the problem and its origins might spark a change of heart sufficient to revive a concern, if not to reinvigorate that constitution, then at least to institute reforms necessary to chain our rulers to the internal morality of law. We expect to have no such impact, but offer our view of current constitutional conditions as, perhaps, a basis for useful discussion.

Conclusion

The Plural Structure of Society and the Limits of Law

W E BEGIN OUR CONCLUSION with some scholarly analysis of constitutional troubles:

> Congress was a classic example of a legislature that . . . preferred to "abdicate" its power rather than "empire build." Major policy proposals did not originate in the legislature; virtually everything important was crafted by the president and his team of technocrats. . . . Still, passing bills was not easy, because it required that the president shower individual legislators with sufficient amounts of pork and other particularistic benefits to buy their support. When, as commonly happened with important policy measures, presidents were unable to cobble together a sufficiently large coalition of legislators . . . their proposals were blocked. As a result, the president often used his sweeping . . . powers to legislate directly, bypassing congress altogether.

This quotation reads like a textbook description of "gridlock" in the United States, including, as it does, reference to presidents' increasing resort to unilateral executive actions to institute and maintain government programs. It is instructive, then, to note that the "sweeping . . . powers" referenced here are the emergency powers of the president of Colombia. As the passage continues, "[B]etween 1970 and 1991, the country existed under some kind of a state of emergency 82 percent of the time."[1]

Most Americans know of Colombia only as the home of drug cartels and guerilla warfare. Of course, such national stereotypes are unfair, but they highlight the troubles experienced by a nation with many proud traditions that is caught in a perpetual constitutional crisis, suffering from a long-standing failure to uphold constitutional morality among those in government and, consequently, the rule of law for society. As in the United States, demands for government action in Colombia are vast. They have been answered by varying institutions, including a constitutional court that has taken it upon itself to legalize recreational drug use and assisted suicide as well as to restructure financial markets to prevent middle-class mortgage foreclosures—surely not the most pressing constitutional matters for a nation in crisis.[2] Americans may protest that our presidents declare no general states of emergency, but rule by decree remains rule by will rather than through law even if the decrees are called executive orders or signing statements.

It is time for those who value the well-being of the American people to consider the potential long-term effects of their own demands for action. It is time to reconsider the decades-long campaign to reshape our society through law conceived as a device for attaining social justice. Constitutionalism and the rule of law it supports cannot survive the continued stress placed upon them by the demands of a nascent commanding constitution foreign to our constitutional culture.

In pursuit of justice, fairness, and distribution of substantive goods through federal action, the formal structures of the American Constitution have been vitiated. The demand has been for a more active and efficient government. Nonetheless, attacks on the Framers' Constitution have not been primarily functional, but normative. From the late nineteenth century on, the separation of powers has been portrayed as illegitimate on account of its being archaic, uncaring, and undemocratic in both its assumptions and its goals. Over time, the Framers' constitutional morality, emphasizing procedure, caution, and restrained defense of one's institutional prerogatives, has dissolved in the face of demands for more and quicker action and more discretionary power in the hands of administrators seeking to "do good."

In keeping with the goals of the Progressives who achieved this transformation, the new dispensation has been a government ruled not by formal structures and procedures but by the pursuit of putatively good policy through broad statements of programmatic goals and the exercise of broad discretionary power. The government of the United States now consists of four separate loci of power (Congress, courts, agencies, and president), each able to create rights and impose burdens through directives having the force of law. This government's central feature is an institutionally weak legislature whose members achieve near life tenure by declaring general policy preferences that then are codified, operationalized, and even institutionalized by administrative experts and judges.

Unfortunately, the result has not been the smooth, efficient, and fair application of wise rules predicted by Progressives. Rather, as the Constitution has come to be treated as a set of vague guidelines wrapped in inconvenient, dispensable procedures, true law has become rare while quasi-law has become as omnipresent in its sources as in its effects. We have replaced certain rules allowing the people to go about their business with a vast realm of inchoate policy directives enforced by changing and conflicting rules of action, violation of which can bring retribution of unpredictable extent and severity.

Many evils have been eliminated—almost certainly more quickly than would have been the case under the original dispensation, with its mediating constitution. But the claim that "but for" insistent disregard for constitutional forms and procedures abuses of the past would have gone on unabated, as abuses of the present would become permanent, lacks substantiation. Indeed, as Gerald Rosenberg has shown in his study of the impact of court decisions on social change, actions more in keeping with the Framers' constitutional morality—that is, aimed at changing hearts, minds, and thence laws rather than convincing powerful political figures such as Supreme Court justices to issue new quasi-laws—have been the real motive force behind important gains made by movements such as those for civil rights and desegregation.[3]

Moreover, the cost of bypassing constitutional means of pursuing social change has been very high. Lacking a functioning constitutional morality, ours currently is a regime of profound uncertainty, in which one may find oneself on the wrong side of governmental orders emanating from a variety of sources, requiring an unpredictable variety of forms of action or inaction, facing penalties that depend on one's popularity, the popularity of one's activities, and/or one's power to bargain effectively with government actors. It is in this context that presidents have sought, and been accorded, increasing, unilateral powers.

Unable even to control their own subordinates in the executive and "independent" branches, presidents nonetheless have sought to solidify power in their own hands in the name of coherent public policy, efficiently administered—and in pursuit of a legacy of "greatness." The result increasingly has been arbitrary rule by plebiscitary presidents, hemmed in only by weak political opposition. Whatever one's policy preferences, such a turn of events should be profoundly troubling to all believers in self-government.

Progressives have sought to replace the Framers' constitutional morality with a new one, characterized by a code of administrative conduct emphasizing adherence to set procedures. But neither that code nor the virtues it demands are in keeping with either the written or the unwritten constitutions of the United States. In setting forth their visions for the future Mill and especially Wilson looked to the European administrative state, with its emphasis on class structures and centralized powers, neither of which fit American circumstances or self-conceptions. American constitutional culture does not lend itself to trust in administrative officers within an inquisitorial process leaving common citizens with only governmental patrons as their protectors. Yet, after decades of Progressive rule, we no longer live in our traditional system of mediating constitution and common law. As a result, our system has become fundamentally disordered and law has come to be seen as merely the current bargain, subject to change whenever any center of power divines a new policy preference and summons the will to reshape the law in its pursuit.

Our long history of procedural due process thus far has prevented a complete descent into lawlessness. But, as habits of law-abidingness among both rulers and ruled become more attenuated, the protections of law will become ever more precarious until we truly live in a nation under the will of some chief officer addressing "emergencies" through decrees having the force of law. At such a time, whether that officer is elected or not will make little difference to those who live in fear of unknowable dictates that may negate their plans or even subject them to punishment for what they had thought permissible. This is the price a society pays when it chooses expediency in pursuit of specific ends (however noble) over the rule of law.

The Impracticality of "Practical" Reforms

What, then, shall be done? Times of disorder may spawn many plans of reform. Unfortunately, during such times reforms, especially those of the most seemingly practical kind, often have no real chance at success. The drive to "do something" runs up against the brute fact that we have been doing all kinds of things, generally with the goal of improving our lot, that have produced increasing disorder. Thus, serious reform with any real chance at long-term success requires admitting that reforms on the table, as it were, will do us no good.

We already have mentioned some impractical reforms; others seem both obvious and obviously impractical. We limit ourselves here to outlining and rejecting the most obvious.

First, there can be no simple return to the original dispensation. The people as constituted by the current, incomplete and highly discordant unwritten constitution will no longer accept, as an operational reality, the Framers' Constitution. They no longer will accept a government ruled by the restraints of constitutional mediation, or limitations on power instantiated through textual enumeration, separation of powers, and federalism. Habituation toward demanding national "action" is too strong and insistent for any governing coalition dedicated to restoring the Framers' Constitution to form, let alone achieve its goals. And rejection of the institutions, beliefs, and practices of our traditional society is sufficiently widespread among the people to prevent an easy or quick reversal of this process.

Second, a straightforward "reboot" of the administrative state would be too adverse to the political self-interest of today's political actors for them to allow it, let alone make it happen. While a constitutional structure bringing active, centralized government under the rule of Congress and, through this, the rule of law might, in theory, provide the certainty that is the minimal good necessary for a decent society over the long term, there is no coherent push for such reforms. Moreover, members of the American Congress would not accept reconfiguration of the administrative state in a fashion abiding by the formal structures and procedures of the Framers' Constitution. Such reforms would require that Congress bring executive agencies under its own power and responsibility, and this would require that its members direct the actions of administrators with genuinely limited discretion and, more important, write laws binding down those administrators through clear statutory language of definite scope and limit. The time, trouble, and political responsibility of such a system have been explicitly rejected by Congress time and again as it has chosen instead to cede lawmaking power to other centers of power along with the power to prosecute violations through administrative procedures not bound by law.[4]

Third, attempts at technical fixes to the rule of quasi-law, even were they to be adopted, would do little to improve our constitutional order. We have seen balanced budget amendments, calls for line-item veto powers, and various proposals to limit the discretionary power of agency personnel. Such policies would serve only as new paper barriers to be broken through in the continuing pursuit of "good" public policy within our antiformalist political culture.

Finally, a new, formal constitution is beyond the possibility of acceptance in the United States. The people and those in government harbor sometimes laudable and sometimes merely cynical or sentimental attachment to the symbol of the Framers' Constitution. In addition, the justifiably quite limited legitimacy of our current political and intellectual elites renders them unfit to proffer any new proposals. Thus, while the Framers' Constitution is no longer followed in fact, its civil religious status renders dead in the water any attempt to remodel our frame of government, including along the parliamentary lines called for so many times by Progressives and their successors.

Thus, it would appear that we are doomed to continue moving toward a situation in which varying quasi-laws send citizens conflicting messages, in answer to which the president exercises ever greater discretionary, even prerogative power; in which the president feels the need and the right to exercise and extend this power to bring order to a system ever closer to the edge of lawlessness; in which members of the congressional "lawmaking" body see their job as helping powerful constituents navigate the realm of quasi-law; and in which courts seek to protect grandly stated individual rights of their own formulation through their own pronouncements—pronouncements that, because of their quasi-legal character, cannot provide individuals with the rules of action they need to guide and protect their everyday conduct.

Under this new dispensation, the people may see themselves as in some sense free. They will continue to be allowed to vote, to sue, and to complain to public functionaries in defense of their "rights." But there will be no stable rules on which to rely. And voting, a rather abstract right at its best, will come to resemble more and more a combination popularity contest and plebiscite, with the actual machinery and practices of self-government relegated to the bureaucratic process.

Reconsidering the Social Order

None of this is to say that we are somehow doomed to descend into lawless tyranny. It is to say that to reform our constitutional order we first must reform our understanding of that order. And a constitutional order depends in significant measure upon the social and cultural order on which it sits. The manner in which we interpret and apply our constitution—written and unwritten—depends in large measure on how we perceive the goals of our society and the role of a constitution and law more generally in securing those goals. Sadly, for generations now Americans have seen their society and their goals through a set of myths and through misunderstandings of their own character and of the nature of society itself.

The Progressive vision of society, to take one central example, for many decades has been seen as collectivist in nature and intent. That is, devoted as it is to restructuring social institutions, Progressivism has been seen by its opponents as intent on lessening the role and scope of autonomy set aside for individuals in favor of an activist state. But this view misses the central goal of Progressivism, at least as justified and developed from the New Deal onward. That goal is to provide individuals with the conditions necessary to achieve full autonomy.

It is true that an active government may be designed to collectivize all persons within its jurisdiction. Whether emanating from the left or the right side of the political spectrum, such a government would take control over (if not title to) the economic means of production, moral and religious authority, and social discourse, as well as political organization. Whatever the nature of the promised utopia, and however much it is claimed that the citizens will enjoy a new freedom in that far-off paradise, the claim to be "making free" a people under such conditions is disingenuous. But in the United States, and throughout the democratic West, activist governments in recent decades have seen themselves and their programs in a very different light.

As we have pointed out, in responding to charges that he was regimenting the American citizenry, Franklin Delano Roosevelt argued that the New Deal actually was freeing people from regimentation imposed by powerful economic institutions and actors, and promised freedom from want as well as other forms of insecurity.[5] And so those with political power today (and not only Progressives) argue that government action is necessary to empower individuals to lead fully free lives. Regulation may be conceived as the means by which individual autonomy is increased through minimizing the effects of its misuse by others, and even by oneself. After all, the argument goes, one's choices may be constrained by fear of bad consequences or by irrational beliefs as well as by the threat of punishment.

The rights state may be designed with an emphasis on individual autonomy. The problem for such a vision is that it presents no coherent stopping point for regulation. Its service to individual autonomy requires constant oversight by a government looking out for concentrations of power and sources of danger potentially restricting individual choice. The government must constantly recalibrate its regulations to protect individuals from new evils, forms of discrimination, and concentrations of power. But such a regulatory tendency, while it undermines the effectiveness of the regime and even the rule of law, remains focused on maximizing individual autonomy.

It is in this context that we can better understand the social vision at the root of the commanding constitution. In this vision, society is in essence a collection of individuals. This is not to say that Progressives deny the existence, or even the "constitutive" or "encumbering" importance of various institutions such as families, churches, unions, various social and economic clubs, or local political groups. But they see the ideal national association as a collection of more or less fully formed individuals joined by common interests and the ultimate expression of human dignity as the exercise of individual choice.[6] Precisely because associations may influence and restrict the autonomy and life choices of individuals, then, an individualist society requires a higher, more inclusive association designed to protect individuals from them, namely, the central government.

A Progressive/individualist society may be seen as a geographical unit within the jurisdiction of a particular government that has as its duty the protection of that unit from outside forces and the protection of individuals within the society from various aggregations of power, whether rooted in race, class, ethnicity, sex, sexual orientation, family structure, or economic power. Debates, then, will concern how much power the central state should have to reconstruct these associations to make them more open to various types of individuals (and their choices) and how to limit associations' capacity to take collective action in the public square.

Current left versus right debates tend to center on which associations to subject to how much reconstitution in the name of what types of individual rights. Those considered on the political right tend to be more restrictive in their list of essential categories of individuals or characteristics that must be included and more suspicious of governmental methods; there is here a particular desire that the government establish market-based mechanisms regulated so as to provide desired outcomes. Those considered on the left tend to emphasize equality more, to be more demanding regarding who must be included in all groups, more accepting of governmental control over economic exchanges, and intolerant of "irrational" or intolerant individual choices. Yet left and right share a vision of the central government as shaper of other institutions in service to individual autonomy.

The civic republican challenge to procedural liberalism stems from the intrinsic contradictions of a system devoted to protecting individuals by interfering with those individuals' natural inclination to form restrictive associations. As the administrative procedures of an increasingly commanding government come to shape more and more of subjects' lives, the civic republican charges that this power should be used to achieve justice rather than mere neutrality becomes increasingly relevant. But its effect has not been to undermine procedural liberalism. Instead, civic republicanism has democratized and juridicized liberalism. Emphasizing the need for substantive equality of honor and status as well as life opportunities, civic republicanism has subjected an increasing proportion of actions, whether by governments, associations, or persons, to claims of right to be adjudicated in some form of court.[7]

Of course, as civic republicans have stated, the demands of law as justice cannot be met within the limitations of procedural liberalism; a neutral state is not capable of instantiating justice through law. But this, too, is merely an extension of the logic of Progressivism. Progressives' administrative process itself lacks essential elements of the rule of law. Civic republicanism merely emphasizes the role of law as justice in empowering rulers to "do the right thing" in reshaping society and norms of individual conduct. The problem is that constitutionalism and the rule of law, both of which are necessary for development of any stable social order capable of maintaining even minimal justice, are undermined by law as justice. Pursuit of full, substantive justice through governmental directives involves too much oversight and too much administrative discretion for law to remain viable over the long run. It ends in arbitrary power.

The Reality of American Associational Pluralism

Unseen amidst the storm and stress of contemporary conflicts over the status of particular rights and the proper role of the state in vindicating individual autonomy has been an appreciation for the common conceptual problem at their root. The problem in brief is the myth of American individualism. Individualism is not, in practice, a coherent point of view; it cannot sustain a working political association. Neither is individualism the heart, as it is so often portrayed, of American culture.

All societies consist of various collections of thick constitutive associations rooted in familial, religious, professional, economic, and other attachments. These associations may exist in tension with political associations that seek to maintain public peace through some set of limitations on associational powers. Alternatively, these associations may be made subservient to a political center that structures and/or destroys them according to some common set of principles—including, of course, the principle of individual autonomy. Any such principle, if read into the law as a definition of justice to which any "true" law conforms, will produce a commanding constitution and, over time, undermine the rule of law. This is particularly true of individualism in the United States.

Americans have come to see individualism as deeply rooted in our society, if not in human nature itself. But this individualism, to the extent it is real, is as much a product as a cause of recent political realities. Tocqueville, of course, warned of the dangers of an individualism that would separate Americans from one another, insulating them from public life as they followed narrower, private pursuits. But he saw this tendency as one that was kept in check by the associational life fostered by administrative decentralization. In this light Progressivism may be seen as more a cause of than a correction to contemporary social atomism because its administrative structures have crowded out of the public square the associations in which most Americans once lived most of their lives. Any effective long-term response to our current dilemma, then, must begin by crystallizing elements in our lived tradition that belie the individualist myth, opening the way to build on practices in keeping with a thicker, more embedded and associational society.

The associational vision at the heart of the Framers' mediating Constitution is fundamentally different from that of individualism. It sees society as a collection of associations including families, unions, clubs, schools, and religious groups, and—as a number of important groups among many—various forms of government. Persons certainly exist in such a society, and remain its most essential component. But they do not exist as mere free-floating monads. Rather, each person is a member of a variety of overlapping associations that vie for the attention of persons (e.g., various clubs), or include them as integral parts of themselves (e.g., families). In either instance, they are essential for the development and the very survival of persons as full human beings.

In this context, a mediating constitution distributes and controls power within the government but is more concerned to keep the peace among fundamental associations than to impose a particular order on them. The government itself may be relatively active or passive, depending on the powers given to it. But those powers will be aimed at protecting associations from improper conduct on the part of other associations, fostering associational cooperation, and preventing violations of procedural rights, including the procedural rights of individual persons.

The individualist myth is at odds with the conception of persons and social order dominant in the founding era. It also contradicts the sociability at the core of every person's (and every society's) normative reality. We offer here the barest sketch of a large and growing literature showing the extent to which our society has been constituted not by "rugged individualists" but by persons acting within and among strong, active associations.

Most readers are aware of Tocqueville's description of the character of Americans and their public life. A summary passage may suffice here:

> The political associations that exist in the United States are only a single feature in the midst of the immense assemblage of associations in that country. Americans of all ages, all conditions, and all dispositions constantly form associations. They have not only commercial and manufacturing companies, in which all take part, but associations of a thousand other kinds, religious, moral, serious, futile, general or restricted, enormous or diminutive. The Americans make associations to give

entertainments, to found seminaries, to build inns, to construct churches, to diffuse books, to send missionaries to the antipodes; in this manner they found hospitals, prisons, and schools. If it is proposed to inculcate some truth or to foster some feeling by the encouragement of a great example, they form a society. Wherever at the head of some new undertaking you see the government in France, or a man of rank in England, in the United States you will be sure to find an association.[8]

The vast literature analyzing, bemoaning, and seeking reasons behind the decline in associational life in the United States should not blind us to its reality in former times and throughout much of our history (even, to an extent too little recognized, up until today).[9] Reasons for this concern are many and generally rooted in the determination, attributable to Tocqueville himself, that associations constitute a necessary bulwark against tyranny, especially in times of increasing equality.[10] Isolated individuals facing a commanding state must bow to power where associations may resist and potentially reach reasonable accommodations.

The role of associations in forming the character of individual persons and in bringing them together to achieve particular ends and forge a corporate identity necessary for a vibrant public life is too often lost or seen as irrelevant to the political concerns involved in the building of the American administrative state.[11] But it is important to note that this associational personality was central to the constitutional culture that produced the American republic.

At the political and constitutional level, Donald Lutz, among others, has shown the continuity of American traditions stemming from the Calvinist church covenants by which groups of dissenters in early modern England joined in seeking to protect their way of life in the face of official Anglican intolerance. These agreements bound members together in religious, social, and economic life. They also set up structures for internal self-government that were transplanted more or less directly to the new world. In addition to its technical, textual, and legal origins in preceding documents and practices, then, the Framers' Constitution had a spiritual and normative patrimony stretching back through religious, social compacts to church covenants.[12]

At a more cultural level, Barry Alan Shain has shown the deep communitarianism of American colonial communities. Intrusive family, church, and local political and social structures inculcated a reformed Protestant virtue ethic. Their members internalized conceptions of liberty and the ends of public life that supported a latent federalism in which close-knit local communities formed larger, thinner associations in limited ways for limited purposes.[13]

While individualism was a part of the American character, it never was a dominant part of that character. As David Hackett Fischer has shown, colonists differed significantly, according to their geographic origins, in their folkways and character traits. Most colonists were significantly communitarian, although some "warrior culture" colonists from the English-Scottish borderlands brought with them individualistic habits requiring communal responses from other groups, even as they moved off into less settled territories. Fischer shows the persistence of folkways within the varying communities throughout the American colonies, and their instantiation in everything from settlement patterns to religious beliefs to customs regarding death. Particular persons were formed within communal traditions and ways of life. And Fischer shows that early folkways have endured in American regional cultures.[14]

Strong local traditions persisted for many decades in the United States and fostered vigorous self-government. William Novak has shown the great extent of local concern and regulation for the common good. Local governments were involved in protecting the lives and welfare of the people through common law methods and local ordinances—including fire regulations, sanitary codes, inspection and licensing rules, and morals regulations regarding prostitution and drunkenness—until late in the nineteenth century. It was at this time that ideological programs, in particular the drive for national prohibition, began taking attention and power away from the locality.[15]

Ironically, the very strength of local communities in the American colonies contributed to their downfall under the pressures of administrative centralization. Founding communities had been just that—small, tight-knit groups intent on pursuing common goals and a common way of life. These colonial groups even established a protofederalist system as, for example, when communities in what is now Connecticut set up, on their own, a local confederacy of communities to better secure limited goals such as their common defense.[16] But this very formative strength and importance left municipalities relatively unprotected in facing centralizing tendencies because Americans almost never felt the need to seek municipal charters, and this, in turn, caused the atrophy of the legal rights and customs that otherwise would have defended local corporate groups against state-instituted drives toward centralization.[17] The decline of local self-government was only exacerbated by court opinions beginning in the late nineteenth century insisting on construction of a "national market" in the area of commercial regulation, resulting in the reconstruction of various local and state institutions to make them more favorable to a supposedly laissez-faire nationalist model.

Myths of the open frontier West certainly promoted a more individualistic ethos. The reality was more mixed, with settlements often taking shape in and through communities and frontier towns seeking the security of common ties as protection from "individualistic" outliers.[18] And the self-perception of Americans as individualists had a dark side. This myth was part and parcel of the hostility toward Irish immigrants and their supposed loyalty to a "foreign prince" in the person of the pope—an attitude with significant consequences for localism and religious liberty.[19] Moreover, as Richard Hofstadter pointed out long ago, Progressivism in significant measure grew out of the mugwump reaction to immigrants and other communitarian forces. Repelled by ethnic politics and various foreign customs, Progressives sought to inculcate greater "Americanism" in public life, in part through programs of national action, efficiency, and discipline. The goal was a national, secularizing WASP culture.[20] That goal has not been achieved, but clearly our unwritten constitution has been altered and atomized in the attempt.

Progressive Atomism and the Inevitable Quest for Community

In his groundbreaking book *The Quest for Community*, sociologist Robert Nisbet notes that people cannot exist as mere individuals. Whatever their race, class, religion, or country of origin, people gravitate toward others in pursuit of friendship and recognition. Historically, it has been in the family, religious congregation, and local community that people have found the social connections they need to lead meaningful lives. But, lacking such associations, they will seek ersatz communities, including within ideological structures (including Marxism and fascism, but also less overtly totalitarian systems) that bring them together in grand projects centered on state action.[21]

For decades, Progressive reforms and policies have pushed Americans to act more on abstract principle than on custom and practical virtue in ordering their social lives and to look to the federal government more than local associations as the guarantor of their well-being. Basic social institutions like family, church, and local associations have been subjected to reformative governmental actions in the name of freedom, defined as individual autonomy. The individual increasingly has been seen as the true and only building block of society, whose integrity was to be protected through social policies protecting it from harm as its will was gauged and, where a majority general will was found, put into action.

As Nisbet notes, already in the first half of the twentieth century increasing focus on individual autonomy and security as goods to be provided by the national government undermined more local associations by taking from them their practical reasons to exist. But people never did become mere individuals. Ethnic ties, for example, never fully disappeared, and the drive for desegregation and civil rights for racial minorities did not end with a call to equal treatment and meritocracy. Indeed, it has become increasingly clear that merit itself is and must be in significant part a social construct for the simple reason that societies' goals and requirements differ, leading them to value different merits. Thus, conflict over the distribution of goods cannot be finally settled.

Through its national pursuit of politicized justice in all aspects of society, the federal government has taken into itself the means and powers of other associations. It has not achieved its goals, but it has succeeded in making itself the locus of debate and competition. Where before people would pursue various goods in myriad cultural, social, and political contexts, for many today national politics and structures have become the primary source of benefits and the primary focus of conflict. This trend has heightened tensions and ideological conflict while undermining the ability of the federal government to maintain domestic tranquility and the basic elements of ordered liberty.

The commanding constitution's model is of individuals acting upon, and being acted upon by, the central state. The constitution would set the outlines of acceptable, just conduct, and reorder society to meet them. Individuals would be served by being freed from unjust associations to pursue their own desires and vocations in safety. This model never was and never can be accurate because people congregate, forming associations of one kind or another, no matter how hard the federal government may make it for those associations to govern themselves.

The civic republican turn in law and politics rests on recognition of people's social nature, and on an attempt to harness this communalism for political ends. In accordance with this approach, individuals have been encouraged to judge the most basic social institutions in light of abstract and idealized theories of justice and equality. Likewise, law no longer aims to free individuals from their communities, but rather to reorder those communities to make them more just by civic republican standards.

What all this means, of course, is that people within their communities must look to the central state, whether through its legal or its administrative structures, in pursuit of support and recognition so that they and their communities may survive and flourish. No longer mediating among associations, the federal government seeks to command associations to take certain shapes and stances. But people's associations, whether rooted in race, ethnicity, or economic activity, are not mere pliant creatures to be acted upon; where they survive they seek to make the government their patrons in concrete fashion, winning subsidies, official recognition, and official action against those they believe threaten their own rights and interests.[22]

We have seen in Chapter 2 how the attempt to make the central state responsible for providing a good life to its citizens through provision of material goods has produced tyranny and anarchy in various postcolonial societies. Adding recognition and dignity to the list of goods to be provided by the state exacerbates the problems of commanding constitutionalism. Disagreements over the nature and requirements of human dignity delegitimize state actions in this area, at least among sizeable dissenting groups.[23] The postcolonial model of a central government promising to provide all good things to the people only to become a battleground among warring factions and the plaything of powerful political figures, thereby losing its capacity to govern, should greatly concern anyone examining the trajectory of American public law and policy.

Practical Constitutional Virtue

Our cultural unwritten constitution has been damaged by decades of conflict and abuse. It will not be restored through adoption of one or even several reforms. Nor will our operational constitution be "fixed" through even fundamental changes in formal law. Lacking an appropriate constitutional morality, those who govern will continue to do so through quasi-law, with all the consequences attendant thereto.

What is required, then, is a renewal of culture and renewed recognition, among those in and out of government alike, of the duties of officeholders. Such renewal is, of course, the work of decades. What is more, it entails changes in conduct before changes in form can take hold. As we noted in our introduction, renewal would entail specific actions responding to changing circumstances in a fashion designed not to maintain the current, failing system but rather to bring a transition back to a smaller, better organized federal government capable of ruling under law.

Rather than a specific formal reform, then, Americans need to develop a consistent opposition to further centralization of power, regardless of how beneficial or even necessary a particular program may seem. Rather than "open up" the federal government to participation by nongovernmental associations (be they political, economic, ethnic, or religious in form), we must close off the means of access for outside actors to affect government conduct outside the political process, even as we cut off administrators' ability to shape the character of civil associations through the use of discretionary power.

Among possible vehicles for such a program would be an overhaul of current administrative rulemaking procedures not in their detail but in their fundamental nature. Where today agencies almost always make rules "informally," through a largely self-directed "notice and comment" procedure, the original Administrative Procedure Act seemed to call for formal rulemaking, including evidentiary hearings, in almost all instances. A return to this methodology through legislative direction would do much to restore discipline to the bureaucratic process and remind all its participants that regulating industries, civil associations, and individual persons is serious business, requiring care and clear recognition of statutory requirements.

Like most reforms, however, overhauling administrative rulemaking would be possible only after members of Congress in particular develop new habits and convictions. Certain things need to be done: Congress must stop delegating lawmaking authority. It must stop passing massive omnibus spending bills to "keep the government running" by ceding its responsibility not just to set priorities but to make law, including laws determining just how federal monies will be spent. Presidents must veto legislation they believe will damage the constitutional order, including legislation that is, in fact, a bundle of vague directives and budgetary line items masquerading as law. Presidents must not use the stroke of their pens to make the quasi-laws of the land. And judges must let go of the delusion that they are philosophers, instead embracing their crucial role in adjudicating under law, looking to the methodologies of history and humble grammar in interpreting the laws that must be their masters if they are to do their duty.

As always in a republic, the focus of reform must be in the legislature. Only a legislature filled with people who understand their own primary role in making law and their responsibility to make that law according to the formal dictates of the Constitution will show the fortitude and perseverance necessary to institute real reforms. Development of such habits and convictions would have to take place over time, in part through much less systemic acts aimed at curbing the size and scope of our federal government, not because good things should not be done but because they should be done by the more fundamental associations of our society, which can act through personal interaction outside law without endangering (indeed, while supporting) liberty. We must again pursue goods through what Vincent Ostrom termed democratic rather than our current monarchical administration.

The Limits of Law and the Promise of Associational Pluralism

As there is no simple going back to an older operational constitution, given the significant changes in our unwritten constitution, it would be difficult to argue that the unwritten constitution itself is open to easy reform. However, we submit that there are valuable lessons to be drawn from the last several decades regarding the relationship between ideology and law, and between administrative centralization and social structure. It seems clear to us that the drive for a national "community" devoted to a specific conception of justice embodied in a specific legal code undermines the institutions, beliefs, and practices necessary for ordered liberty and the rule of law.

Both the mediating constitution and the associational vision supporting it have their roots deep in historical practice. We submit that these roots remain vital and their outgrowths available today. Individualism always has been more ideology than historical fact. The natural drive for self-assertion, like all natural drives, may be taken to its extreme and so undermine the balancing forces of community and the common good. Incorporated into law and constitutionalism, this drive has undermined the common rules necessary for peace, order, and the possibility of freedom and virtue. But persons remain sociable beings inclined to form associations when there is some purpose to doing so.[24]

What, then, is to be done? More important than any particular policy is the attitude toward law and policy making that must be recaptured. A concern to do no further harm to what is left of local and associational life—of which America retains far more than is generally acknowledged—is of primary importance. We also must reintroduce into public debates a general concern that policies, including those emanating from the bench, be formulated and evaluated according to their impact on local and associational self-government. Both these attitudes require rejection of the false neutrality of Rawlsian "public reason." As important, they require a concern to renew common understanding and valuation of the self-restraining virtue associated with law-abidingness and constitutional morality. This last virtue is of primary importance, for with it comes renewed understanding of the limits of law and its capacity to do good.

We understand and sympathize with the desire to end various forms of human suffering in the quickest, most efficient manner possible. When one sees the effects of poverty, discrimination, and other lamentable events and conduct, one naturally wants to do away with them, preferably for good. But the question is not whether the evil we see is indeed an evil. The question is how best we may address that evil, given our limited resources, the limited power of the tools we have at hand, and the damage rash, overreaching actions may do to the social order the most vulnerable among us rely upon most for their well-being.

Law has come to be seen as a tool for the reconstruction of society in a manner intended to address, if not eliminate, social ills. The problem is that the "tool" of law is not, in fact, a tool in any meaningful, practical sense. Laws are not discrete objects capable of achieving narrowly defined ends. Law rests on common, cultural assumptions relating to our common identities, the legitimacy of various associations, and even our duties to one another. If laws are aimed at undermining or reshaping such assumptions, there will be conflict—possibly violent conflict—and a loss of common feeling. While such a price may be worth paying in some circumstances, it should not be understated in debating whether and especially how to act.

The structure of our current regime of quasi-law attests to the fact that law simply is not capable of remolding society to fit our desires. Persons and associations react to laws. They or their members seek to overcome or avoid laws that impede their access to desired ends. The result is new, unforeseen, and even harmful institutional arrangements. Lawmakers in turn may seek to break down these arrangements, moving toward the use of arbitrary power as they reduce the diversity of institutional and associational opportunities for the development of human personalities.

Laws are capable of allowing for the formation of associations that can better address the needs of their members and serve the public good. The speed and efficiency with which social problems will be addressed by such means will disappoint many observers. But they have the benefit of being rooted in the social consensus necessary for ameliorating abuses without spawning large-scale conflict. They also better serve to maintain the mediating structures necessary to moderate among disputing parties, encourage our nobler, social instincts, cabin power, and help maintain balance in society.

Recognition of the intrinsic limits of law's efficacy, hence its proper scope, may be part of a resuscitation of more natural, social institutions and the fellow feeling necessary to foster genuine public spirit and private compassion. One might draw from this volume the conclusion that the life of public virtue is impossible in the extended republic—that a nation must be a collection of strangers, governed only by mechanisms and calculations of interest rather than by virtuous citizens. This is not our conclusion. Virtue remains essential within the compound, federal republic. But that virtue, the habits and duties necessary to maintain a stable, just, and peaceful order among the associations making up our public life, is different from the virtues of local life. As the charity of a poor person must of necessity be more limited (though if anything more virtuous) than that of the rich person, so the virtue of a public actor on the national stage must be different, more limited, and in particular more restrained than that of one who acts within one's own locality.

Like all associations, that of the national government has particular goods toward which its members must act if they are to fulfill their duties. The ends of a national government are more abstract and limited than the ends of more local associations. The virtues of actors in this sphere, therefore, are more characterized by restraint, deliberation, and procedural propriety than by energy and determination.

The exception here truly does prove the rule. For it is in foreign policy, where action by a single, energetic political actor is most necessary, that we have seen the greatest accretion of power to the center, and the greatest danger to self-government. We should not take that limited sphere within which dangerous power must be suffered to exist (though not embraced) as our national model. It would be better for us to recur to a public morality in which national leaders are praised for refusing power rather than for seizing it, for restraining themselves rather than asserting themselves, for respecting the limits of tradition rather than "innovating" at the expense of the people's reasonable expectations.

The results would not be an impoverished national public sphere, but rather a regeneration of various smaller, more local spheres in which more of us may find fulfilment. The freedom of particular persons, as well as the development of their fuller humanity, would be fostered within a constitutional order recognizing the claims to self-government of a multiplicity of associationss, in a variety of which particular persons may participate at various times in their lives—some of them fully immersive, and some not. A richer life is available to most of us at the local level if we are willing to disempower the center from usurping the roles of our fundamental associations. Obviously, any renewal of our culture will be long and painful in coming; what took a few generations to tear down through a combination of centralized planning (much of it well-intentioned) and ideological hostility from both sides of the political spectrum cannot quickly or easily be rebuilt. Only the virtue of restraint, practiced at the center of power, can foster the rule of law and the local self-government necessary for us to join with our fellows in forming our own and our common characters in the associations in which persons by nature live.

It may be the case that radical reforms become necessary to reconstitute proper political authority and the rule of law in the United States. It may be that no nation of over three hundred million people can be governed so as to maintain ordered liberty. If this is true, then the "nation" must become some form of loose confederation eschewing attempts to regularize, let alone standardize, incomes or ways of life, or it must split into several nations, or lose its freedom. But such decisions can be made wisely only after renewing our understanding of what government is, what law is, and what each can accomplish within a political community that recognizes the priority of social over political life.

Notes

Introduction

1. Akhil Reed Amar, *America's Unwritten Constitution: The Precedents and Principles We Live By* (New York: Basic Books, 2012), xi.
2. Ibid.
3. The most telling critique of the empirical accuracy and logical consistency of this theory of moral abstraction remains Keith E. Whittington, "Dworkin's 'Originalism': The Role of Intentions in Constitutional Interpretation," 62 *Review of Politics* 197 (2000).
4. Amar, *America's Unwritten Constitution*, 245, 247.
5. Ibid. (emphasis in original).
6. Ibid., 248, 451.
7. Ibid., ix.
8. Ibid., 238–239.
9. We note that Amar ignores a vast literature examining the language and intent of that amendment, literature that demonstrates that the amendment was drafted as a limited grant of power, predominantly to Congress rather than the courts, providing procedural protections aimed specifically at helping freed slaves achieve equality before the law, most importantly through access to the courts. Alas, such access was denied through unlawful violence, political gamesmanship, and judicial decisions ignoring the text and historical context of the amendment. The classic text here is Raoul Berger, *Government by Judiciary: The Transformation of the Fourteenth Amendment* (Cambridge, MA: Harvard University Press, 1977).
10. Amar, *America's Unwritten Constitution*, 84, 81.

11. See, for example, Erwin Chemerinsky and Samuel Kleiner, "Obama Has the Law—and Reagan—on His Side on Immigration," *New Republic,* November 18, 2014, http://www.newrepublic.com/article/120328/obama -immigration-executive-action-why-it-will-be-legal.

12. Aristotle, *Nicomachean Ethics,* trans. Terence Irwin, 2nd ed. (Indianapolis, IN: Hackett, 1999), 23–24.

13. Russell Kirk, *Enemies of the Permanent Things* (New Rochelle, NY: Arlington House, 1969), 168. Alexis de Tocqueville referred to much the same phenomenon in his discussion of mores or "habits of the heart" and their cultural roots in volume 2 of *Democracy in America,* though one should not overlook the equally important discussion of physical, social, and legal characteristics on Americans' society and ability to maintain free government. Alexis de Tocqueville, *Democracy in America,* ed. Phillips Bradley (New York: Vintage, 1990).

14. Those skeptical of this conception of an unwritten constitution might consider the failures of the 1935 constitution of the Philippines. Closely patterned on the American Constitution, this governing document failed to provide a pattern of effective governance. Philippine political society, being marked by ethnic, religious, and political conflict, with a hybrid indigenous, Spanish, and American legal and cultural heritage, a physical makeup as an island archipelago, and a plethora of postcolonial resent-ments, was not accepting of the demands imposed by a complex, limiting constitution like that of the United States. See, for example, Stanley Karnow, *In Our Image: America's Empire in the Philippines* (New York: Ballantine, 1989). We take up a discussion of constitutionalism in post-colonial societies in Chapter 2.

15. Certainly not a common term, "constitutional morality" has appeared in Clinton Rossiter, *The American Presidency* (New York: Harcourt, Brace and World, 1956), and in Willmoore Kendall and George W. Carey, *The Basic Symbols of the American Political Tradition* (Washington, DC: Catholic University of America Press, 1995).

16. Vincent Ostrom, *The Intellectual Crisis in American Public Administration* (Montgomery: University of Alabama Press, 1973).

17. Ibid., 88–89.

18. Ibid., 34.

19. Ibid., 133.

20. Carl J. Friedrich, *Constitutional Government and Democracy* (New York: Little, Brown, 1941).

21. John Rawls, *A Theory of Justice* (Cambridge, MA: Harvard University Press, 1971).

22. Richard A. Epstein, *The Classical Liberal Constitution* (Cambridge, MA: Harvard University Press, 2014).

23. Cass R. Sunstein, *Designing Democracy: What Constitutions Do* (Oxford: Oxford University Press, 2002).

Chapter 1: The Rule of Law

1. See our discussion of Michael J. Sandel, below, and of Louis Michael Seidman in Chapter 2.

2. "Magna Charta," article 39, in *The American Republic: Primary Sources,* ed. Bruce P. Frohnen (Indianapolis, IN: Liberty Fund, 2002), 145. "Disseized" refers to confiscation of lands.

3. Stephen E. Gottlieb, Brian H. Bix, Timothy D. Lytton, and Robin L. West, *Jurisprudence Cases and Materials: An Introduction to the Philosophy of Law and Its Applications,* 2nd ed. (Dayton, OH: LexisNexis, 2001), chapter 1.

4. Bruce P. Frohnen, "The One and the Many: Individual Rights, Corporate Rights and the Diversity of Groups," 107 *West Virginia Law Review* 789 (2005), 817–818.

5. Lois Schwoerer, *The Declaration of Rights, 1689* (Baltimore, MD: Johns Hopkins University Press, 1981), 9–18.

6. For current purposes we leave aside developments of the notion of "King in Parliament," with its historically important bringing together of executive and legislative roles in the making of law, with the effective role of the executive being transferred, over time, from monarch to prime minister.

7. Ronald A. Cass, *The Rule of Law in America* (Baltimore, MD: Johns Hopkins University Press, 2001), xi: "In a fundamentally just society, the rule of law serves to channel decision making in attractive ways, to make decisions more predictable, and to increase the prospects for fair administration of public power." H. L. A. Hart, "Positivism and the Separation of Laws and Morals," 71 *Harvard Law Review* 593 (1958), 604: "The relationship is vertical between the commanders or authors of the law conceived of as essentially outside the law and those who are commanded and subject to the law. . . . [R]ules provide facilities for the realization of wishes and choices. They do not say (like commands) 'do this exercise whether you wish it or not,' but rather 'if you wish to do this, here is the way to do it.' Under these rules we exercise power, make claims, and assert rights."

8. Alexander Hamilton, John Jay, and James Madison, *The Federalist,* ed. George W. Carey and James McClellan (Indianapolis, IN: Liberty Fund, 2000), no. 47 (Madison), 257–258 (emphasis in original).

9. We will argue below, however, that the ability to enact unjust laws is limited by what Lon Fuller terms law's "internal morality" as well as by political and structural limitations on the power to legislate. Lon L. Fuller, *The Morality of Law* (New Haven, CT: Yale University Press, 1964).

10. Russell Kirk, *The Roots of American Order* (Wilmington, DE: Intercollegiate Studies Institute, 2003), 4–6.

11. Jeremy Bentham, *Fragment on Government* (Cambridge: Cambridge University Press, 1988).

12. H. L. A. Hart, *The Concept of Law*, 2nd ed. (New York: Clarendon Press, 1997), 6.

13. Ibid., 19–20.

14. Ibid., 83, 206–207.

15. Ibid., 94–95, 60–61.

16. Ibid., 619–620.

17. Ibid., 617, 619.

18. H. L. A. Hart, *Law, Liberty, and Morality* (Stanford, CA: Stanford University Press, 1963), 19.

19. H. L. A. Hart, Book Review 78 *Harvard Law Review* 1281 (1965) 1291 (reviewing Lon Fuller, *The Morality of Law* (1964).

20. Hart, "Positivism and the Separation of Laws and Morals," 624, 618.

21. Hart, *Concept of Law*, 158, 207.

22. Hart, *Morality of the Criminal Law*, 1291.

23. Hart, "Positivism and the Separation of Laws and Morals," 623–624.

24. We note Hart's statement that a generalized refusal on the part of judges to abide by the rule of recognition "would be treated by a preponderant majority as a subject of serious criticism and as a wrong" and would constitute a change of regime. Hart, *Concept of Law*, 146.

25. Ibid., 116.

26. H. L. A. Hart, *Punishment and Responsibility: Essays in the Philosophy of Law*, 2nd ed. (New York: Oxford University Press, 2008), 1017, 1023.

27. Hart, *Concept of Law*, 273.

28. Hart, "Positivism and the Separation of Laws and Morals," 618.

29. Hart, *Law, Liberty, and Morality*, 20–22.

30. Hart, *Concept of Law*, 162.

31. Ibid., 171–172.

32. Ibid., 171.

33. We discuss legitimacy issues in the modern administrative state in Chapter 6.

34. See, for example, Brian Tamanaha, *On the Rule of Law: History, Politics, Theory* (Cambridge: Cambridge University Press, 2004), 102–104.

35. Charles Taylor, *The Ethics of Authenticity* (Cambridge, MA: Harvard University Press, 1992), 38–39.
36. Lynn E. Wardle, "Sexual Orientation: Law and Policy: Parenthood and the Limits of Adult Autonomy," 24 *St. Louis University Public Law Review* 169 (2005), 171.
37. Planned Parenthood v. Casey, 505 U.S. 833 (1992), 851.
38. Academics, too, insist on the link between autonomy and human dignity; Michael Neumann, for example, insists on the necessity of privacy rights for human dignity, though he denies that this is a moral claim. See Michael Neumann, *The Rule of Law: Politicizing Ethics* (Burlington, VT: Ashgate, 2002), 56.
39. "[C]itizens' reasoning in the public forum about constitutional essentials and basic questions of justice [must be] guided by a political conception the principles and values of which all citizens can endorse." John Rawls, *Political Liberalism,* 2nd ed. (New York: Columbia University Press, 2005), 3.
40. Ibid.
41. See, for example, Ronald S. Beiner, "Introduction: The Quest for a Post-liberal Public Philosophy," in *Debating Democracy's Discontent,* ed. Anita L. Allen and Milton C. Regan, Jr. (Oxford: Oxford University Press, 1998), 11–12.
42. Edward C. Lyons, "Reason's Freedom and the Dialectic of Ordered Liberty," 55 *Cleveland State Law Review* 160 (2007), 181–182.
43. Ibid., 193 (emphasis in original).
44. Michael J. Sandel, *Justice: What's the Right Thing to Do?* (New York: Farrar, Straus and Giroux, 2009, 179.
45. Ibid., 261.
46. Ibid., 264, 267.
47. Ibid., 204.
48. PGA Tour, Inc. v. Martin, 532 U.S. 661 (2001).
49. Sandel, *Justice,* 204.
50. Ibid., 206–207.
51. Ibid., 268.
52. Obergefell v. Hodges, 576 U.S. __ (2015).
53. Goodridge v. Dep. of Public Health, 798 N.E.2d 941 (Mass. 2003).
54. Indeed, the authors disagree among themselves concerning its legitimacy.
55. Sandel, *Justice,* 259.
56. Ibid., 189.
57. Ibid., 189–190.
58. Oliver O'Donovan and Joan Lockwood O'Donovan, eds., *From Irenaeus to Grotius: A Sourcebook in Christian Political Thought* (Grand Rapids, MI:

Wm. B. Eerdmans, 1999), 300. We can, of course, choose to pursue only wealth, physical pleasures, and the like, and so doing will make us greedy, lustful, and so on. But we are capable of acting in accordance with natural goods such as honesty, justice, and love—and are at our best when we do so. We would note that there is no necessity that any adherent of natural law accept the existence of a personal deity; one of us has no such belief yet recognizes an intrinsic structure to existence.

59. Heinrich Rommen, *Natural Law: A study in Legal and Social history and Philosophy* (Indianapolis, IN: Liberty Fund, 1998, 172.

60. William N. Eskridge, "The Marriage Cases: Reversing the Burden of Inertia in a Pluralist Constitutional Democracy," 97 *California Law Review* 1785 (2009), 1790.

61. Thomas Aquinas, *The Summa Theologiae of Saint Thomas Aquinas,* trans. Fathers of the English Dominican Province, vol. 4, *Prima Secundae,* Q. 71–114, Latin-English ed. (New York, NY: NovAntiqua, 2010), Q. 95 a. 2 co., citing Augustine, *De Gratia et Libero Arbitrio I, 5 ("non videtur esse lex, quae iusta non fuerit").*

62. Aquinas, *Summa Theologiae,* Q. 95 a. 2 co., citing Augustine, *De Gratia et Libero Arbitrio I, 5 ("non videtur esse lex, quae iusta non fuerit")* (emphasis added).

63. Ibid. *("inquantum habet de iustitia, intantum habet de virtute legis").*

64. Ibid. *("omnis lex humanitus posita intantum habet de ratione legis, inquantum a lege naturae derivatur").*

65. Ibid., Q. 96 a. 4 co. See also Rommen, who notes that it would be incorrect to see natural law as dictating a purely utilitarian weighing of costs and benefits arising from disobedience to a law. Rommen also points out that, for disobedience to be licit, the law in question must not merely be unjust as, say, a law imposing high taxes for the funding of foolish projects might be deemed unjust. Only a law that undermines the fundamental order of society is unjust in the true, full sense. Rommen, *Natural Law,* 42, 227–228.

66. Aquinas, *Summa Theologiae,* Q. 91 a. 4 co.

67. Russell Kirk, *Rights and Duties: Reflections on Our Conservative Constitution* (Dallas, TX: Spence, 1997), 132.

68. Rommen, *Natural Law,* 47.

69. Bruce P. Frohnen, "The Bases of Professional Responsibility: Pluralism and Community in Early America," 63 *George Washington Law Review* 931 (1995).

70. Harold J. Berman, *Law and Revolution: The Formation of the Western Legal Tradition* (Cambridge, MA: Harvard University Press, 1983).

71. A. W. B. Simpson, "The Common Law and Legal Theory," in *Folk Law:*

Essays in the Theory and Practice of Lex Non Scripta, vol. 1, ed. Alison Dundes Renteln and Alan Dundes (Madison: University of Wisconsin Press, 1994), 126.

72. Ibid., 123, 128.

73. Quoted in ibid., 125–126.

74. Riggs v. Palmer, 115 N.Y. 506 (1889).

75. Karl N. Llewellyn, "Remarks on the Theory of Appellate Decision and the Rules or Canons about How Statutes Are to Be Construed," 3 *Vanderbilt Law Review* 395 (1950), 401–406.

76. Antonin Scalia, *A Matter of Interpretation: Federal Courts and the Law* (Princeton, NJ: Princeton University Press, 1998), 96–97.

77. Kristen Rundle, "The Impossibility of Exterminatory Legality," 59 *University of Toronto Law Journal* 65 (2009), 65; Cass, *Rule of Law in America,* 14–15.

78. Lon L. Fuller, *The Morality of Law* (New Haven, CT: Yale University Press, 1964), 47–48.

79. Rundle puts it thus: "[T]he conception of the person implicit in legality— as a responsible agent, capable of following rules, and answerable for his defaults—does make a real moral difference to lives of those who live within the constraints of law." Rundle, "Impossibility of Exterminatory Legality," 118.

80. Fuller, *Morality of Law,* 4.

81. Ibid., 46–49.

82. Lon L. Fuller, *The Principles of Social Order: Selected Essays of Lon L. Fuller,* ed. Kenneth I. Winston (Oxford: Hart, 2001), 46.

83. Hart, *Concept of Law,* 207.

84. Hart, *Morality of the Criminal Law,* 1285–1286.

85. Hart, *Concept of Law,* 204–205; Aristotle, *Nicomachean Ethics,* trans. Terence Irwin, 2nd ed. (Indianapolis, IN: Hackett, 1999), 25.

86. Alasdair MacIntyre, *Dependent Rational Animals: Why Human Beings Need the Virtues* (Chicago: Open Court, 1999), 65–66.

87. Fuller, *Morality of Law,* 14, 32.

88. Cass, *Rule of Law in America,* xi, 19.

89. Aquinas, *Summa Theologiae,* Q. 91 a. 3 co.

90. Aristotle, *Nicomachean Ethics,* 34.

91. Fuller, *Morality of Law,* 161–162.

92. Aristotle, *Nicomachean Ethics,* 42.

93. Ibid., 118.

94. Colleen Murphy, "Lon Fuller and the Moral Value of the Rule of Law," 24 *Law and Philosophy* 239 (2005), 241.

95. Fuller, *Morality of the Law,* 39.
96. Murphy, "Lon Fuller and the Moral Value of the Rule of Law," 243.
97. Aristotle again provides a useful summary: "[W]hat is decent is just, but is not what is legally just, but a rectification of it. The reason is that all law is universal, but in some areas no universal rule can be correct; and so where a universal rule has to be made, but cannot be correct, the law chooses the [universal rule] that is usually [correct], well aware of the error being made." Aristotle, *Nicomachean Ethics,* 144–145.
98. Aquinas, *Summa Theologiae,* Q. 95 a. 4 co.
99. Tamanaha, *On the Rule of Law,* 96.
100. Arthur Schlesinger Jr., "The Inevitability of Violence," in *The Causes of the Civil War,* ed. Kenneth Stampp (New York: Touchstone, 1992), 165.
101. Rundle, "Impossibility of Exterminatory Legality," 71, 75, 96–97.
102. Murphy, "Lon Fuller and the Moral Value of the Rule of Law," 253, 257–258.
103. Fuller addresses this issue by distinguishing between the morality of aspiration (best seen in aesthetic terms, for him) and the morality of duty, for which law serves as the best analogy. Fuller, *Morality of Law,* 9–11, 15.
104. Note, for example, our discussion of the damage laws against prostitution might bring to society.
105. Bertrand de Jouvenel, *On Power: The Natural History of its Growth* (Indianapolis, IN: Liberty Fund, 1993), 350-51.

Chapter 2: Constitutions

1. Barry Nicholas and Ernest Metzger, *Introduction to Roman Law* (Oxford: Oxford University Press, 2008), 17–18. The term *constitutio* also was widely used in the early Catholic Church, and throughout the Middle Ages, to denote important documents laying down rules of worship and conduct. The term remains in use today in reference to critical papal pronouncements.
2. Günter Frankenberg, "Comparative Constitutional Law," in *The Cambridge Companion to Comparative Law,* Eds. Mauro Bussani and Ugo Mattei (Cambridge: Cambridge University Press, 2012), 171.
3. H. L. A. Hart, *The Concept of Law,* 2nd ed. (New York: Clarendon Press, 1997), 02. Alec Stone Sweet, "Constitutionalism, Legal Pluralism, and International Regimes," 16 *Indiana Journal of Global Legal Studies* 621 (2009), 625
4. Louis Michael Seidman, "Should We Have a Liberal Constitution?" 27 *Constitutional Commentary* 541 (2010).

5. Ibid., 543–544.

6. James Bryce, "The Action of Centripetal and Centrifugal Forces on Political Constitutions," in *Studies in History and Jurisprudence* (London: Oxford University Press, 1901), 231.

7. Ibid., 318. Bryce notes that Hamilton agreed with Montesquieu "that a nation's form of government ought to be fitted to it as a suit of clothes is fitted to its wearer."

8. Vincent Ostrom, *The Intellectual Crisis in American Public Administration* (Montgomery: University of Alabama Press, 1973).

9. Michael Oakeshott, *Lectures in the History of Political Thought* (Exeter, UK: Imprint Academic, 2007), 2:471.

10. Ibid., 2:483–484.

11. Ibid.

12. Richard B. Friedman, "What Is a Non-instrumental Law?," 21 *Political Science Reviewer* 85 (1992), 87–88. Friedman notes Oakeshott's schema, in which the fundamental basis for legal analysis is the assumption that individuals are defined by their capacity for choice. Given this basis, it is no surprise that Oakeshott distinguishes between voluntary, compulsory but noninstrumental, and compulsory, instrumental societies. The last, telocratic, society is one in which individuals are made to act in furtherance of state-selected goals.

13. Oakeshott, *Lectures,* 2:496.

14. See generally Bruce D. Porter, *War and the Rise of the State* (New York: Free Press, 2008).

15. Michael Oakeshott, *On Human Conduct* (Oxford: Clarendon Press, 1975), 128.

16. Oakeshott, *Lectures,* 2:484 (emphasis in original).

17. See Friedman, "What Is a Non-instrumental Law?," 97. Friedman argues that Oakeshott's definitions do not prevent the state from seeking substantive ends. For example, in outlawing arson (lighting a fire in a particular, unlawful manner), the state may be seeking to prevent deterioration of the urban core of a city, but this is categorically different from drafting citizens into a fire brigade to improve conditions there.

18. Orestes Brownson, *The American Republic: Constitution, Tendencies, and Destiny* (Rockville, MD: Manor, 2007), 103.

19. Philip A. Hamburger, "Natural Rights, Natural Law, and American Constitutions," 102 *Yale Law Journal* 907 (1993), deals with the significantly limited incorporation of morals into the American Constitution. This is not to say that there is no role for law in ameliorating harm and injustice, consistent with a society's background normative understanding.

Note, for example, Edmund Burke's *Sketch of a Negro Code,* intended
to lay out a means by which slavery in the British Caribbean might be
rendered consistent with the natural rights of all persons—including
slaves. The resulting code, as Burke indicated he knew full well, would
have put slavery on the road to extinction; see Bruce P. Frohnen,
"Multicultural Rights?," 52 *Catholic University Law Review* 39 (2003).

20. Nicholas and Metzger, *Introduction to Roman Law,* 1.
21. Ibid., 14, 15.
22. Ibid., 28.
23. Ibid.
24. Ibid., 52.
25. Bertrand de Jouvenel, *On Power* (Indianapolis, IN: Liberty Fund, 1993), 228.
26. Nicholas and Metzger, *Introduction to Roman Law,* 54–55.
27. Cicero, *De Legibus,* book 1, quoted in Jouvenel, *On Power,* 222.
28. Ibid., 342.
29. Ibid., 334.
30. Philip A. Hamburger, *Law and Judicial Duty* (Cambridge, MA: Harvard University Press, 2008), 70–71.
31. Ibid. We would not want to be seen as underestimating the importance of coronation oaths. As Brian Tamanaha notes, through these oaths monarchs "confirmed, time and again, that they were bound by the law, whether customary, positive, natural, or divine, not just admitting but enforcing the proposition that fidelity to the law was an appropriate standard against which to evaluate regal conduct. This routine helped render a self-imposed obligation into a settled general expectation." Brian Tamanaha, *On the Rule of Law: History, Politics, Theory* (Cambridge: Cambridge University Press, 2004), 22.
32. Jouvenel, *On Power,* 214–215.
33. Kenneth Pennington, *The Prince and the Law, 1200–1600: Sovereignty and Rights in the Western Legal Tradition* (Berkeley: University of California Press, 1993), 92.
34. Brian Tierney, "Hierarchy, Consent, and the Western Tradition," 15 *Political Theory* 646 (1987), 649.
35. Pennington, *Prince,* 45.
36. Bruce P. Frohnen, "The One and the Many: Individual Rights, Corporate Rights and the Diversity of Groups," 107 West Virginia Law Review 789 (2005), 820.
37. Bertrand de Jouvenel, *Sovereignty* (Indianapolis, IN: Liberty Fund, 1998), 224.
38. Ibid., 224.

39. Ibid.

40. Ibid., 225.

41. Brian Tierney, *The Crisis of Church and State, 1050–1300.* (Englewood Cliffs, NJ: Prentice-Hall, 1964), 85.

42. Ibid., 151.

43. Filippo Sabetti, "Local Roots of Constitutionalism," 33 *Perspectives on Political Science* 70 (2004). Sabetti provides an overview of a plethora of local charters establishing constitutional government in places like Sicily and binding monarchs in a manner similar to that of Magna Carta well before that charter's promulgation.

44. Bruce P. Frohnen and Kenneth L. Grasso, eds., *Rethinking Rights: Historical, Political, and Philosophical Perspectives* (Columbia: University of Missouri Press, 2009), 111.

45. Harold J. Berman, *Law and Revolution: The Formation of the Western Legal Tradition* (Cambridge, MA: Harvard University Press, 1983), 313.

46. Ibid., 205.

47. Ibid.

48. Pennington, *Prince*, 92–93.

49. Tierney, *Crisis of Church and State,* 83.

50. Rob Meens, "Politics, Mirrors of Princes and the Bible: Sins, Kings and the Well-Being of the Realm," 7 *Early Medieval Europe* 345 (1998).

51. Joseph Canning, *A History of Medieval Political Thought: 300–1450* (Boca Raton, FL: Taylor and Francis, 2006), 163.

52. Frohnen, "One and the Many," 815.

53. Pennington, *Prince*, 211.

54. George W. Carey, *The Federalist: Design for a Constitutional Republic* (Urbana: University of Illinois Press, 1994), 133.

55. Pennington, *Prince*, 187.

56. Alexis de Tocqueville, *The Old Regime and the Revolution,* trans. Alan S. Kahan, vol. 1 (Chicago: University of Chicago Press, 2004).

57. Porter, *War and the Rise of the State,* 12.

58. This mistranslation likely stems from the notion that basic laws "constitute" a political community. See, for example, James Bernard Murphy and Richard Oliver Brooks, *Aristotle and Modern Law* (Burlington, VT: Ashgate, 2003), 218.

59. Aristotle, *The Politics,* trans. Carnes Lord (Chicago: University of Chicago Press, 1984), III.1, 1274b29–38.

60. Ibid., IV.11, 1294a30–39.

61. Ibid., III.6, 1278b11–12 (emphasis in original). See also III.7, 1279a25–6 (regime and governing body "signify the same thing").

62. Giovanni Sartori, *The Theory of Democracy Revisited* (Chatham, NJ: Chatham House, 1987), 1:278.
63. Aristotle, *Politics,* IV.8, 1294a8–28.
64. Sartori, *Theory of Democracy,* 279.
65. Aristotle, *Politics,* III.3, 1276a26–31.
66. Ibid., III.9, 1280a31–45.
67. Sartori, *Theory of Democracy,* 281.
68. Ibid., 286.
69. Ibid., 285.
70. Ibid., 281, 282.
71. Ibid.
72. Alexander Hamilton, John Jay, and James Madison, *The Federalist,* ed. George W. Carey and James McClellan (Indianapolis, IN: Liberty Fund, 2000), no. 9 (Hamilton), 37.
73. Ibid., 37–38.
74. Sartori, *Theory of Democracy,* 306.
75. Ibid. (emphasis in original; citations omitted).
76. *Federalist,* no. 9 (Hamilton), 38.
77. Sartori, *Theory of Democracy,* 271, points out that the major benefit of constitutional mechanisms is to prevent rulers from carrying out any plans they might have to slaughter their (perceived or real) opponents.
78. Aristotle, *Politics,* V.8, 1307b29–35.
79. Ibid., V.8, 1307b35–1308a1–25.
80. Sweet, "Constitutionalism," 639–640.
81. Ibid., 641.
82. Daryl J. Levinson, "Parchment and Politics: The Positive Puzzle of Constitutional Commitment," 124 *Harvard Law Review* 657 (2010), 659–660.
83. Chimène I. Keitner, *The Paradoxes of Nationalism: The French Revolution and Its Meaning for Contemporary Nation Building* (Albany: State University of New York Press, 2007), 54.
84. Thomas Gold Frost, *The French Constitution of 1793* (New York: A. E. Chasmar, 1888).
85. "Declaration of the Rights of Man and of the Citizen," in *The Constitution and Other Select Documents Illustrative of the History of France, 1789–1907,* ed. Frank Maloy Anderson (New York: Russell and Russell, 1908), 59–61.
86. Ibid., 59.
87. Ibid.
88. Jean-Jacques Rousseau, *On the Social Contract,* in *On the Social Contract and Discourses* (Indianapolis, IN: Hackett, 1983), especially book 2.

89. Robespierre, quoted in Jouvenel, *On Power*, 250.
90. Ibid., 254–257.
91. Paul R. Hanson, *Contesting the French Revolution* (West Sussex, UK: Wiley-Blackwell, 2009), 174.
92. Jouvenel, *On Power*, 53.
93. Ibid., 242–243, 248.
94. Napoleon quoted in Ibid., 251. None of this is to deny the essential accuracy of Tocqueville's observation that administrative centralization under the monarchy already had undermined local liberty by the time of the Revolution. But it was the National Assembly, and only it, that could deliver the final, killing blow.
95. Louis Michael Seidman, "Let's Give Up on the Constitution," *New York Times,* December 30, 2012, A19.
96. Sweet, "Constitutionalism," 629–630.
97. Ibid., 630n31.
98. Arch Puddington, "Freedom in the World 2012: The Arab Uprisings and Their Global Repercussions," in *Freedom in the World* (Lanham, MD: Rowman and Littlefield, 2012), 28.
99. Ibid., 2. More countries registered declines than exhibited gains over the course of 2011 in political rights and civil liberties.
100. Ibid., 8. Nations listed here included The Gambia, Ethiopia, Burundi, Rwanda, and Djibouti, but political oppression also increased in Ethiopia, Uganda, and Sudan.
101. "Ethiopia Using Aid as Weapon of Oppression," *BBC News,* BBC, May 8, 2011.
102. Alayna Hamilton, "Political Oppression in Sub-Saharan Africa," *Topical Review Digest: Human Rights in Sub-Saharan Africa* (Denver, CO: University of Denver, 2012), 49, https://www.du.edu/korbel/hrhw /researchdigest/africa/PoliticalOppression.pdf.
103. Paul Collier and Anke Hoeffler, "Coup Traps: Why Does Africa Have So Many Coups d'Etat?" (paper presented at the annual meeting of the American Political Science Association, Centre for the Study of African Economies, Oxford University, August 2005), 11, http://users.ox.ac .uk/~econpco/research/pdfs/Coup-traps.pdf.
104. Sweet, "Constitutionalism," 623.
105. Constitution of the Republic of Sudan, 1998, Part I, Provision 11.
106. See, for example, Steven D. Roper, "A Comparison of East European Constitutional Rights," 5 *International Journal of Human Rights* 2 (2001), 30.
107. Frohnen and Grasso, *Rethinking Rights,* 12–16. Note we are not advo- cating for any particular policy here, in particular that nations hand over

their natural resources and/or economies to multinational corporations. We merely note that taking on the role of provider undermines any possible role as arbiter.

108. Gerald Dworkin, *The Theory and Practice of Autonomy* (Cambridge: Cambridge University Press, 1988), 164.

109. Jouvenel, *On Power*, 329.

110. Ibid., 350–351.

Chapter 3: The Framers' Constitution

1. Alexander Hamilton, John Jay, and James Madison, *The Federalist*, eds. George W. Carey and James McClellan (Indianapolis, IN: Liberty Fund, 2000), no. 10 (Madison), 44.

2. Alexander Hamilton to Marquis de Lafayette, 6 January 6, 1899, quoted in James Bryce, *Studies in History and Jurisprudence* (London: Oxford University Press, 1901), 398.

3. Thus, Publius argues in *Federalist* 39, "The first question that offers itself is, whether the general form and aspect of the government be strictly republican? It is evident that no other form would be reconcileable with the genius of the people of America; with the fundamental principles of the revolution; or with that honourable determination which animates every votary of freedom, to rest all our political experiments on the capacity of mankind for self-government. If the plan of the convention, therefore, be found to depart from the republican *character*, its advocates must abandon it as no longer defensible." *Federalist*, no. 39 (Madison), 193.

4. See, for example, James Allen Smith, *The Spirit of American Government* (New York: MacMillan, 1907). For a discussion of Smith's influence on succeeding historians, see George W. Carey, introduction to the new edition of Willmoore Kendall and George W. Carey, *The Basic Symbols of the American Political Tradition* (Washington, DC: Catholic University of America Press, 1995), x–xiii.

5. Ibid.

6. Bruce Frohnen, ed., *The American Republic: Primary Sources* (Indianapolis. IN: Liberty Fund, 2002), 189.

7. See George W. Carey, "Natural Law, Natural Rights, and the Declaration of Independence," in *Rethinking Rights: Historical, Political, and Philosophical Perspectives*, ed. Bruce P. Frohnen and Kenneth L. Grasso (Columbia: University of Missouri Press, 2009), 80.

8. *Federalist*, no. 10 (Madison), 45.

9. *Federalist,* no. 9 (Hamilton), 37.

10. See, for example, Frohnen, *American Republic,* 4–32.

11. See, for example. Edmund Burke, "Speech on Moving Resolutions for Conciliation with the Colonies," *Select Works of Edmund Burke,* ed. Francis Canavan (Indianapolis, IN: Liberty Fund, 1999), I: 221, 225–226.

12. *Federalist,* no. 39 (Madison), 194.

13. We are aware, of course, that the Founders' definition of "the people" excluded many whose consent we today would deem essential to the very definition of a republic. However, one should keep in mind that even the vaunted "direct democracies" of ancient Greece were hardly representative of all inhabitants—most of those inhabitants being disenfranchised and even enslaved under the constitutions of that place and time. Clarity of analysis requires, however, that we recognize the continuities in forms of government and their appropriate terminology, even as minimal self-awareness requires that we recognize the limits placed on our right to condemn, let alone dismiss the possibility of learning from, those whose political and other failings one day may be seen as no greater than our own. On the definition of "the people" and its importance to democratic politics and their legitimacy, see Joseph Schumpeter's classic text, *Capitalism, Socialism, and Democracy* (New York: Harper and Row, 1950), 243–247.

14. "Address of the Minority of the Pennsylvania Convention," in Frohnen, *American Republic,* 275.

15. Ibid., 276.

16. See, for example, ibid., 271.

17. *Federalist,* no. 10 (Madison), 43.

18. Ibid., 46.

19. Ibid., 45.

20. *Federalist,* no. 39 (Madison),193–199.

21. Donald Lutz, "Religious Dimensions in the Development of American Constitutionalism," 39 *Emory Law Journal* 21 (1990), 23–24 (citation omitted).

22. "Mayflower Compact," in Frohnen, *American Republic,* 11.

23. James Wilson was joined by both John Adams and Thomas Jefferson in noting people's primary loyalty to what Jefferson referred to as their "little republicks." See Bruce P. Frohnen, *The New Communitarians and the Crisis of Modern Liberalism* (Lawrence: University Press of Kansas, 1996), 218–219 and citations therein.

24. The Virginia Plan, Frohnen, *American Republic,* 231.

25. Most important here is the list in Article I, Section 8, of congressional powers, including that of funding armed forces, and also powers aimed at

providing commonality of basic commercial prerequisites such as coinage, copyright, and bankruptcy laws.

26. Alexis de Tocqueville, *Democracy in America*, ed. Phillips Bradley (New York: Vintage, 1990), 1:59.

27. Corfield v. Coryell, 4 Wash. (C.C. 3d) 6 Fed. Cas. 546, No. 3,230 C.C.E.D.Pa. (1823).

28. Assertions by the Supreme Court were made in this era to a novel supremacy, serving only to worsen the conflict, particularly given the intrinsic weakness of courts in areas of pronounced substantive disagreement. See especially Ableman v. Booth, 62 U.S. 506 (1859).

29. Tocqueville, *Democracy in America*, 1:59.

30. James Wilson, "State House Yard Speech," in *The Collected Works of James Wilson,* ed. Kermit L. Hall and Mark David Hall (Indianapolis, IN: Liberty Fund, 2007), 1: 150..

31. One useful summary of the battles over definitions of "commerce among the states" may be found in Richard A. Epstein, *The Classical Liberal Constitution* (Cambridge, MA: Harvard University Press, 2014).

32. Ibid., 150.

33. Ibid., 152–153.

34. Ibid., 158.

35. Ibid., 210.

36. Relevant developments in private law regarding corporate charters, real estate deeds, and trust instruments also show the limited purpose of the Necessary and Proper Clause, tying it to the need to grant "parties entrusted with the care of other individuals . . . sufficient power to discharge their duties, but not so much as to abuse that relationship." Epstein, *Classical Liberal,* 211. See also Philip Hamburger, *Law and Judicial Duty* (Cambridge, MA: Harvard University Press, 2008), 335n12. Hamburger argues that the clause actually was intended to be restrictive. English rulers and state governments at the time of the American Revolution had acted outside their own laws, justifying their actions on grounds of necessity. Bowing to the circumstances but concerned about the precedential value of such acts, participants in the Philadelphia Convention saw this clause as a way of "taming" necessity. The Necessary and Proper Clause, while leaving "Congress, like Parliament" with "absolute discretion as to what" in particular was necessary, nonetheless obliged Congress to "conduct itself under the Constitution, which required that its acts done of necessity had to be within the scope of what was 'necessary and proper' for carrying out more grounded constitutional powers."

37. For such an argument, see Epstein, *Classical Liberal.*
38. *Federalist,* no. 33 (Hamilton), 161. Of course, *The Federalist* was written before the Tenth Amendment, highlighting the sense in which that amendment was needed to emphasize key conceptions intrinsic to a government of enumerated powers, but all too likely to be overlooked or minimized.
39. See, for example, *Federalist* 45: "The powers delegated by the proposed Constitution to the Federal Government are few and defined. Those which are to remain in the State Governments are numerous and indefinite. The former will be exercised principally on external objects, as war, peace negotiation, and foreign commerce . . . The powers reserved to the several states will extend to all the objects, which, in the ordinary course of affairs, concern the lives, liberties and properties of the people, and the internal order, improvement, and prosperity of the state. Regarding international relations, we deem the 'solution' sufficiently obvious as to need no explication beyond reference to the decision to have a unitary executive with significant powers in foreign and military affairs, as spelled out in Article II." *Federalist,* no. 45 (Madison), 241.
40. *Federalist,* no. 51 (Madison), 270.
41. *Federalist,* no. 47 (Madison), 249.
42. Ibid., 252 (emphasis in original).
43. See George W. Carey, *The Federalist: Design for a Constitutional Republic* (Urbana: University of Illinois Press, 1994), 36–42.
44. Charles de Secondat Montesquieu, *Spirit of the Laws,* trans. Anne M. Cohler, Basia C. Miller, and Harold Stone (Cambridge: Cambridge University Press, 1989), 157.
45. Ibid., 158.
46. Scott Gordon, *Controlling the State* (Cambridge, MA: Harvard University Press, 1999), 139.
47. *Federalist,* no. 57 (Madison), 297.
48. See, for example, ibid., no. 57, where Publius refers to the "manly spirit" necessary if members of Congress are to be kept from passing partial legislation exempting themselves and their friends.
49. The charter colonies of Connecticut and Rhode Island were content to stick with their charters as "amended" over the decades. But these charters also provided for a distinct separation of powers.
50. Georgia Constitution, quoted in *Federalist,* no. 47 (Madison), 255.
51. Mass. Const., art. I, § XXX, http://press-pubs.uchicago.edu/founders /print_documents/v1ch1s6.html.
52. Thomas Jefferson, *Notes on the State of Virginia,* quoted in *Federalist,* no. 48 (Madison), 258–259 (emphasis in original).

53. James McClellan and M. E. Bradford, *Jonathan Elliot's Debates in the Federal Convention of 1787 as Reported by James Madison* (Richmond, VA: James River Press, 1989), 3:33. All subsequent citations to the proceedings of the Philadelphia Constitutional Convention are to this volume.

54. Ibid., 299.

55. Ibid., 322, 327.

56. Ibid., 80, 60, 323, 438.

57. Ibid., 326.

58. Ibid., 113, 296–297.

59. Ibid., 297, 298.

60. Ibid., 299, 342.

61. *Federalist,* no. 48 (Madison), 257.

62. *Federalist,* no. 71 (Hamilton), 371.

63. *Federalist,* no. 48 (Madison), 256–257.

64. *Federalist,* no. 49 (Madison), 263–264.

65. *Federalist,* no. 50 (Madison), 265.

66. *Federalist,* no. 51 (Madison), 267, 268.

67. The judiciary is strengthened—i.e., placed to a great degree outside the control of the legislature or the president—through the constitutional provision that judges hold their office during "good behavior." Publius makes this clear in essays 51 and 78.

68. *Federalist,* no. 51 (Madison), 269.

69. *Federalist,* no. 73 (Hamilton), 381.

70. *Federalist,* no. 51 (Madison), 271.

71. Ibid., 268.

72. Ibid., 269.

73. *Federalist,* no. 78 (Hamilton), 403.

74. Ibid., 404.

75. Ibid., 403 (emphasis in original).

76. Ibid., 404.

77. Ibid., 405.

78. Hamburger, *Law and Judicial Duty,* 179–180.

79. Ibid., 309. See also Ibid., 101: "The duty of common law judges was to decide in accord with the law of the land, and because the constitution was the highest part of this law, the judges in the course of doing their duty had to hold unconstitutional customs and acts unlawful and void." Today's "judicial review," then, is an exaggerated form of a thin slice of the duty of a judge.

80. Ibid., 211. As Hamburger points out, the sovereign status of the monarch

precluded courts from finding his acts "unreasonable," but not from siding with his subjects when required by the law of the land.

81. Ibid., 237–239.

82. Ibid., 584–585, 397–398, 594–596.

83. Ibid., 255, 579.

84. *Federalist,* no. 78 (Hamilton), 404. Publius notes one difference, namely, that in conflicts between statutes effect is to be given to the law coming later in time, but that in instances where a constitutional provision is concerned, its status as fundamental law gives it precedence.

85. For example, in Massachusetts v. Mellon; Frothingham v. Mellon, 262 U.S. 447 (1923) the court noted: "[W]e have no power per se to review and annul acts of Congress on the ground that they are unconstitutional. That question may be considered only when the justification for some direct injury suffered or threatened, presenting a justiciable issue, is made to rest upon such an act. Then the power exercised is that of ascertaining and declaring the law applicable to the controversy. It amounts to little more than the negative power to disregard an unconstitutional enactment, which otherwise would stand in the way of the enforcement of a legal right."

86. See, for example, *Federalist,* no. 81 (Hamilton), 417–418, where Publius denies any power of the Supreme Court to decide cases on the basis of any "spirit" of the Constitution.

87. See, for example, the sources and discussion provided in Robert Lowry Clinton, *Marbury v. Madison and Judicial Review* (Lawrence: University Press of Kansas, 1989), 20–27.

88. Thomas Jefferson to Abigail Adams, September 11, 1804, quoted in *The Constitution of the United States,* 2nd ed., ed. Michael Stokes Paulsen et al. (St. Paul, MN: West, 2013), 159.

89. Jefferson to William Charles Jarvis, September 28, 1820, quoted in ibid., 160.

90. James Madison to unknown addressee, 1834, quoted in ibid., 160.

91. Jefferson to Jarvis, September 28, 1820, quoted in ibid., 160.

92. Hayburn's Case, 2 U.S. 408 (1792).

93. Marbury v. Madison, 5 U.S. 137 (1803).

94. Madison to unknown addressee, 1834 quoted in Paulsen, *Constitution,* 160.

95. In addition to the well-known reference to the court as the "least dangerous branch," note *Federalist* 81, in which Publius points out the multiple checks, impeachment most of all, on any court attempt to usurp power through "creative" interpretation.

96. Hamburger, *Law and Judicial Duty,* 148.

97. Ibid., 108–109.

98. Thomas Tillinghast, quoted in ibid., 519.
99. Again, we refrain from extensive discussion of the role of traditional religion in this calculus of virtue. We disagree among ourselves as to the necessity of religion in undergirding judicial duty over time. Most important, constitutional morality is not directly dependent on particular theological conceptions.
100. *Federalist,* no. 55 (Madison), 291.
101. Ibid.
102. George Washington to the Presbyterian ministers of Massachusetts and New Hampshire, November 2, 1789, quoted in *The Sacred Rights of Conscience,* ed. Daniel L. Dreisbach and Mark David Hall (Indianapolis, IN: Liberty Fund, 2009), 358.
103. See, for example, Akhil Reed Amar, *The Bill of Rights: Creation and Reconstruction* (New Haven, CT: Yale University Press, 2000).

Chapter 4: Progressives and Administrative Governance

1. Ralph Charles Henry Catterall, *The Second Bank of the United States* (Chicago: University of Chicago Press, 1903), 2:206.
2. Ibid., 2:333.
3. Richard Hofstadter, *The American Political Tradition and the Men Who Made It,* (New York: Alfred A. Knopf, 1973).
4. Dwight Waldo, *The Administrative State: A Study of the Political Theory of American Public Administration,* 2nd ed. (New York: Holmes and Meier, 1984). This work, including the extended preface of the second edition, offers a broad survey of administrative theory and reforms principally from Woodrow Wilson's 1887 essay on administration (see below) to the early 1980s with an eye to discovering their underlying ideology.
5. We are mindful that Progressivism was far from being a monolithic movement. However, there are strands of thought in Progressives' writings on administration, the separation of powers, and accountability of the government to the people that, as we will indicate below, remain consistent over the decades. For an overview of the underlying social transformation that led to Progressivism and its role in reshaping American institutions and politics during the initial decades of the twentieth century, see Robert H. Wiebe, *The Search for Order, 1877–1920* (New York: Hill and Wang, 1967).
6. For the Progressives this centralization involved making the voters' task manageable. This involved a number of organization reforms along with the short ballot. Above all, however, this involved increasing the authority

of the executive with clear lines of responsibility. On the degree to which centralization became a "dogma" in administrative circles, see Waldo, *Administrative State*, chapter 8, and Vincent Ostrom, *The Intellectual Crisis in American Public Administration* (Montgomery: University of Alabama Press, 1973), chapter 2.

7. For this purpose we use Mill's *Considerations on Representative Government*, in John Stuart Mill, *Three Essays*, (New York: Oxford University Press, 1975). This work ranks among the finest in the literature dealing with the perennial issues of representative government. Of particular interest in light of modern developments are Mill's treatment of the role of experts and his discussion of his proposed reforms, which were intended to elevate the intellectual and moral character of representatives. His teachings here should be understood in the broader context of his social and political thinking. See Joseph Hamburger, *John Stuart Mill on Liberty and Control* (Princeton, NJ: Princeton University Press, 1999).

8. Mill, *Considerations on Representative Government*, 213, 214.

9. Ibid., 215, 216, 217.

10. Ibid., 217, 218.

11. Ibid., 218–219.

12. Ibid. (emphasis in original).

13. Ibid.

14. Ibid.

15. Ibid., 221.

16. Ibid., 221, 222.

17. Ibid., 223, 227, 223.

18. Ibid., 225.

19. Ibid., 223, 226.

20. Ibid., 227–228.

21. Ibid., 229.

22. Ibid., 167, 168.

23. Ibid., 170, 233.

24. Ibid., 234, 236. There is something of a paradox here. Those who are most competent and capable are under the control of those who are less so, which, as we shall see, is the case in the Progressive theories. Precisely what constitutes an expert is never fully set forth, but these "skilled persons" are pictured as highly knowledgeable, dedicated, and virtuous, possessing a keen insight into the "public interest." Given this, the question arises: why shouldn't experts rule, rather than the people or an assembly representing the people? See Waldo, *Administrative State*, chapter 6: "Who Should Rule."

25. Mill, *Considerations on Representative Government*, 236, 237.
26. Ibid., 231.
27. Ibid., 241, 242.
28. Ibid.
29. Ibid., 246.
30. Ibid., 257, 260, 263, 259, 264.
31. See Ostrom, *Intellectual Crisis*, especially 75–77.
32. Woodrow Wilson, "The Study of Administration," 2 *Political Science Quarterly* 197 (June 1887), 202, 201.
33. Ibid., 200–201.
34. Ibid., 207, 208.
35. For a fine treatment of this conflict within early Progressive thought, see Peter Levine, *The New Progressive Era* (Lanham, MD: Roman and Littlefield, 2000), chapter 1.
36. Wilson, "Study of Administration," 209.
37. Ibid., 216.
38. Ibid., 216, 210.
39. Ostrom, *Intellectual Crisis*, 75–76.
40. See our discussion of Ostrom in the introduction.
41. Wilson, "Study of Administration," 217, 217.
42. Ibid., 215.
43. Ibid., 213.
44. Ibid.
45. The most frequent and basic criticism of the constitutional system by those who share the Progressive vision concerns the separation of powers. An excellent overview of the mainstream criticism and resulting reforms proposed over the years may be found in Donald L. Robinson, ed., *Reforming American Government: The Bicentennial Papers of the Committee on the Constitutional System* (Boulder, CO: Westview Press, 1985). Wilson was initially somewhat ambivalent about the handiwork of the Framers. While he suggests in his essay that the Framers may not have anticipated major difficulties, his criticism is muted. Later, of course, he is more outspoken in pointing to what he believes are serious shortcomings, the most basic directly related to the separation of powers.
46. Wilson, "Study of Administration," 218–219 (emphasis in original).
47. Ibid., 220.
48. Frank J. Goodnow, *Politics and Administration: A Study in Government* (New York: Russell and Russell, 1900), 7.
49. Ibid., 9, 18, 38, 39.
50. Ibid., 16.

51. Ibid., 72, 79.
52. Ibid., 82.
53. In this context it should be noted that Progressives were very much in favor of the city manager/council form of governance, at least for municipal governments of medium and small size. As perception matters, at this level there is a consensus on what function the government ought to perform, as well as a consensus on the need for expert administration. In this environment the politics/administration distinction could readily be drawn. On the rapid growth during the twentieth century of the council-manager plan, see Richard J. Stillman II, *The Rise of the City Manager* (Albuquerque: University of New Mexico Press, 1974).
54. Goodnow, *Politics and Administration,* 87, 88.
55. Ibid., 38.
56. As we note below, the politics/administration concept has given way to other analytical perspectives. As Dwight Waldo notes, by the early 1930s Luther Gulick had seriously questioned the worth of drawing a wall between politics and administration since policy formation and execution involved the exercise of discretion at virtually all points. Moreover, as Waldo also notes, by the late 1940s Herbert Simon had developed a new conceptual framework that focused on decision making, distinguishing between "the factual and the valuational." Waldo, *Administrative State,* xviii.
57. Goodnow, *Politics and Administration,* 15.
58. Ibid., 25.
59. Ibid., 25, 107.
60. Ibid., 111, 113.
61. Ibid., 259–260, 114, 118.
62. Ibid., 131, 133.
63. Herbert Croly, *The Promise of American Life* (New York: MacMillan, 1909).
64. Herbert Croly, *Progressive Democracy* (New York: MacMillan, 1914).
65. Croly, *Promise of American Life,* 319, 351.
66. Ibid., 319, 320.
67. Ibid., 324–325
68. Ibid., 325, 327.
69. Ibid., 328, 329.
70. Ibid., 330.
71. Ibid., 332, 338, 339.
72. Ibid., 340.
73. Croly, *Progressive Democracy,* 355, 349–350.

74. Ibid., 350, 351, 362.

75. Ibid., 353.

76. Ibid., 358, 359.

77. Ibid., 360.

78. Ibid., 361.

79. Ibid., 363, 364, 365.

80. Ibid., 368.

81. Ibid., 368, 370, 371, 373.

82. Mill would formally accord experts a wider role in the legislative process by allowing them to introduce measures that the representative assembly could either accept or reject. The measures would receive popular endorsement, and that only indirectly, once they were approved by the assembly. The experts play a more ambiguous role in Wilson and Goodnow, but Croly seems to acknowledge that they would have considerable policy input, but almost entirely through their influence on "political" supervisors, i.e., through those directly or indirectly accountable to the people. We discuss this issue more fully below.

83. Croly, *Promise of American Life*, 24, 208, 23.

84. Pendleton Herring, *Public Administration and the Public Interest* (New York: Russell and Russell, 1936), 4, 23.

85. Ibid., 18, 381, 380.

86. Ibid., 377, 380, 383.

87. Ibid., 380, 383, 398, 384.

88. Ibid., 386, 43.

89. Ibid., 24, 386.

90. Ibid., 386.

91. Ibid., 387, 395.

Chapter 5: Progressive Reformers and the Framers' Constitution

1. Herbert Croly, *The Promise of American Life* (New York: MacMillan, 1909), 320–325; Pendleton Herring, *Public Administration and the Public Interest* (New York: Russell and Russell, 1936), 383–386.

2. Notable exceptions to this view are James Burnham, *Congress and the American Tradition* (Chicago: Regnery, 1959), and Willmoore Kendall, "The Two Majorities," 4 *Midwest Journal of Political Science* 317 (1960).

3. For an overview of the theories of presidential power, see Joseph E. Kallenbach, *The American Chief Executive* (New York: Harper and Row, 1966), chapter 7. A new "unitary executive theory" emerged full blown

with the presidency of George W. Bush. This theory asserts a scope of presidential power beyond that envisioned by either Wilson or Roosevelt. See, for example, Eric A. Posner and Adrian Vermeule, *The Executive Unbound* (Oxford: Oxford University Press, 2011). A trenchant critique of this theory is found in Gene Healy, *The Cult of the Presidency* (Washington, DC: Cato Institute, 2008).

4. Woodrow Wilson, *Congressional Government* (New York: Meridian Books, 1960), 30, 31.

5. Ibid., 53. On the impact of the Civil War and in particular the civil religion set forth by Abraham Lincoln on the American constitutional tradition, see Willmoore Kendall and George W. Carey, *The Basic Symbols of the American Political Tradition* (Washington, DC: Catholic University of America Press, 1995, chapter 8.

6. Wilson, *Congressional Government*, 55, 45, 44.

7. Ibid., 48, 49.

8. Ibid., 50–51.

9. Ibid., 203.

10. Ibid., 195, 95–96.

11. Ibid., 195, 198, 206.

12. Ibid., 201.

13. Ibid., 215.

14. Woodrow Wilson, "Cabinet Government in the United States," in *Woodrow Wilson: Essential Writings and Speeches of the Scholar-President,* ed. Mario R. DiNunzio (New York: New York University Press, 2006), 218.

15. Wilson, *Congressional Government*, 23.

16. It is perhaps ironic that John C. Calhoun was among the first to see the potential of political parties to overcome the constitutional separation of powers. See his *A Disquisition on Government,* in *Union and Liberty,* ed. Ross M. Lence (Indianapolis, IN: Liberty Fund, 1992), 27–28.

17. Woodrow Wilson, *Constitutional Government in the United States* (New York: Columbia University Press, 1908), 60, 89.

18. Ibid., 60, 68.

19. Robert A. Dahl, for instance, argues that mandates for given policies cannot be derived from presidential elections. Indeed, he holds that those theories that see the president as embodying the will of the people or articulating the "general will" perpetrate a *"psuedodemocratization* of the presidency" and are detrimental to genuine democracy. Robert A. Dahl, "Myth of the Presidential Mandate," 3 *Political Science Quarterly* 355 (1990), 370 (emphasis in original).

20. Fred I. Greenstein, "Change and Continuity in the Modern Presidency," in *The New American Political System,* ed. Anthony King (Washington, DC: American Enterprise Institute, 1978), 45–46.

21. David K. Nichols, *The Myth of the Modern Presidency* (University Park: Pennsylvania State University Press, 1994), 6.

22. On pre–New Deal institutional developments, see generally Stephen Skowroneck, *Building a New American State: The Expansion of National Administrative Capacities, 1877–1920* (New York: Cambridge University Press, 1982).

23. Alexis de Tocqueville, *Democracy in America,* ed. Philips Bradley (New York: Vintage, 1990), 1:325–326 (emphasis in original).

24. See Nichols, *Myth of the Modern Presidency,* 72, and citations provided therein.

25. See, for example, President Grover Cleveland, *Veto of Texas Seed Bill,* in *The American Republic: Primary Sources,* ed. Bruce P. Frohnen (Indianapolis, IN: Liberty Fund, 2002), 410.

26. Theodore Roosevelt, *An Autobiography* (New York: Scribner's, 1920), 357.

27. Robert J. Cornell, *The Anthracite Coal Strike of 1902* (Washington, DC: Catholic University Press, 1957), 238.

28. See, for example, William H. Harbaugh, "The Constitution of the Theodore Roosevelt Administration and the Progressive Era," in *The Constitution and the American Presidency*, ed. Martin L. Fausold and Alan Shank (Albany: State University of New York Press, 1991), 71–74.

29. Paul D. Moreno, *The American State from the Civil War to the New Deal* (Cambridge: Cambridge University Press, 2013), 166. We would note our disagreement with Moreno's interpretation of the text, meaning, and character of the Framers' Constitution while acknowledging our general concurrence with his summary of the Wilson wartime presidency, in ibid., 163–176.

30. The definition of "the people" also was expanded by the Nineteenth Amendment, though women's suffrage did not entail any necessary alteration in the character of the Constitution itself; a larger voting public may recognize and support the Constitution's mediating character, should it so choose.

31. See, for example, Martin Shefter, *Political Parties and the State* (Princeton, NJ: Princeton University Press, 1994), especially chapter 3. Shefter emphasizes the hostility of Progressive reforms (and especially their mugwump antecedents) to political parties. We would emphasize that the "direct" application of voter preferences to political actors in the Progressive mind always was to be subject to interpretation and actualization by expert administrators.

32. For a favorable treatment of this expansion of judicial power, see Moreno, *American State*, 66–68, 102–105. On the origins and limitations of Privileges and Immunities, see Raoul Berger, *Government by Judiciary: The Transformation of the Fourteenth Amendment* (Cambridge, MA: Harvard University Press, 1977).

33. See our discussion in Chapter 3.

34. The claim was made, of course, as it still is, that this change was dictated by the language of the Fourteenth Amendment. For a critique of this view, see Berger, *Government by Judiciary*. We are aware of the various controversies concerning the proper interpretation of this amendment, but would note that they are largely irrelevant to our thesis. Should one believe doctrines such as substantive due process or a wide definition of the privileges and immunities of citizens be called for in that amendment, this would justify the courts' opinions; it would not change the transformative effect of those opinions. For an argument that the Fourteenth Amendment should be read to establish a new dispensation of increased judicial as well as congressional powers applying the Bill of Rights against state governments, see Akhil Reed Amar, *The Bill of Rights: Creation and Reconstruction* (New Haven, CT: Yale University Press, 2000).

35. For a balanced treatment of the issues involved in substantive due process cases, and the grounding of early examples in the genre, see Victoria E. Nourse, "A Tale of Two Lochners: The Untold Story of Substantive Due Process and the Idea of Fundamental Rights," 97 *California Law Review* 751 (2009). Critiques of such cases generally fall into two camps: those dismissing them as heavy-handed policy making in favor of large businesses and those applying a kind of Protestant/Scottish natural law ethos to economic and social regulation. Either, in our view—or, for that matter, an entirely accurate reading of the requirements of a free market—strays from the requirements of judicial duty.

36. Even basic care in legislative drafting was abandoned in the heat of the moment; New Deal legislation, especially in the early days, was extraordinarily sloppy. See, for example, Melvin I. Urofsky, *The Warren Court: Justices, Rulings, and Legacy* (Santa Barbara, CA: ABC-Clio, 2001), 4.

37. See William E. Leuchtenberg, *The FDR Years: On Roosevelt and His Legacy* (New York: Columbia University Press, 1995), chapter 2. See also Moreno, *American State*, 221–222, 231–232, and citations provided therein.

38. Funding for unemployment insurance was provided by the federal government in exchange for adherence to detailed federal rules. Collectively known as the Social Security cases, Supreme Court decisions

in Helvering v. Davis, 301 U.S. 619 (1937), Steward Machine Company v. Davis, 301 U.S. 548 (1937), and Carmichael v. Southern Coal & Coke Co., 301 U.S. 495 (1937), sustained the constitutionality of a federal scheme collecting taxes from employers and employees for certain old-age benefits and for payments to states who would use them to provide unemployment compensation.

39. Graham G. Dodds, *Take up Your Pen: Unilateral Presidential Directives in American Politics* (Philadelphia: University of Pennsylvania Press, 2013), 164–167.

40. 5 U.S.C. §§551–559, 701–706.

41. Perhaps the greatest change in Supreme Court doctrine enabling institutionalization of Progressive reforms was the atrophy of the nondelegation doctrine spelled out most famously in A. L. A. Schechter Poultry Corp. v. U.S. 295 U.S. 495 (1935). We discuss this development at some length in Chapter 6.

42. Franklin Delano Roosevelt, address, Chicago, October 14, 1936, quoted in Moreno, *American State*, 271.

43. Theodore J. Lowi, *The End of Liberalism: The Second Republic of the United States*, 2nd ed. (New York: Norton, 1979), especially chapter 5.

44. Donald L. Robinson, ed., *Reforming American Government: The Bicentennial Papers of the Committee on the Constitutional System* (Boulder, CO: Westview Press, 1985), 76, 69.

45. This view is well articulated in James MacGregor Burns, *The Deadlock of Democracy* (Englewood Cliffs, NJ: Prentice-Hall, 1963). Burns places primary blame for "deadlock" on James Madison's belief in the need for "checks and balances." Burns, *Deadlock of Democracy*, 21.

46. For a discussion of revisionist treatments of the New Deal, minimizing its impact, as well as a defense of FDR's state-building, see Leuchtenberg, *FDR Years*, chapter 8.

47. Moreno, *American State*, 296–309. This phase included the revived court-packing scheme and FDR's attempts at systemic administrative reorganization.

48. An excellent compilation of the major proposed reforms of the Constitution is to be found in Robinson, *Reforming American Government*.

49. C. Douglas Dillon, "The Challenge of Modern Governance," in Robinson, *Reforming American Government*, 26.

50. Committee on the Constitutional System, "A Statement of the Problem," in Robinson, *Reforming Government*, 69–70.

51. Ibid., 69.

52. Lloyd N. Cutler, "To Form a Government," in Robinson, *Reforming Government*, 12.

53. Bruce Ackerman, "The New Separation of Powers," 113 *Harvard Law Review* 633 (2000), 643-88.

54. Charles Hardin, "Toward a New Constitution," in Robinson, *Reforming American Government*, 149.

55. Today it may seem somewhat ironic that among the specific powers the Framers did not want the president to possess was that of declaring war, a power that was a prerogative of the British monarch. In this area the separation of powers has broken down almost completely. See our discussion in Chapter 6.

56. Robinson, *Reforming American Government*, 189.

57. One of the earliest works to advance this thesis was James Allen Smith's *The Spirit of American Government* (New York: MacMillan, 1907). This thesis gained almost universal acceptance in Progressive circles.

58. In this regard our bicameralism, and in particular the composition of the Senate, has been a significant target of criticism. Bicameralism technically is not a part of the separation of powers doctrine, though in the American context it is an auxiliary precaution and an integral part of the doctrine in practice.

59. Robert A. Dahl, *A Preface to Democratic Theory* (Chicago: University of Chicago Press, 1956). It would be difficult to overstate the impact of this work on political scientists, particularly those concerned with the American political system or, more generally, with democratic theory. As Ronald M. Peters has noted, words such as "skillful," "admirable," "sophisticated," "unusually intelligent," "compelling," and, among other accolades, "systematic" have been used to describe it. The work was also portrayed as holding out "the promise of fruitful further researches" and as pointing "political theory to a possible new stage in its development." Ronald M. Peters, "Political Theory, Political Science, and the Preface: A Review of Robert A. Dahl: *A Preface to Democratic Theory*," 7 *Political Science Reviewer* 145 (1977).

60. Dahl, *Preface*, 31.

61. Ibid., 30. This view of the Framers' intentions accords essentially with that set forth by the earlier Progressives. Not only was the system designed to provide for "deadlock," but it was also structured to protect select minorities. As Douglass Adair observed, by 1950 a majority of leading American history textbooks incorporated the view that the Founding Fathers "were intent on protecting the property of the few at the expense of the many." Douglass Adair, "The Tenth Federalist Revisited," in *Fame and the*

Founding Fathers: Essays by Douglass Adair, ed. Trevor Colbourn (New York: W. W. Norton, 1974), 76.

62. Burns, *Deadlock of Democracy.*

63. Alexander Hamilton, John Jay, and James Madison, *The Federalist,* eds. George W. Carey and James McClellan (Indianapolis, IN: Liberty Fund, 2000), no. 10 (Madison), 43.

64. Ibid., 270.

65. Burns, *Deadlock of Democracy,* 21.

66. Ibid., 20.

67. Obvious questions arise with respect to both Dahl's and Burns's analyses of the Framers' intentions with respect to the separation of powers. Why would the Framers, who were intent upon establishing a stronger national government, construct a system that would be so easily deadlocked? And, if they were intent upon protecting specific privileged minorities, could they not have constructed a system that would more effectively and reliably secure this end? Indeed, as we will show, the Framers' intentions, by all evidences, were entirely different from those attributed to them by Dahl and Burns.

68. We have noted the partial exception of the Seventeenth Amendment, and add to this the observation that the amendment was adopted in the midst of numerous other statutory and other reforms, of which it was a not inconsiderable, but hardly the decisive, part.

69. "The Founder's Constitution," in *The Popular Sources of Political Authority: Documents on the Massachusetts Constitution of 1780,* ed. Oscar Handlin and Mary Handlin (Cambridge, MA: Harvard University Press, 1966), http://press-pubs.uchicago.edu/founders/print_documents /v1ch1s6.html.

70. On this point see Healy, *Cult of the Presidency.* This work traces the growth of presidential powers and the emergence in the public mind of the "heroic presidency."

71. Clinton Rossiter, *The American Presidency* (New York: Harcourt, Brace and World, 1956), 28–30.

72. Edward Corwin, *The President: Office and Powers, 1787–1957* (New York: New York University Press, 1957), 29–30.

73. We recognize, of course, the much-discussed decline of party strength and multiple criticisms of the lack of voter participation, particularly in primary elections. We would note simply that these entirely predictable results of a system that depends too much on continued interest among citizens with intraparty differences and on particular policy positions citizens find too divorced from their daily concerns nonetheless serve to center attention

and political legitimacy on the presidency. For a classic statement of dissatisfaction with modern parties and their inability to institute programmatic governance, see E. E. Schattschneider, *The Semisovereign People: A Realist's View of Democracy* (Belmont, CA: Wadsworth, 1975).

74. Wilson, *Constitutional Government*, 68.

75. Obviously, one can find exceptions to this general statement, rooted in particularly unpopular presidential policies, programs, or actions. But such instances—for example—the Republican Party's repudiation of Nixon after the Watergate scandal are highly unusual and generally noted as such.

76. The view that the popular will finds expression through the legislature is, for instance, the implicit premise of Publius's argument in *Federalist* 10.

77. Robert Nisbet, *The Quest for Community* (San Francisco: ICU Press, 1990), 153 (emphasis in original).

78. Ibid., 222.

79. Much this same point is made by James Burnham in *Congress and the American Tradition*. See also Kendall, "Two Majorities."

80. Dahl, *Preface*, 84. In a sense this aspect of Dahl's polyarchy resembles what Joseph Schumpeter called the "classical theory of democracy," which he defined as follows: "the democratic method is that institutional arrangement for arriving at political decisions which realizes the common good by making the people itself decide issues through the election of individuals who are to assemble in order to carry out its will." Schumpeter went on to point up the insurmountable difficulties involved in pursuing this type of democracy. Schumpeter, *Capitalism, Socialism, and Democracy* (New York: Harper and Row, 1950), 269.

81. *Federalist*, no. 62 (Madison), 323.

82. Ibid., 323–324.

83. Ibid., 324.

84. A compelling argument can be made in keeping with Hamilton's views expressed in *Federalist* 9, that popular government was possible only after the emergence of a "constitutional liberalism" that embraced the rule of law and curbed the mutability of laws. See, for example, Giovanni Sartori, *The Theory of Democracy Revisited* (Chatham, NJ: Chatham House, 1987), 2: chapter 11.

Chapter 6: The New Dispensation and the Rule of Quasi-Law

1. Eric A. Posner and Adrian Vermeule, *The Executive Unbound: After the Madisonian Republic* (Oxford: Oxford University Press, 2011), 61.

2. Lon L. Fuller, *The Morality of Law,* (New Haven, CT: Yale University Press, 1964), 39.

3. Joel Kotkin points out that "Google employs 50,000, Facebook 4,600, and Twitter less than 1,000 domestic workers. In contrast, GM employs 200,000, Ford 164,000, and Exxon over 100,000. Put another way, Google, with a market cap of $215 billion, is about five times larger than GM yet has just one fourth as many workers." High-tech subsidies, of course, include those for "green energy corporations." Joel Kotkin, "America's New Oligarchs—Fwd.us and Silicon Valley's Shady 1 Percenters," *Daily Beast,* May 14, 2013, http://www.thedailybeast.com/articles/2013/05/14/america-s -new-oligarchs-fwd-us-and-silicon-valley-s-shady-1-percenters.html.

4. Joel Kotkin, *The New Class Conflict* (Candor, NY: Telos Press, 2014), Kindle edition.

5. Theodore J. Lowi, *The End of Liberalism: The Second Republic of the United States,* 2nd ed. (New York: Norton, 1979), chapter 5.

6. Peter B. Oh, "Veil-Piercing Unbound," 93 *Boston University Law Review* 89 (2013), 95.

7. Abdullahi A. An-Nacim, "Symposium: The Competing Claims of Law and Religion: Complementary, Not Competing, Claims of Law and Religion: An Islamic Perspective," 39 *Pepperdine Law Review* 1231 (2013), 1251–1252.

8. Linda D. Jellum, "The Impact of the Rise and Fall of *Chevron* on the Executive's Power to Make and Interpret Law," 44 *Loyola University of Chicago Law Review* 141 (2012), 147–148.

9. Frederick Schauer, "The Best Laid Plans," 120 *Yale Law Journal* 586 (2010), 618.

10. There must be general rules; the rules must be promulgated; the rules must typically be prospective, rather than retroactive; the rules must be clear; the rules must not require contradictory actions; the rules must not require actions that are impossible to perform; the rules must remain relatively constant over time; and there must be a congruence between the rules as declared and the rules as administered. Fuller, *Morality of Law,* 46–49.

11. This category seems too obvious and voluminous to discuss in detail, but consider the vast number of so-called earmarks, by which members of Congress provide federal funding to special interests in their districts.

12. Indeed, Lowi argues that properly drafted laws could be enacted so as to bring the administrative state under the rule of law. See *End of Liberalism,* especially chapter 11.

13. Note, for example, the Defense Appropriations bill, subjected to Obama's multitude of objections in his signing statement. As with most contemporary

abuses of the lawmaking process, riders and omnibus legislation have deep historical roots, but have been expanded exponentially in recent decades. See ibid. We discuss defense spending and signing statements at greater length below.

14. Morris P. Fiorina, *Congress: Keystone of the Washington Establishment* (New Haven, CT: Yale University Press, 1989).

15. Here the acquiescence of the courts in the stretching of congressional power under the Commerce Clause is, of course, crucial.

16. A. L. A. Schechter Poultry Corp. v. United States, 295 U.S. 495 (1935).

17. David Rosenbloom, "Administrative Law and Regulation," in *Handbook of Administrative Law,* 3rd ed., ed. Jack Rabin, W. Bartley Hildreth, and Gerald J. Miller (Boca Raton, FL: CRC Press, 2012), 642–643.

18. Kenneth Culp Davis argues that the "objective of requiring every delegation to be accompanied by meaningful statutory standards had to fail, should have failed, and did fail." Kenneth Culp Davis, "A New Approach to Delegation," 36 *University of Chicago Law Review* 713 (1969), 719.

19. Lowi, *End of Liberalism,* 124.

20. Ibid., 96; Interstate Commerce Act of 1887, Pub. L. No. 49–41, February 4, 1887, Enrolled Acts and Resolutions of Congress, 1789–, General Records of the United States Government, 1778–1992, Record Group 11, National Archives.

21. Lowi, *End of Liberalism,* 124.

22. Ibid., 101, quoting Federal Trade Commission Act, 15 U.S.C. § 41–58, as amended (2011).

23. Ibid., 97, citing Louis L. Jaffe and Nathaniel Nathanson, *Administrative Law: Cases and Materials* 2nd ed.(Boston, MA: Little, Brown and CO., 1961), 60–61. It is true that section 1 of the ICC legislation made the vague demand that prices be "reasonable and just," but at least these terms were defined through the listing of forbidden charges provided in section 2.

24. Ibid., 102.

25. Ibid., 117, quoting Occupational Safety and Health Act, 29 U.S.C. § 651 (2011).

26. Occupational Safety and Health Act, 29 U.S.C. § 651(b) (2011).

27. Lowi, *End of Liberalism,* 118, quoting Occupational Safety and Health Act, 29 U.S.C. § 655 (2011).

28. Ibid., 111. We note the increasing role of "public interest" groups in such processes, expanding influence to ideologically motivated activists and their legal and political representatives.

29. The Consumer Product Safety Act of 1972, 15 U.S.C. § 2051(b)(1) (2008).

30. Clean Air Act, 42 U.S.C. § 7401(b)(1) (2008).

31. American Association of Law Libraries *Federal Register Pages Published Annually,* http://www.llsdc.org/assets/sourcebook/fed-reg-pages.pdf

32. See especially Whitman v. American Trucking Ass'ns, Inc., 531 U.S. 457 (2001) (reiterating the "intelligible principle" standard).

33. See Administrative Procedure Act (APA), Pub. L. No. 79–404, 60 Stat. 237, 5 U.S.C. § 500 et seq. (2011).

34. Chevron, U.S.A., Inc. v. Natural Res. Def. Council, Inc., 467 U.S. 837 (1984); Sec. & Exch. Comm'n v. Chenery Corp., 318 U.S. 80 (1943).

35. Philip Hamburger, *Is Administrative Law Unlawful?* (Chicago: University of Chicago Press, 2014), 130.

36. Ibid., chapter 24.

37. Ibid., 6.

38. INS v. Chadha, 462 U.S. 919 (1983).

39. Louis Fisher, "Signing Statements: Constitutional and Practical Limits," 16 *William and Mary Bill of Rights Journal* 183 (2007), 196.

40. Alexander Hamilton, John Jay, and James Madison, *The Federalist,* ed. George W. Carey and James McClellan (Indianapolis. IN: Liberty Fund, 2000), no. 62 (Madison), 323–324.

41. Nina E. Olson, "We Still Need a Simpler Tax Code," *Wall Street Journal,* April 10, 2009, A13. In this 2009 article, Olson reported that more than 3,250 changes had been made to the tax code since 2001.

42. *Federalist,* no. 62 (Madison), 324 (emphasis in original).

43. See Philip K. Howard, *The Death of Common Sense* (New York: Random House, 1994), 12.

44. Ibid., 37.

45. Ibid., 12.

46. Ibid., 14.

47. An extensive discussion of the hazards to American citizens from the state's use of vague and overbroad criminal laws is provided in Harvey Silverglate, *Three Felonies a Day: How the Feds Target the Innocent* (New York: Encounter, 2011).

48. R. Craig Kitchen, "Negative Lawmaking Delegations: Constitutional Structure and Delegations to the Executive of Discretionary Authority to Amend, Waive, and Cancel Statutory Text," 40 *Hastings Constitutional Law Quarterly* 525 (2013), 555–556..

49. Sam Baker, "HHS Finalizes Over 1,200 Waivers under Healthcare Reform Law," *TheHill,* January 6, 2012, http://thehill.com/blogs/healthwatch /health-reform-implementation/202791-hhs-finalizes-more-than-1200 -healthcare-waivers.

50. Patient Protection and Affordable Care Act, Pub. L. No. 111–148, Title I, Section 1332, 42 U.S.C.A. § 18052 (2011).

51. No Child Left Behind Act, Pub. L. No. 107–110, 20 U.S.C.A. § 7861 (2011).

52. Lyndsey Layton, "U.S. to Grant Waivers for No Child Left Behind," *Washington Post,* August 8, 2011, http://articles.washingtonpost.com /2011–08–08/local/35269406_1_education-reform-education-secretary -arne-duncan-standards.

53. Department of Education, "ESEA Flexibility," last updated July 9, 2013, http://www2.ed.gov/policy/elsec/guid/esea-flexibility/index.html. California and Iowa both at one time had been turned down for waivers by the Department of Education.

54. David J. Barron and Todd D. Rakoff, "In Defense of Big Waiver," 113 *Columbia Law Review* 265 (March 2013).

55. Ibid., 279.

56. Richard A. Epstein, "Government by Waiver: The Breakdown of Public Administration," *Forbes,* November 23, 2010, http://www.forbes.com/sites /richardepstein/2010/11/23/government-by-waiver-the-breakdown-of -public-administration/.

57. Ibid.

58. Ibid.

59. Ibid.

60. Ibid.

61. Lowi, *End of Liberalism,* 111.

62. Frank J. Macchiarola notes the rise and increasing use of consent decrees beginning in the 1970s. Frank J. Macchiarola, "The Courts in the Political Process: Judicial Activism or Timid Local Government?," 9 *St. John's Journal of Legal Commentary* 703 (1994), 707. James A. Kushner notes the widespread use of consent decrees, including the fact that as of 2004 one in ten school districts and over four hundred correctional institutions were operating under a consent decree. James A. Kushner, "The Unintended Consequences of Consent Decrees and the Case of the Century Freeway Litigation: Keith v. Volpe," 36 *Southwestern University Law Review* 301 (2007), 302.

63. Fuller, *Morality of Law,* 39–40.

64. Ronald F. Wright, "Trial Distortion and the End of Innocence in Federal Criminal Justice," 154 *University of Pennsylvania Law Review* 79 (2005).

65. Floyd R. Gibson, "American Buffalo: Vanishing Acquittals and the Gradual Extinction of the Federal Criminal Trial Lawyer," 156 *University of Pennsylvania Law Review* 226 (2007).

66. Philip A. Hamburger, *Law and Judicial Duty* (Cambridge, MA: Harvard University Press, 2008), 618, 615.
67. Unaware of "judicial duty," and believing its exercise in nullifying legislation to be "judicial review," legal scholars look in vain for the constitutional grounding of judicial review. Ibid., 616.
68. Ibid., 339–340.
69. Ibid.
70. Ibid., 19–30.
71. Missouri v. Jenkins, 495 U.S. 33 (1990), 56–57.
72. We note, for example, the well-known doubts of Justice Ruth Bader Ginsburg regarding the reasoning of *Roe.* See, e.g., "Judge Ginsburg Still Voices Strong Doubts on Rationale behind Roe v. Wade Ruling," *New York Times,* November 29, 2010, http://www.nytimes.com/2005/11/29/politics/ginsburg.html.
73. Dred Scott v. Sandford, 60 U.S. 393 (1857).
74. To speak of a "fundamental" right suggests that rights may vary in their importance and brings to mind the court's use of "strict scrutiny" and "heightened scrutiny" of legislation involving, inter alia, race and gender. This practice, which accords a different judicial treatment to individuals based on their attributes, is justified on existing social conditions and attitudes, distinctly nonjudicial considerations best taken into account by the legislative branch.
75. Lochner v. New York, 198 U.S. 45, 117 (1905).
76. Roe v. Wade, 410 U.S. 113, 174 (1973) (Rehnquist, J., dissenting).
77. See Hamburger, *Law and Judicial Duty,* 321–322, citing the quotation of Blackstone by "the young law student William Plumer" in New Hampshire during the founding era.
78. *Roe,* 410 U.S., 164.
79. Ibid., 137.
80. See, e.g., Stenberg v. Carhart, 530 U.S. 914 (2000) striking down Nebraska's "partial birth abortion" ban on the grounds that a woman has a fundamental right to choose the safest means of abortion medically available.
81. See generally David D. Meyer, "*Gonzales v. Carhart* and the Hazards of Muddled Scrutiny," 17 *Journal of Law & Politics* 57 (2008).
82. *Federalist,* no. 70 (Hamilton), 362.
83. Todd F. Gaziano, "The Use and Abuse of Executive Orders and Other Presidential Directives," 5 *Texas Review of Law and Policy* 267 (Spring 2001), 276.
84. Perhaps the most interesting place where this attribution has been made is the C-SPAN Classroom website, dedicated to educating young people

about their government. See C-SPAN Classroom, *Roles of the President,* http://www.cspanclassroom.org/pdf/ws_rolesofthepresident.pdf.

85. Gaziano, "Use and Abuse," 273. Presidential directives of various sorts date to the founding. The name refers simply to written instructions or declarations issued by the president.

86. Tara L. Branum, "President or King? The Use and Abuse of Executive Orders in Modern-Day America," 28 *Journal of Legislation* 1 (2002), 22.

87. Paul Begala, quoted in Alissa C. Wetzel, "Beyond the Zone of Twilight: How Congress and the Court Can Minimize the Dangers and Maximize the Benefits of Executive Orders," 42 *Valparaiso Law Review* 385 (2007), 416.

88. Taft, quoted in Branum, "President or King?," 26n106.

89. Ibid., 26n156.

90. Wetzel, "Beyond the Zone," 398.

91. Branum, "President or King?," 21–22.

92. Ibid., See, e.g. Mississippi v. Johnson, 71 U.S. 475 (1866).

93. Gaziano, "Use and Abuse," 271.

94. Ibid. The directive also purported to put people on notice of possible prosecution for violating rules of neutrality, in effect creating federal criminal law in this area, something Washington did not have the constitutional power to do.

95. Branum, "President or King?," 24.

96. Ex parte Merryman, 17 F. Cas. 144 (C.C.D. Md. 1861). Chief Justice Taney's order in the case was ignored, and then rendered moot by a subsequent executive order freeing most political prisoners. See Abraham Lincoln, "Executive Order No. 1—Relating to Political Prisoners, February 14, 1862, online by Gerhard Peters and John T. Woolley, *The American Presidency Project,* http://www.presidency.ucsb.edu/ws/index.php?pid=69792 .

97. Ex parte Milligan, 71 U.S. (4 Wall.) 2 (1866).

98. Wetzel, "Beyond the Zone," 394.

99. A. L. A. Schechter Poultry Corp. v. United States, 295 U.S. 495, 529 (1935).

100. Youngstown Sheet & Tube Co. v. Sawyer, 343 U.S. 579, 659 (1952)

101. Ibid., 638; Jackson concurrence.

102. Wetzel, "Beyond the Zone," 411–412.

103. Ibid., 420.

104. Ibid., 426–427.

105. Branum, "President or King?," 36.

106. Ibid., 26–30. Agencies created by executive order include the Federal Emergency Management Agency (FEMA).

107. Wetzel, "Beyond the Zone," 427.

108. Gaziano, "Use and Abuse," 292.

109. Ibid., 293–294.

110. John F. Manning and Matthew C. Stephenson, *Legislation and Regulation* (Rochester, NY: Foundation Press, 2010).

111. "Patient Protection and Affordable Care Act's Consistency with Longstanding Restrictions on the Use of Federal Funds for Abortion," Exec. Order No. 13535, 75 *Fed. Reg.* 15599 (March 29, 2010). The reader may note the frequency of examples of quasi-lawmaking regarding so-called social issues, and abortion in particular. We would posit that these issues are ripe for such treatment because they are, in fact, deeply and hotly contested, making the normal, constitutional path to (legislative) policy change fraught with difficulty. They are the successors to New Deal economic issues precisely because of their tendency to produce "gridlock"—which the Constitution is designed to use as a means of delay until deliberation produces acceptance of any change by a disinterested majority bordering on consensus, but which Progressives find unacceptable because it prevents instantiation of the policy preferences they deem democratic, egalitarian, and just.

112. Mimi Hall, "Both Sides of Abortion Issue Quick to Dismiss Order," *USA Today,* March 24, 2010, www.usatoday.com/news/washington /2010–03–24-abortion_N.htm.

113. "Obama White House Abortion Executive Order and Statement on Healthcare Bill," *Los Angeles Times,* March 31, 2010, http://latimesblogs .latimes.com/washington/2010/03/obama-abortion-statement-stupak -.html?utm_source=twitterfeed&utm_medium=twitter.

114. Ibid.

115. We note here that even the passage of the act is highly suspect in terms of constitutional morality, because both houses of Congress did not pass the same legislation; rather, one house passed the legislation and the other passed an earlier version, then a resolution adopting amendments thereto. Ewen MacAskill, "Barack Obama's Healthcare Bill Passed by Congress," *Guardian,* March 22, 2010, http://www.guardian.co.uk/world/2010/mar/22 /us-healthcare-bill-passes-congress.

116. Fuller, *Morality of Law,* 39.

117. Sofia E. Biller, "Flooded by the Lowest Ebb: Congressional Responses to Presidential Signing Statements and Executive Hostility to the Operation of Checks and Balances," 93 *Iowa Law Review* 1067 (2008), 1069.

118. Gaziano, "Use and Abuse," 289–290.

119. Foreign Intelligence Surveillance Act (FISA), Pub. L. No. 95–511, 92 Stat. 1783, 50 U.S.C. § 36 (1978).

120. Louis Fisher, "Signing Statements," 206–207.
121. Andrew Jackson, "Special Message," May 30, 1830, online by Gerhard Peters and John T. Woolley, *The American Presidency Project,* http://www .presidency.ucsb.edu/ws/?pid=66775.
122. Fisher, "Signing Statements," 189.
123. Ibid., 189–190, 185–188.
124. Ibid., 192. A number of these signing statements provided an alternative presidential reading of the statute at odds with that found in Congress's legislative history, asserted limits on the statute's implementation in accordance with presidential interpretation of constitutional requirements, and directed executive branch personnel to implement the statute in a specific manner. Biller, "Flooded by the Lowest Ebb," 1078.
125. Biller, "Flooded by the Lowest Ebb," 1073, 1095.
126. Walter Dellinger, assistant attorney general, memorandum to Bernard N. Nussbaum, counsel to the president, "The Legal Significance of Presidential Signing Statements," 17 *U.S. Op. Off. Legal Counsel* 131 (1993), http://www.justice.gov/olc/signing.htm.
127. Biller, "Flooded by the Lowest Ebb," 1075–1076.
128. Todd Garvey, *Presidential Signing Statements: Constitutional and Institutional Implications* (CRS Report No. RL33667) (Washington, DC: Congressional Research Service, 2012), 7–8, http://www.fas.org/sgp/crs /natsec/RL33667.pdf. Congress ratified the Clinton action with legislation in 2000 (Title XXXII of the National Defense Authorization Act for Fiscal Year 2000, Pub. L. No. 106–65).
129. Garvey, *Presidential Signing Statements,* 6–8.
130. Dellinger, "Legal Significance of Presidential Signing Statements."
131. Ibid.
132. Walter Dellinger, assistant attorney general, Department of Justice, memorandum to Honorable Abner J. Mikva, counsel to the president, "Presidential Authority to Decline to Execute Unconstitutional Statutes," 18 *U.S. Op. Off. Legal Counsel* 199 (1994), http://www.justice.gov/olc /nonexcut.htm.
133. Detainee Treatment Act of 2005, Pub. L. No. 109–148 § 1003(a), 119 Stat. 2680, 2739 (codified as amended at 42 U.S.C.A. § 2000dd (West 2001 & Supp. 2006)).
134. Ibid.
135. Statement on Signing the Department of Defense, Emergency Supplemental Appropriations to Address Hurricanes in the Gulf of Mexico, and Pandemic Influenza Act of 2006, 41 *Weekly Comp. Pres. Doc.* 1918 (December 20, 2005).

136. Fuller, *Morality of Law*, 39, states that unpublished rules and ad hoc governmental actions are not law.

137. Garvey, *Presidential Signing Statements*, 11.

138. Fisher, "Signing Statements," 201.

139. By way of contrast, Bush I issued 146 signing statements containing 232 challenges during his single term; Reagan in two terms issued 71 statements. Biller, "Flooded by the Lowest Ebb," 1080.

140. Julian G. Ku, "Unitary Executive Theory and Exclusive Presidential Powers," 12 *University of Pennsylvania Journal of Constitutional Law* 615 (2010), 615–616, 621.

141. Garvey, *Presidential Signing Statements*, 9.

142. Ku, "Unitary Executive Theory," 619–620.

143. Ibid., 620, quoting President Obama's signing statement.

144. It may well be the case that Congress was here overstepping its proper bounds, attempting to legislate treaty terms when its role in such negotiations properly is limited to the Senate's power of rejecting any proposed treaties; our point remains, however, that the president chose to both sign and contradict the law.

145. Statement by the President on H.R. 4310, January 3, 2013 (on signing the National Defense Authorization Act for Fiscal Year 2013), http://www.whitehouse.gov/the-press-office/2013/01/03/statement-president-hr-4310.

146. Ibid.

147. Philip Hamburger, "Are Health-Care Waivers Unconstitutional?," *National Review*, February 8, 2011, http://www.nationalreview.com/article/259101/are-health-care-waivers-unconstitutional-philip-hamburger. Hamburger makes several further points, in particular regarding the question of whether waivers are even authorized under the ACA. See also Hamburger, *Administrative Law*, chapter 5.

Conclusion

1. David Landau, "Political Institutions and Judicial Role in Comparative Constitutional Law," 51 *Harvard International Law Journal* 319 (2010), cited in *Comparative Constitutional Law*, 3rd ed., ed. Vicki C. Jackson and Mark Tushnet (St. Paul, MN: Foundation Press, 2014), 777.

2. Ibid.

3. Gerald N. Rosenberg, *The Hollow Hope: Why Courts Can't Bring About Social Change*, 2nd ed. (Chicago: University of Chicago Press, 2008).

4. Recall our discussion of Morris P. Fiorina and Theodore J. Lowi in Chapter 6.

5. See our discussion in Chapter 5.

6. Here we merely note the vast literature on communitarianism, in which claims to protect "constitutive" groups fall afoul of the requirements, especially face-to-face contact within ongoing relationships, necessary for associations to actually constitute characteristic habits of their members. See Alasdair MacIntyre, "Why I Am Not a Communitarian," in *After MacIntyre,* ed. John Horton and Susan Mendus (Notre Dame, IN: University of Notre Dame Press, 1995).

7. Michael J. Sandel, *Justice: What's the Right Thing to Do?* (New York: Farrar, Straus and Giroux, 2009).

8. Alexis de Tocqueville, *Democracy in America,* ed. Philips Bradley (New York: Vintage, 1990), 2:106.

9. A prototypical example is Robert D. Putnam, *Bowling Alone* (New York: Simon and Schuster, 2001).

10. Tocqueville, *Democracy in America,* 2:106–107.

11. John C. Turner, *Rediscovering the Social Group* (Oxford: Blackwell, 1989). Turner points out the natural and beneficial character of what he terms the "category shift" from individual to social identity. Whether in a family, profession, or other social group, individual members who are fully engaged become "subjectively the exemplars or representatives of society or some part of it, the living, self-aware embodiments of the historical, cultural and politico-ideological forces and movements which formed them. Indeed, psychologically speaking, they do not 'represent,' they 'are'; they become self-conscious society." Individuals take on the interests, the perspectives, and the habits of thought and mind of the groups in which they are engaged. Turner argues that this shift in social identity "is not a loss or submergence of the self in the group . . . nor any kind of regression to a more primitive or unconscious form of identity . . . In many respects [it] may be seen as a gain in identity, since it represents a mechanism whereby individuals may act in terms of the social similarities and differences produced by the historical development of human society and culture." People do not "disappear" when they act as group members; they become part of a "team," the interests of which they make their own, within whose habits of conduct they know how to act so as to serve the common good—and with it their own.

12. See especially Donald S. Lutz, *The Origins of American Constitutionalism* (Baton Rouge: Louisiana State University Press, 1988). We in no way mean to imply that healthy, liberty-enhancing communalism must be Calvinist in character, only that this was the particular form of communalism dominant in early America.

13. Barry Alan Shain, *The Myth of American Individualism* (Princeton, NJ: Princeton University Press, 1996).
14. David Hackett Fischer, *Albion's Seed* (Oxford: Oxford University Press, 1989).
15. William Novak, *The People's Welfare: Law and Regulation in Nineteenth-Century America* (Chapel Hill: University of North Carolina Press, 1996).
16. "The Fundamental Orders of Connecticut," in *The American Republic: Primary Sources*, ed. Bruce P. Frohnen (Indianapolis, IN: Liberty Fund, 2002), 12–14.
17. This is a major theme of Bruce P. Frohnen, "The One and the Many: Individual Rights, Corporate Rights and the Diversity of Groups," 107 *West Virginia Law Review* 789 (2005).
18. See, for example, the discussion of ready-made communal organizations on the Western frontier provided in Daniel J. Boorstin, *The Americans: The Democratic Experience* (New York: Vintage, 1974), part 1.
19. This was the argument used by Protestant activists seeking to prevent Catholics in areas in New York and other states from securing public funding for parochial schools more friendly to their faith than the pervasively Protestant "public" schools already receiving such funds. See Philip A. Hamburger, *Separation of Church and State* (Cambridge, MA: Harvard University Press, 2004).
20. Richard Hofstadter, *The Age of Reform* (New York: Vintage, 1955), chapter 4.
21. Robert Nisbet, *The Quest for Community* (San Francisco: ICU Press, 1990).
22. For a positive statement of this theory, see Charles Taylor and Amy Gutmann, *Multiculturalism and "The Politics of Recognition"* (Princeton, NJ: Princeton University Press, 1992).
23. One thinks here of religious dissenters from recent decisions requiring public approbation of same-sex unions. Again, whatever one thinks of the underlying policies (one might, for example, substitute race for sexual orientation here), the fact remains that the state's legitimacy is undermined when it chooses to forge rather than follow consensus. For evidence of the depth of legitimacy issues in this area one need only review the instances of public violence precipitated by charges of racially motivated police killings of African Americans during 2015 in Ferguson, Baltimore, Cleveland, and Los Angeles, as well as the antipolice violence ensuing thereafter. Again, whatever one's view of the merits (and it seems clear that there is blame on all sides), our point is the continuing salience of "group" issues and the depth of antagonisms surrounding them,

which have not been solved through actions under the commanding constitution.

24. This is the theme of George W. Carey, "The Constitution and Community," in *Community and Tradition: Conservative Perspectives on the American Experience,* ed. George W. Carey and Bruce P. Frohnen (Lanham, MD: Rowman and Littlefield, 1998), 63.

Acknowledgments

The untimely death of my dear friend and colleague George Carey came after a lifetime of important work on the nature of American constitutionalism, and after he and I had mapped out the arguments and much of the content of the present book. Unfortunately, it came before George had a chance to put down in writing any recognition of debts he incurred in its preparation. I can only convey his often-expressed gratitude for the work of his many fine students and his love and appreciation for his family, especially his daughter, Michelle, and his wife, Claire. I should like to express my own gratitude to Claire, especially for her assistance with this book.

On behalf of both authors, I thank the two anonymous reviewers and all at Harvard University Press for their kindness and professionalism. In particular, thanks are owed to Mike Aronson, who shepherded the manuscript through its early stages, and Thomas LeBien for overseeing completion of the project.

I also must acknowledge a number of good friends for their support, helpful advice, and valuable feedback related to this book. I would like in particular to thank Joe Fornieri, Allan and Harriette Fox, Grace Goodall, Ken Grasso, Philip Hamburger, Dick Helmholz, Annette Kirk, Ed Lyons, and Horst Mewes. For their efforts in maintaining a supportive atmosphere at Ohio Northern University I thank President Dan DiBiasio, Provost Dave Crago, Dean Rick Bales, Associate Dean Bryan Ward, and former Acting Dean Steve Veltri.

As always, I owe a great debt, never to be repaid, to Rob Waters. My brother-in-arms throughout my adult life, he has persisted in providing me with meaningful insights, editorial suggestions, and intellectual prodding—as well as the occasional well-chosen caustic remark.

To Antonia, Michaela, and Augustine, who constantly demonstrate life's meaning and value, I merely restate my undying love.

—BPF

Index